The Significance

Willard Van Orman Quine was one of the mo̶ . ̶wentieth-century American analytic philosophy. Although he wr ...ınantly in English, in Brazil in 1942 he gave a series of lectures on logic and its philosophy in Portuguese, subsequently published as the book *O Sentido da Nova Lógica*. The book has never before been fully translated into English, and this volume is the first to make its content accessible to Anglophone philosophers. Quine would go on to develop revolutionary ideas about semantic holism and ontology, and this book provides a snapshot of his views on logic and language at a pivotal stage of his intellectual development. The volume also includes an essay on logic which Quine also published in Portuguese, together with an extensive historical-philosophical essay by Frederique Janssen-Lauret. The valuable and previously neglected works first translated in this volume will be essential for scholars of twentieth-century philosophy.

WALTER CARNIELLI is Professor of Philosophy of Logic and Foundations of Mathematics at the State University of Campinas. His publications include books on computability theory, modal logics, paraconsistent logics, and combinations of logics.

FREDERIQUE JANSSEN-LAURET is a lecturer in philosophy at the University of Manchester. She is co-editor of *Quine and His Place in History* (2015), and her work on Quine, logic, and ontology has appeared in *Synthese* and *The Monist*.

WILLIAM PICKERING is a translator and editor of academic works in the areas of logic and linguistics, and holds a Ph.D. in linguistics from the State University of Campinas. He has lectured and published on the applications of complex systems theory in linguistics.

The Significance of the New Logic

WILLARD VAN ORMAN QUINE

Translated and edited by

WALTER CARNIELLI
State University of Campinas, Brazil

FREDERIQUE JANSSEN-LAURET
University of Manchester, United Kingdom

WILLIAM PICKERING
State University of Campinas, Brazil

CAMBRIDGE
UNIVERSITY PRESS

University Printing House, Cambridge CB2 8BS, United Kingdom

One Liberty Plaza, 20th Floor, New York, NY 10006, USA

477 Williamstown Road, Port Melbourne, VIC 3207, Australia

314-321, 3rd Floor, Plot 3, Splendor Forum, Jasola District Centre, New Delhi - 110025, India

79 Anson Road, #06-04/06, Singapore 079906

Cambridge University Press is part of the University of Cambridge.

It furthers the University's mission by disseminating knowledge in the pursuit of education, learning and research at the highest international levels of excellence.

www.cambridge.org
Information on this title: www.cambridge.org/9781316631164
DOI: 10.1017/9781316831809

© Cambridge University Press 2018

Quine's *The Significance of the New Logic* was originally published in Portuguese as *O Sentido da Nova Lógica* (São Paulo: Livraria Martins Editora, 1944) and his essay "The United States and the Revival of Logic" was originally published in Portuguese as "Os Estados Unidos e o Ressurgimento da Lógica" in A. C. P. e Silva (Ed.), *A Vida Intelectual nos Estados* Unidos (São Paulo: União Cultural Brasil-Estados Unidos, 1945).

First published in English, with additional material, by Cambridge University Press in 2018; translations by Walter Carnielli, Frederique Janssen-Lauret, and William Pickering.
First paperback edition 2020

A catalogue record for this publication is available from the British Library

ISBN 978-1-107-17902-8 Hardback
ISBN 978-1-316-63116-4 Paperback

Contents

Acknowledgments

We would like to thank Dr. Douglas Quine, who holds the copyright to *O Sentido da Nova Lógica* and who kindly agreed to the publication of its translation, as well as to thank the União Cultural Brasil Estados Unidos for granting permission to translate *Os Estados Unidos e o Ressurgimento da Lógica*. We are grateful to Dr. Douglas Quine and Ms. Margaret Quine McGovern for the cover photograph. We are also indebted to Hilary Gaskin and Sophie Taylor of Cambridge University Press for their efficiency and continuous support. The authors acknowledge, respectively, support from research grants from the National Council for Scientific and Technological Development (CNPq), the Coordination for the Improvement of Higher Education Personnel (CAPES), and the São Paulo Research Foundation (FAPESP). We are also indebted to colleagues, especially to Alfredo Roque Freire, and to the staff at the Centre for Logic, Epistemology, and the History of Science of the State University of Campinas, who supported us in this project. Lastly, we are grateful to Alfredo Roque Freire for compiling the index.

Editors' Introduction

Walter Carnielli, Frederique Janssen-Lauret, and William Pickering

"So I was embarked on my fourth book, *O Sentido da Nova Lógica*," says Quine in his *The Time of My Life: An Autobiography* (Quine 2000, 173). In 1942, he was writing his lectures out in full, in what he modestly considered to be his faulty Portuguese: "I was getting portions [of the book] mimeographed so that the students could study them, and furthermore I wanted to leave my lectures in Brazil as a book so as to have more impact than could be hoped for through a small group in the classroom."

The study of logic was introduced in Brazil through the scholastically oriented philosophy courses taught in Jesuit schools. Not entirely disconnected from this tradition, the positivist influence on the understanding of logic in Brazil was strengthened at the end of the nineteenth century. The influence of positivist philosophy was so strong in this era that the Brazilian national flag, adopted in 1889, carries a positivist motto: *Ordem e Progresso*, or "Order and Progress."

The first book written in Brazil that makes reference to mathematical logic was *As Idéas Fundamentaes da Mathemática* by Manuel Amoroso Costa, published in 1929 (Amoroso Costa 1929). However, it was only in 1940 that a book exclusively dedicated to symbolic logic went to print in the country. This book, *Elementos de Lógica Matemática* by Vicente Ferreira da Silva (Ferreira da Silva 1940), placed logic as the basis of philosophical activity.

A lawyer with a keen interest in existentialist philosophy, Ferreira da Silva ended up acting as assistant to Quine during his stay and helped him with the editing of *O Sentido*. Quine knew Ferreira da Silva from reviewing his 116-page booklet, which Quine referred to as "an introduction to modern logic and, secondarily, to logical empiricism." Quine's review criticized Ferreira da Silva's proposal to divide meaningful from meaningless propositions, a mode of division that "has no apparent advantage over the more usual one, which subsumes the valid under the true and the invalid (or contravalid) under the false and extrudes the meaningless from the category of propositions altogether" (Quine 1941, 110).

However, the true inauguration of the contemporary phase of Brazilian logic occurred with the visit of Willard Van Orman Quine, in a course taught at the Free School of Sociology and Politics of São Paulo from June to September 1942. Quine's visit significantly contributed to an increased interest in logic among Brazilians and resulted two years later in the publication of the course material, in Portuguese, as *O Sentido da Nova Lógica*.

O Sentido is divided into four chapters: I – Theory of Composition, II – Theory of Quantification, III – Identity and Existence, and IV – Class, Relation, and Number. As Quine explains in the book's preface (Quine 1944, 9), the specific logical systematization used in the book results from an effort to reconcile three ideals: rigor in theoretical details, convenience in practical applications, and simplicity in presentation. This last ideal, he added, was the main objective.

In the first chapter of the book, "Theory of Composition," after "an illuminating introduction," as one reviewer put it (Bennett 1945, 509), Quine claims that it is convenient to consider logic as containing two parts: the theory of deduction and the theory of classes. The theory of deduction is divided into two other parts: composition theory and quantification theory. The purpose of this first part of the book is to provide the necessary means of preparation for a technical study of more advanced topics.

The second chapter of the book, "Theory of Quantification," takes on the work of Gottlob Frege, which according to the author was responsible for most of the content of modern logic; this includes the creation of quantification theory, which governs the use of prefixes called quantifiers.

The third chapter, "Identity and Existence," emphasizes the contrast between object and symbol. Here Quine deals with the concept of identity, for him a notion so simple and fundamental that it hardly admits explanation in clearer terms. Only one kind of existence is accepted – material existence in the case of physical objects. Quine tries to clarify certain confusions related to the concept of identity, and presents what he considers the fundamental principles of identity, such as the principle of the substitutivity of identity, the principle of the transitivity of identity, the principle of the symmetry of identity, and the principle that every object is identical to some object. An argument is presented for the elimination in logic of all substantives other than pronouns. In this part, Quine also deals with the topics of sense, synonymy, and necessity.

The last chapter of the book, "Class, Relation, and Number," aims to clarify how mathematics depends on abstract objects such as numbers, functions, and relations, and how these are reducible to notions of classes and attributes.

From 1936 to 1939, Quine had taught courses in mathematical logic in the Department of Mathematics at Harvard as Faculty Instructor (in 1941 he was promoted to Associate Professor). The result of these courses was his book *Mathematical Logic* of 1940. According to Quine, he was still strongly influenced by *Principia Mathematica* at the time, and as early as 1940, when he prepared *Mathematical Logic* for publication, he considered that Frege's *Begriffsschrift* (1879) was the "true beginning of mathematical logic." It was this influence that was passed on to the Brazilian logicians.

In his Brazilian publications, Quine argued that the discovery of the paradoxes and of the possibility of defining other notions (such as the infinitesimal and the imaginary numbers) on the basis of more fundamental concepts, had contributed to what he called the resurgence of logic. This view was fundamental to the turn of logic in Brazil, as was Quine's presentation – the first in Portuguese – of Kurt Gödel's incompleteness theorem of 1931, summarized by Quine as "Given any systematization of logic, there will be logical truths, and even arithmetical truths, that are provably unprovable" (Quine 1944, 20).

This turn occurred ten years later, in the 1950s, with the work of Brazilian logicians such as Edson Farah, Newton Carneiro Affonso da Costa, Jacob Zimbarg, and Benedito Castrucci at the University of São Paulo, Mario Tourasse Teixeira at UNESP in Rio Claro, Leonidas Hegenberg at the Aeronautics Technology Institute of São José dos Campos, and Jorge Barbosa of the Fluminense Federal University in Rio de Janeiro. It is the students of these men who today occupy a central position in logic research in Brazil and are responsible for the consolidation of the Brazilian school of logic.

Quine, in his course in São Paulo, not only argued that the limitations of Aristotelian logic justified the need for a new logic, but also that the need for a new logic had become urgent with the development in mathematics of the "higher infinity" of infinite numbers and classes. If, on the one hand, mathematical paradoxes simultaneously threatened but also stimulated the development of modern logic, only a more sophisticated logic could establish the foundations of mathematics and avoid the emergence of new paradoxes. In this context, the interest in new types of logic (such as paraconsistent logic) that developed in the Brazilian community, even though distantly connected to the figure of Quine, does not sound so strange.

It is inevitable to compare the topics covered by Quine in his *O Sentido da Nova Lógica* with Alfred Tarski's *Introduction to Logic and the Methodology of Deductive Sciences*, first published in Polish in 1936, then in German in 1937, and finally in English, in an expanded version, in 1941 (Tarski 1941; see also Murawski 1998). This is hardly a surprise if we look closely at the transcriptions and translations of the conversations between Carnap, Tarski, and Quine on nominalism and finitism (Frost-Arnold 2013). Tarski's work, as much as Quine's book of 1944, helped shape the reception of the methodology of deductive sciences in the twentieth century.

On July 30, 1942, Quine gave a public lecture, which he described as "well attended," at the United States–Brazil Cultural Union in São Paulo. Entitled *Os Estados Unidos e o Ressurgimento da Lógica* (The United States and the Revival of Logic), this talk highlights the symbolic tools of mathematical logic and makes a commendable defense of modern logic, which Quine considered a revolutionary and promising movement. This lecture, published in Quine 1945 and Quine 2004, and mentioned in the preface to *O Sentido da Nova Lógica*, is a quite natural complement to Quine's textbook and is translated in this volume.

Quine's unique Brazilian book was not received without criticism. For instance, Bennett 1945 warns of the risk that the reader might think that all important problems in logical theory have been disposed of, and adverts that "the book is not equipped with exercise material, nor designed for classroom drill" (509). The reviewer also regrets that "the confident tone and clear, enthusiastic and well organized statements commend the book to all thoughtful readers – who read Portuguese" (510).

Those interested in this phase of Quine's work now no longer have cause for regret. The translation we offer of *O Sentido da Nova Lógica* fills a gap that has long been noticed by scholars, and should also contribute to clarifying how this remarkable book was seminal not only for the consolidation of the study of logic in Brazil, but for the later research of Quine himself. As N. C. da Costa recognizes in his review, "Quine's book was very important for the development of logic and its philosophy in Brazil; several Brazilian logicians and philosophers, in effect, began their logic studies with Quine's book" (da Costa 1997, 688).

As for the role of this book in the development of Quine's views, his account of the problem of interpreting modal logic, and in particular of the failure of intersubstitutivity of co-referential names in modal contexts (a question that has inspired a vast literature), also originates with his work in Brazil, as reported on p. 173 of his autobiography (Quine 2000):

> I thus questioned [in my classes], in particular, the coherence of admitting bound variables into contexts governed by modal operators of necessity and possibility. Eager to put these latter bits of *O Sentido* before English readers, I dictated

a translation of my Portuguese to an English stenographer in São Paulo under the title "Notes on Existence and Necessity."

This volume thus includes several passages that appeared in English in "Notes on Existence and Necessity" (published in 1943, a year before *O Sentido*). With regard to these passages, we have incorporated Quine's own words into the translation insofar as we think they are faithful to the original Portuguese. Footnotes and comments indicate these passages and note where Quine's published English text diverges from the Portuguese equivalent.

There are three types of footnote in this volume. Quine's original notes are indicated with Roman numerals (i, ii, iii, etc.); his notes from the second edition alphanumerically (a, b, c, etc.); and our own editorial notes with Arabic numerals (1, 2, 3, etc.) at the end of the book.

The translation of *O Sentido* is based on the first edition of 1944, the second edition of 1996 being simply a reprint of the first in modernized orthography. Quine did provide a preface to the second edition, however, and a translation of this short text has been included in the present volume. With regard to the translation of the São Paulo lecture, we have used the reprinted version of 2004 (Quine 2004), as we were not able to obtain a copy of the original published version (Quine 1945).

Quine's Portuguese was far from faulty. He had attended a second-year Portuguese class at Harvard after a stay in the Azores, and had listened to much short-wave radio from Brazil before he flew to Rio in 1942. However, it has been a challenge to translate a book written in Portuguese back into the native language of the author. This is especially true of an author such as Quine, who helped to shape philosophical and technical terms in the English language and is also known for his clear, lively, and elegant style. The book by Quine in Portuguese is well written in a correct but somewhat flowery style, perhaps influenced by his assistants. However, this style is now more than seven decades away from contemporary language. In the face of these difficulties, we have tried to deliver, if not a Quinean piece, at least a text as clear and concise as possible. Quine would certainly have approved, if not of the result, at least of the efforts.

References

Amoroso Costa, Manuel. 1929. *As Idéas Fundamentaes da Mathemática*. Rio de Janeiro: Papelaria e Litho-Typographia Pimenta de Mello.
Bennett, Albert A. 1945. Review of Willard Van Orman Quine, *O Sentido da Nova Lógica*. *Bulletin of the American Mathematical Society*. Vol. 51, No. 7, 509–510.

da Costa, Newton C. 1997. A Review of *O Sentido da Nova Lógica* by W. V. Quine. *The Journal of Symbolic Logic*. Vol. 62, No. 2 (June), 688.

Ferreira da Silva, Vicente. 1940. *Elementos de Lógica Matemática*. São Paulo: Cruzeiro do Sul.

Frege, Gottlob. 1879. *Begriffsschrift: Eine der aritmetischen nachgebildete Formelsprache des reinen Denkens*. Halle: Louis Nebert.

Frost-Arnold, Greg. 2013. *Carnap, Tarski, and Quine at Harvard: Conversations on Logic, Mathematics, and Science*. Series Full Circle: Publications of the Archive of Scientific Philosophy. Chicago, IL: Open Court.

Murawski, Roman. January 1998–April 2000. Review of Alfred Tarski, *Introduction to Logic and to the Methodology of the Deductive Sciences* (4th edn., 1944). *Modern Logic*. Vol. 8, No. 1/2, 172–175.

Quine, Willard Van Orman. 1940. *Mathematical Logic*. New York: Norton.

  1941. Review of *Elementos de Lógica Matemática* by Vicente F. da Silva. *The Journal of Symbolic Logic*. Vol. 6, No. 3 (September), 109–110.

  1943. Notes on Existence and Necessity. *Journal of Philosophy*. Vol. 40, 113–127.

  1944. *O Sentido da Nova Lógica*. São Paulo: Livraria Martins Editora.

  1945. *Os Estados Unidos e o Ressurgimento da Lógica*. In: A. C. P. e. Silva (ed.), *A Vida Intelectual nos Estados Unidos*. São Paulo: União Cultural Brasil–Estados Unidos, vol. II. pp. 267–286.

  1996. *O Sentido da Nova Lógica*. 2nd edn. Curitiba: Editora da UFPR.

  2000. *The Time of My Life: An Autobiography*. Cambridge, MA: MIT Press; A Bradford Book.

  2004. Os Estados Unidos e o Ressurgimento da Lógica. *Scientiae Studia*. Vol. 2, No. 3, 381–392.

Tarski, Alfred. 1941. *Introduction to Logic and the Methodology of Deductive Sciences*. Oxford and New York: Oxford University Press.

Willard Van Orman Quine's Philosophical Development in the 1930s and 1940s

Frederique Janssen-Lauret

1 The History of Analytic Philosophy and the Early Quine's Place within It

Willard Van Orman Quine (1908–2000), pioneer of mathematical logic, champion of naturalism in the philosophy of science and epistemology, atheist, materialist, unifier of an austere physicalism with the truth of logic and mathematics, globetrotter, polyglot, Harvard stalwart and celebrated naval officer, was both an establishment figure and a free-thinking radical. Quine's life began shortly after the emergence of analytic philosophy. He was soon to become one of its towering figures. Taught by A. N. Whitehead, interlocutor to Rudolf Carnap, Alfred Tarski, and Ruth Barcan Marcus, teacher of Donald Davidson and David Lewis, Quine was on the scene of the development of modern set theory, logical positivism, modal logic, truth-conditional semantics, and the metaphysics of possible worlds. Hardly a significant new movement in analytic philosophy passed him by. Yet Quine's relationship to many of these movements is surprisingly ill-understood. Everyone knows that the logical positivists, including Quine's mentor, Carnap, sought to place truth and meaning on a proper scientific footing by countenancing only *a priori* analytic and *a posteriori* empirically testable statements as properly significant. Quine, initially a devoted Carnap acolyte, soon developed reservations about the dichotomy between analytic truth by definition and empirically testable synthetic truth. All scientific truths, he famously argued in "Two Dogmas of Empiricism" (Quine 1951), rely upon both at once, and both are revisable under sufficient theoretical pressure. Quine's rejection of the analytic–synthetic distinction was once viewed as revolutionizing the philosophy of science and logic. But, strangely, these days Quine himself is commonly portrayed as a flat-footed positivist, a deflationist, a behaviorist, an anti-metaphysician, whose objections to modal logic turn on superficial scope errors.[1] He has been the victim of his own success, his smooth prose distilled into catchy slogans – "the web of belief," "the myth of the museum," "to be is to be the value of a variable," "no entity without identity," "gavagai!" – liable to be misunderstood out of context. A highly original thinker who set himself against common analytic ways of speaking and thinking, Quine is easily misread because his oeuvre is vast, systematic, and largely unconstrained by many of the conceptual categories laid down by other analytic philosophers. To remedy misconceptions about him caused by out-of-context readings of his work, we must consider Quine's writings and influences from an historical point of view, extending the boundaries of the history of analytic philosophy to include the mid to late decades of the twentieth century.

Most research on analytic philosophy to date has concentrated on the early period, nearly all of it centered around Frege, Russell, and Wittgenstein, occasionally including Carnap and the Vienna Circle. Recently, some historians have ventured into scholarly work on Quine, especially on the early evolution of his position on analyticity (e.g. Creath 1990a, Ben-Menahem 2005, Mancosu 2005, Hylton 2007, Ebbs 2011). Quine's previously unpublished lectures and records of his conversations with Tarski and Carnap, revealing the development of his views in the 1940s, have begun to come out posthumously (Quine 2008a, 2008b, Frost-Arnold 2013). But one significant text has remained entirely unexplored. No one to date has paid any heed to Quine's fourth book on logic and its philosophy, a book written with great urgency as he prepared to bid farewell to logic and philosophy while readying himself for war in 1942, a book that in a letter to Carnap he presented as a major turning-point (Quine 1990b, 299).

How did it come about that none of those meticulous Quine scholars have cited, or even read, this book? Because Quine wrote it in Portuguese, under the title *O Sentido da Nova Lógica*, during a visiting professorship at the Free School of Sociology and Politics of São Paulo. Anglophone philosophers have so far neglected it because they could not read it. An English translation never appeared, apart from a few sections translated by Quine himself, published in the *Journal of Philosophy* in 1943 as "Notes on Existence and Necessity" (Quine 1943). Although generations of Brazilian logicians grew up with *O Sentido da Nova Lógica* (da Costa 1997, 688), and Mario Bunge translated the book into Spanish (Quine 1958), Quine modestly declined to translate it into English, claiming that the insights it contained had been

---

[1] For such portrayals of Quine, see for instance Price 2009, 325–326, Shaffer 2009, 348–361, Tahko 2011, 28. For rebuttals of these, see Janssen-Lauret 2015, 151–154 and Janssen-Lauret 2017, 250–255.

supplanted by later, better worked-out versions (Quine 1997, 8). For contemporary philosophers and historians of analytic philosophy, by contrast, such gradual shifts and their contribution to the development of Quine's mature views are part of the fascination the book holds. A full English translation of it is now finally seeing the light of day. Walter Carnielli, William Pickering, and I have jointly translated the book, which appears in this volume under the title *The Significance of the New Logic*. In this accompanying essay I will draw out the main philosophical contributions Quine made in the book, placing them in their historical context and relating them to Quine's overall philosophical development during the period.

The 1930s and 1940s were a time of great intellectual upheaval in the field of logic and its philosophy. What Quine calls "the new logic" in the title of this book – modern mathematical logic rather than the old Aristotelian paradigm – was gaining momentum throughout Europe and the United States, being put to use in a variety of different ways by analytic philosophers, mathematical logicians, pragmatists, logical positivists, and the Polish School in their attempts to make sense of contemporary developments in science and mathematics. Among the applications Quine mentions in the Introduction to this book are transfinite mathematics, the logicist project, the incompleteness of arithmetic, proof theory, solutions to the set-theoretic and semantic paradoxes, formal theories of truth, and new approaches to ontology. Quine had come to Brazil to introduce these methods and their applications to philosophers and scientists there, for many of whom this was entirely new territory.

Although written as a logic textbook, *The Significance of the New Logic* also contains intriguing philosophical material. It is known, for example, for the first appearances of Quine's doctrine of pure vs. impure designation – including his famous example of the impurely designative occurrence of "Giorgione" in "Giorgione is so-called because of his size" – which he excerpted for "Notes on Existence and Necessity," and of the virtual theory of classes, to which he was later to give a key role in *Philosophy of Logic* (Quine 1970) and *Set Theory and Its Logic* (1963). Much of the emerging historical literature on Quine concentrates on the evolution of the young Quine's semantic holism, his opposition to the analytic-synthetic distinction, and his philosophical relationship with Carnap. Several careful historical-philosophical works chart Quine's development from his earliest worries about analyticity in the 1930s, via the influence of Tarski in the 1940s, to his mature "Two Dogmas" view of 1951 (Creath 1990a, Hylton 2001, Ben-Menahem 2005, Mancosu 2008, Frost-Arnold 2011). Analyticity and Quine's rejection of conventionalism about meaning are among the key themes discussed in this book. Quine clearly considered *The Significance of the New Logic*'s sections on meaning and analyticity to be of consequence, since he selected them for publication in "Notes on Existence and Necessity." The ideas expressed in them also led to an intense exchange of letters between him and Carnap on their semantic differences over the course of 1943 (Creath 1990a, 295–377).

But, I will argue, this book is driven just as much by the philosophy of logic and ontology. These too were major motivating factors for the early Quine, although they have thus far not received as much attention in the historical literature. Much of the content of *The Significance of the New Logic* is best understood by considering Quine as part of a broader historical narrative, which I lay out in section 2; a précis of the main philosophical moves of the book follows in section 3. Quine is presented as an interlocutor not only to Carnap but also to Tarski, to Frege, to Quine's Ph.D. supervisor Whitehead, and to Whitehead's co-author Russell. Their three-volume magnum opus *Principia Mathematica*, inspired by Frege's new mathematical logic and his logicist thesis that mathematics was reducible to logic, had been the subject of Quine's 1932 Ph.D. thesis and of his first book based on that thesis (Quine 1934a). He began to appreciate Frege, whose work was difficult to get hold of in the United States at the time, a few years later. Unlike Carnap, these early analytic philosophers held that, in addition to epistemology and the analysis of language, metaphysical questions about existence and the nature of things were central to philosophy, too. The early Quine, I show, had much in common with Carnap, but not anti-metaphysics. Young Quine inclined, as Tarski had done, toward the modest metaphysics of nominalism, holding out hope for a unified science with a modest, concrete ontology (section 4). In this book Quine also made refinements to, and developed further arguments for, his own ontological views – including his four-dimensionalism – and his theory of ontological commitment (section 5). The crucial work on analyticity, modality, and impure designation familiar from "Notes on Existence and Necessity" is considered in its original Portuguese framing, and revealed to be entwined with Quine's commitment to extensionalism, and his desire to avoid abstract posits such as propositions and modal concepts (section 6). Lastly, I explore how his nominalistic leanings informed his philosophy of logic and mathematics (section 7).

2 The Historical Story: The Early Quine and the Period Leading up to *The Significance of the New Logic*

A deep admiration of *Principia Mathematica* had originally brought Quine to Harvard to work on a Ph.D. with Whitehead. Unfortunately, Whitehead had lost interest in mathematical logic some years before, when he had begun to devote himself to making sense of Einstein's general relativity by way of an involved and idiosyncratic event ontology. The more metaphysically cautious Quine concentrated on purging the *Principia* system of use–mention confusions. He completed his Ph.D. on that topic, under Whitehead's rather lax supervision, in just two years. At the suggestion of Feigl, Quine then secured a postdoctoral grant to travel to the European continent, in search of more like-minded spirits: the philosophers and logicians of the Vienna Circle and Polish School, but most of all Carnap.

Carnap's philosophy was driven first and foremost by a quest to make sense, in a scientifically respectable way, of truth, meaning, and justification as used in the empirical sciences, and in logic and mathematics. In addition, it was driven by anti-metaphysical attitudes. Opposition to metaphysics was common among Carnap's colleagues of the Vienna Circle and the Polish School. It was motivated to an extent by justified fears among those left-leaning intellectuals about metaphysics in the neo-Thomist, Heideggerian, and Hegelian styles finding their way into and fuelling the rise of fascist ideologies on the European continent (Uebel 2016, § 2.3). Carnap also thought of anti-metaphysics as an outgrowth of his semantic and epistemological project, his appeal to mathematical axioms as playing the role of implicit definitions of mathematical terms (Creath 1990b, 5–6). Quine had fallen under Carnap's spell because of his semantics and epistemology. He admired Carnap's attempts to put logic and mathematics on a naturalistically solid footing. He was less taken with Carnap's anti-metaphysical attitudes, which he came to reject some time before he had articulated well-developed objections to Carnap's position on analyticity. Quine shared Carnap's pragmatist sympathies and was not drawn to traditional metaphysics of the Platonist, neo-Aristotelian, or Hegelian kind. Yet he took existence questions arising from science and mathematics seriously. He did not consider them to be rendered meaningless or obsolete by Carnap's program. In this respect he resembled Frege, Russell, and Whitehead, as well as American pragmatists such as Peirce and James, not Carnap. Perhaps Quine had failed to develop an anti-metaphysical streak in part because the metaphysics of his culture of origin was much more sober and naturalistic than that of the cultures surrounding Carnap. Whitehead's event-ontology, James's empiricist anomalous monism, and Russell's project of logical construction, although not entirely

Quine's style, were all informed by those philosophers' respect for empiricism and science. Unlike Carnap, Quine did not have cause to associate metaphysics with dangerous political authoritarianism. He always favored a modest, empirically informed ontology.

In July 1934, some months before delivering the Carnap lectures (1990a [1934]) that he was later to call "abjectly sequacious" (Quine 1991, 266), Quine published his third journal article. It was his first publication on a topic other than mathematical logic. Its title was "Ontological Remarks on the Propositional Calculus," and its aim was to undermine what he describes as Frege's and Wittgenstein's views that sentences are the names of special logical posits, such as propositions or truth values. In 1936, in "Truth by Convention," he first published some of his reservations about analyticity. But those reservations were still fairly mild, elaborating on a suggestion made in the first Carnap lecture that it is easy to add further truths to the category of analytic stipulations (Creath 1990b, 30–31, Ben-Menahem 2005, 252–255). It would take him more than ten years to come to an alternative account of meaning, truth, and justification. As we will see in section 6, by the time of *The Significance of the New Logic* Quine, though expressing some hesitation, continued to draw on the notion of analyticity (see pp. 89–93 below). By contrast, Quine's account of ontology evolved far less hesitatingly, and more quickly. His theory of ontological commitment was almost fully formed by 1939. Two papers dating to that year express a version very close to the mature theory – except for some modifications which this book sheds light on, discussed in section 5. While certain expressions designate objects – these papers say – others, the syncategoremata, are meaningful without designating. If existentially generalizing on some expression is truth-preserving, that indicates that the expression designates an entity. In this way we can dispel apparent difficulties about nonexistence claims lacking subject matter, and meaningfully compare the advantages of nominalistic vs. realistic languages (Quine 1939a, Quine 1966 [1939]). The earlier of the two 1939 papers was not published until 1966, the *Erkenntnis/Journal of Unified Science* volume it was due to appear in having been derailed by the Second World War.

The Nazi occupation that precipitated that war proved catastrophic for Quine's friends, the members of the Polish School and the Vienna Circle. Many of them were Jewish, or left-wing and politically active. Those who could fled to the United States or the United Kingdom. Several of those who could not were murdered by the Nazis, such as the logicians Janina Hosiasson, Adolf Lindenbaum, Moses Presburger, and Mordechaj Wajsberg. The Polish logicians had made a significant impression on Quine. Tarski's name occurs frequently in *The Significance of the New Logic*. Łukasiewicz is also cited in its short bibliography. Another small sign of Polish influence is Quine's use of Kotarbinski's term "gnoseology" (meaning "theory of knowledge"; see the title of Kotarbinski 1966 [1929])[2] to rebut Carnap's conventionalism (see p. 14 below).

Quine had looked on in horror as Hitler occupied more and more of Europe in the late 1930s. He regularly voiced his worries about their European friends in letters to Carnap, who had already emigrated to the United States in 1935 (Quine 1990b, 260–268). Tarski, who was Jewish, arrived in 1939. He held a temporary position at Harvard for some time, partly thanks to Quine's efforts (Quine 1990b, 268). There he discussed logic, meaning, truth, and mathematical finitism with Quine and Carnap in 1940–41. Carnap's shorthand transcripts of their conversations have recently been deciphered, translated, and published (Frost-Arnold 2013). Tarski maintained – with Quine, against Carnap – that some scientifically respectable sense could be made of the old nominalism–Platonism debate (see also Quine 1990b, 295). A truly nominalistic mathematics, not invoking abstract numbers, sets, or expression types, might have to be finitist if there is a finite number of physical things in the universe, which Tarski thought might be the case (Carnap 2013 [1940–41], 153). It follows that certain statements generally held to express analytic mathematical truths, such as those expressing the existence of infinite sets or series, turn out not to be analytic after all. Discussing these ideas with Tarski may well have sparked or encouraged Quine's idea that it is possible not only to add extra analytic stipulations to our theories as he had maintained in 1936 but also to subtract some of them (Mancosu 2005, Frost-Arnold 2013, 84–87). By the early 1940s Quine had not yet completely given up on analyticity; it would take him another ten years to express in print the view that any stipulation is potentially revisable.

As the war raged on in 1941 and 1942, Quine was left with little time for philosophical research (Quine 1996, Preface). Having felt duty-bound to help defeat the Nazis, he had signed up for a technical assignment in the US Navy. His time was wholly taken up by a combination of teaching and preparing for his war work, until he was offered, and accepted, a three-month visiting professorship in São Paulo. A keen amateur linguist already proficient in French and German, Quine had picked up some conversational Portuguese while on sabbatical in the Azores in 1938. He was allowed to defer his commission as a naval officer, and flew to Brazil in May 1942. First, he delivered a lecture, "Os Estados Unidos e o Ressurgimento da Lógica," whose translation appears alongside the book in this volume, to the União Cultural Brasil–Estados Unidos. But his primary task was a Portuguese-

---

[2] Thanks to Thomas Uebel for bringing this point and Kotarbinski's book to my attention.

language lecture course aiming to introduce the new logic to Brazil, both its technical advances on the old Aristotelian logic and its potential for scientific and philosophical applications. The philosophy he had lacked the time to work on began once again to fall into place. He received significant help with the Portuguese from his Brazilian assistant, Vicente Ferreira da Silva, whose book on mathematical logic (Ferreira da Silva 1940) he had previously reviewed, and who later became a well-known existentialist (Quine 1997, 6). With Ferreira da Silva's help, Quine began to prepare the lectures for publication in book form. He did so partly because he was keen to publish the new material and to leave a legacy in Brazil, but also because the war had made him fear for the future of the Western world. His three-month appointment and the looming Navy commission left Quine pressed for time. He wrote all night. He lived off deep-fried street food. With days to spare, he finished correcting the proofs for *O Sentido da Nova Lógica* (Quine 1997, 7). Quine's usually consummate attention to detail could not quite withstand the pressure and the sleep deprivation; the book contains some misprints and typographical errors, indicated here in editorial footnotes and corrected in the text. There also appear to be some philosophical loose ends, half-finished trains of thought never quite completed, or picked up in a modified form several years after the war, when Quine's thinking had to an extent shifted. After completing the book, his technical work in the Navy took up nearly all of his time and attention until the war ended. Quine worked, with dedicated groups of mathematicians and cryptanalysts, on translating and analysing intercepted submarine communications – apparently quite successfully, as he was highly commended by his admiral (Lodge, Leary, and Quine 2015, 42).

Meanwhile the publication process of *O Sentido da Nova Lógica* dragged on, much to Quine's annoyance. It was held up by bureaucratic interference, the non-existence of Portuguese-speaking mathematical logicians to serve as plausible manuscript referees, and typesetting troubles. The first edition was finally published in 1944, on the rather brittle paper that resulted from shortages during the Second World War. Copies are now very rare. A second edition followed in 1996, with a new preface by Quine, and a third edition in 2016 (Quine 1996, Quine 2016). Our translation is based on the first edition.

3 *The Significance of the New Logic*: The Book and Its Content

What Quine called "the new logic" was indeed rather new in 1942. Kurt Gödel's incompleteness proof, published in 1931, was only eleven years old.

One year earlier, Susan Stebbing had published the first accessible book on contemporary logic and its philosophy (Stebbing 1930). Tarski's work on truth dated from 1933, but that was the Polish version; Quine and Carnap, who spoke German but no Polish, had had to wait for the German translation of 1935. In his Introduction to this book, Quine described the new logic as a response to Cantor's advances in transfinite arithmetic (see pp. 10–11 below) and to Russell's paradox and the related semantic paradoxes (12–13). The need for a new philosophy of logic had also become apparent. While we might previously have tried to identify logical (and mathematical) truth with provability, Gödel's incompleteness result made that identification impossible (17). Quine proposed instead a conception of logic as a universal science, one compatible with any area of enquiry. Such a universal science would treat all subject matters, and all objects, equally.

The Significance of the New Logic has some areas of overlap with Quine's introductory logic textbook *Elementary Logic* (Quine 1941) and with his expansive and technical *Mathematical Logic* (1940). Like *Elementary Logic* and *Mathematical Logic*, it takes as a point of departure a tripartite division of logic into the theory of composition (sentential logic), the theory of quantification (which, together with sentential logic, yields predicate logic), and the theory of classes. *The Significance of the New Logic* is more ambitious in scope and subject matter than *Elementary Logic*, which only covers the theories of composition and quantification. But it differs from *Mathematical Logic* in being aimed at a non-expert audience. Convinced of the new logic's potential for revolutionizing science and mathematics, Quine took on the task of introducing analytic philosophy neophytes not only to recent advances in philosophical thinking about identity, existence, meaning, modality, and description but also to the theory of classes.

The book's philosophical remarks on statements, in Chapter I which focuses on the theory of composition, have much in common with those in *Elementary Logic*. In both books Quine took statements, the substituends for the ps and qs of sentential logic, to be declarative sentences with timeless verbs and without indexicals, articulating a sort of precursor of his later account of eternal sentences (Quine 1941, 6, §§ 36, 40, and see p. 19 below). In both books he appealed to pragmatic reasons to explain away apparent paradoxes of the material conditional, a strategy we now associate with the later works of Grice. Quine was an early adopter of this style of argument in *Elementary Logic*, although the argument in *The Significance of the New Logic* is worked out in more detail:

In practice we do not utter conditionals when the truth values of their components are already known. But this does not stop us from identifying 'if p then q' with '~ (p • ~ q)', because it is equally obvious that in practice we would not use a compound of the form '~ (p • ~ q)', any more than 'if p then q', when we already know what the truth values of the components are . . . we could provide more information in less space by only affirming 'q' or denying 'p'.

(see p. 32 below; cf. Quine 1941, 21)

In both books he proposed to read 'or' as inclusive, but in this book he adds some further arguments for that conclusion. They include one natural-language case due to Tarski (see pp. 30–31 below), and further appeals to pragmatics:

consider the expression 'x $\leq$ y' . . . 'x < y' and 'x = y' are in themselves mutually exclusive, or incompatible . . . '~ (x < y • x = y)' [is] added to the statement ['~ (~ x < y • ~ x = y)'] with the inclusive sense to produce a statement with the exclusive sense. But this additional conjunct is a known truth (given any x and y) that we can therefore freely insert or omit. To omit it is not to deny it; we never say everything that we know.

(see pp. 29–30 below)

Quine's philosophical reflections on quantification theory in Chapter II do not go far beyond those of *Elementary Logic*, apart from a practical application to insurance calculations also discussed in his "Relations and Reason" (Quine 1939b). New material on the philosophical applications of quantification appears in Chapter III, including several forerunners of arguments made famous by "On What There Is" (Quine 1948). The technical treatment of predicate logic in this book resembles *Mathematical Logic* more than *Elementary Logic*, using truth-table techniques for sentential logic and matrices for quantification theory.

The Significance of the New Logic deploys a simplified version of the symbolism of *Principia Mathematica*, with parentheses to avoid ambiguity, a single (universal) quantifier, and two primitive sentence connectives – the tilde for denial, and the *Principia* dot '•' for conjunction. (Apparently unknown to Brazilian typesetters, the *Principia* dot comes out looking rather square and elongated in the first edition and has transmogrified into an underscore by the second.) All the other operators of predicate logic are defined in terms of those three primitives; the primitive of membership is added in Chapter IV. This system is austere, just one step removed from the simplest possible system, with just one primitive each for the theories of composition, quantification, and classes – that is, the Sheffer stroke, universal quantifier, and membership sign respectively. Quine impressed upon the reader how much can be proved within this tiny, yet powerful, symbolism: in particular, the logicist conclusion of *Principia Mathematica* that 'every mathematical law is an abbreviation of a logical law' (see p. 13 below).

Principia Mathematica also looms large in the philosophy this book contains, both with respect to its treatment of intensionality and its treatment of classes. Quine sought to unite the logico-mathematical power of Frege's work and of *Principia* with his preference for an austere extensional language (also see section 6). Frege had invoked abstract senses. *Principia*, at least according to Quine's interpretation of it, retained some proposition-like entities under the guise of facts (Quine 1981b [1966], 81–82). Quine wanted to steer clear of such posits. The material excerpted for "Notes on Existence and Necessity" is framed differently in this book: as an explicit answer to Frege's use of senses as the referents of phrases in intensional contexts (Frege 1892). Quine felt he had made a great leap forward in *The Significance of the New Logic* by (tentatively) invoking linguistic objects – words, or sentences in quotation marks – instead of senses. Propositional attitudes can then be accounted for – without violating extensionality – as attitudes to sentences, and necessity as ascription of analyticity to a sentence. Progress in this area also informed Quine's account of ontology. Names, too, are on occasion used in intensional contexts where they are not (or not purely) designative – they do not designate a referent (or not only a referent), but a linguistic object. This, combined with Russell's theory of descriptions, implies that ontological commitments cannot be incurred by the use of names but only by bound variables in existential quantifications: 'the pronoun is always the main vehicle of reference to objects; this was made apparent by our reflections on the non-designative occurrence of names . . . now the pronoun, which was already the main vehicle of reference, has become the only one' (see p. 104 below). New arguments in favor of his theory of ontological commitment also appear in this book, forerunners of arguments used in "On What There Is," rebutting Meinongianism and propounding the univocity of ontological vocabulary (see section 5).

The theories of composition and quantification were then, and are now, held to be logic unequivocally. How to classify the third item on Quine's tripartite list, the theory of classes, was less obvious. Frege, Russell, and Whitehead counted the theory of classes as logic, too; that assumption was necessary to their logicist project. But Quine leaned toward considering the theory of classes part of mathematics (Quine 1941, 3). Why, then, did Quine so boldly assert that "Pure mathematics is reducible to logic" in this book (see p. 13 below), having previously attached more qualifiers to the logicist thesis (Quine 1941, 3, Quine 1981a [1940], 5)? There is no explicit answer in this book. To an extent, this is one of its loose ends not fully tidied up before Quine was rushed to the end of his stay in Brazil, and thus to the end of the book. An implicit answer may lie in Quine's virtual theory of classes (see pp. 129–131 below).

Frege's original version of the theory of classes had seemed simple, elegant, and intuitive. But it was famously inconsistent. Assuming that for any specified condition a corresponding class exists, it entailed the existence of self-membered classes – for instance, the class of all classes – as well as non-self-membered ones – for instance, the class of all elephants. Russell's paradox loomed: The class of all non-self-membered objects both is and is not a member of itself (see p. 12 below). A variety of restrictions on the conditions that determine a class were proposed. *Principia Mathematica*'s version deployed the theory of types to yield the necessary restrictions, and reduced arithmetic to logic in that way. Yet it was criticized for relying on two arguably non-logical axioms: the axiom of reducibility and the axiom of infinity, which states that there are infinitely many things in the world. (As we saw above, this was an assumption Tarski had denounced as intolerable at Harvard in 1941, and the young Quine had been inclined to agree.) In *The Significance of the New Logic*, Quine opted for a restriction he attributed to von Neumann:

> certain classes cannot belong to classes. We call *elements* all objects that are members of classes . . . the new *restricted principle of abstraction* will be that, given any matrix whose free pronoun is 'x', there is a class whose members are exactly the *elements* (instead of 'objects', as earlier) that satisfy the matrix.
>
> *(see p. 113 below)*

But Quine also added the virtual theory of classes – concisely expressed in a single section (see pp. 128–131 below) – which he regarded as a breakthrough because it allowed him to simulate quantification over classes or sets. Initially, the class membership notation had been introduced with variables of quantification on either side, as in 'x ε y'. But to say that x is a member of y is, *prima facie*, to affirm the existence of both x and y. The virtual theory of classes sidesteps the question of the existence of classes by dropping the primitive predicate of membership altogether. Instead, certain set-theoretic principles are taken to be definable in terms of schematic predicate letters, such as 'f = g' for '(x) (fx ≡ gx)' (for monadic f and g; '(x) (y) (fxy ≡ gxy)' for dyadic f and g, and so on up). The underlying principle is that statements of the form 'y is a member of the class of f things' – 'y ε x̂fx' – are translated into the form 'fy', so that no variables range over classes.

A virtual theory of classes will be weaker than the full theory of arithmetic (see pp. 130–131 below). But for any finite collection of objects, each of which can truly be said to satisfy some predicate, statements involving those predicates can be translated into set-theoretic language by means of the virtual theory. Tarski, the year before, had instilled in Quine a desire to find a finitist mathematics, one that applied exactly to the things contained within the physical world. It may be that Quine was hopeful that his virtual theory of classes could help provide the physicalistic, finitist mathematics Tarski had longed for, avoiding Russell and Whitehead's implausible claim that the existence of an infinite number of objects was *a priori* or analytic. The war intervened, and by the time Quine returned to set theory, his commitment to nominalism had waned. Finitist mathematics no longer seemed philosophically viable. Later on, Quine put the virtual theory to good use elsewhere, in support of his position that logic proper, unlike set theory, has no ontology (Quine 1970, 66–68). That position, too, had already been apparent in *The Significance of the New Logic*, where he credited to Tarski the insight that "Whatever logic asserts is what can be asserted about the objects of any of the sciences" (see p. 13 below). Quine took it to imply that logic cannot have an ontology of its own. "The theory of classes, in contrast with logic in the strict sense, implies an ontology" (see p. 111 below). His philosophy of logic was always deeply entwined with his views on ontology, although the latter grew more permissive over the years (e.g. his views on mathematical ontology discussed in section 7 below). In this early period, Quine – perhaps partly under the influence of Tarski, whose name is frequently mentioned in this book – still entertained the possibility of a nominalistic ontology.

4 The Early Quine's Nominalistic Tendencies

Even when he still favored Carnap's views on language and epistemology, the young Quine had been unimpressed with the positivistic contention that meta-physical claims lack meaning in any scientifically respectable sense. Positivists held that all metaphysical claims and their negations were pseudo-statements, not verifiable and therefore not capable of being, properly speaking, true or false. Quine had not adhered to that doctrine even in 1934, in his "Ontological Remarks on the Propositional Calculus." Having raised the metaphysical-sounding question "What manner of things are these, whose names are sen-tences?" (1934b, 472), he did not, as a positivist would have done, dismiss it as meaningless and unanswerable. He considered some possible answers to the question – facts, propositions – before providing his own answer: There are no such entities. To the positivist, a negative answer to an ontological question is as bad as a positive one. A pseudo-statement and its negation are equally nonsensical; the nominalist is just as much of a metaphysician as the realist. Even at this early stage, while still a self-professed Carnapian, Quine was flouting positivistic proscriptions. Just like Frege or Russell, he engaged in ontological enquiry. Five years later, while still in thrall to Carnap in many respects, he addressed positivist anti-metaphysics outright, and rebutted it: "We are tempted at this point to dismiss the whole issue between nominalism and realism as a metaphysical pseudoproblem. But in thus cutting the Gordian knot we cut too deep" (Quine 1939a, 704). And by the time Quine came to Brazil, he had explicitly made it part of his mission to explain the new logic's utility in making ontology scientifically respectable again, aiming to answer "even questions of an ontological nature such as 'What is there?' and 'What is real?'" (see p. 17 below), and to overturn "the conclusions of the Vienna Circle," as Chisholm notes in his review of Quine's lecture (Chisholm 1947, 484).

What alternative to positivist anti-metaphysics did Quine propose? A common theme throughout Quine's body of work, early and late, is a modest, frugal, naturalistic account of metaphysics, concentrating especially on assessing what existence claims we have reason to believe based on our best scientific theories (Janssen-Lauret 2015, 147–154, Janssen-Lauret 2017, 250–255). But what kinds of things he admitted as modest, empirically based posits varied over the years. In these early works, Quine still harbored hope that some form of nominalism, some philosophical view "admitting only concrete objects" (see p. 105 below), might win the day. He still thought that a unified science drawing only upon nominalistic resources might materialize, even though it appeared difficult to achieve. As he had said in 1939: "nominalism can be formulated thus: it is possible to set up a nominalistic language in which all of natural science can be expressed" (1939a, 708).

The later Quine is sometimes interpreted as a nominalist because of his aversion to positing such things as properties, propositions, and possibilia. But by that point, Quine himself had relinquished the label of "nominalist." He took several of the positions he held to be incompatible with nominalism, especially his commitment to abstract objects, owing to quantification over numbers in physics (Quine 1981), and his diffidence about the distinction between concrete and abstract objects, following advances in field theory (Quine 1976, 499). Even in the earlier works his nominalist leanings were rather tentatively expressed.[3] In *The Significance of the New Logic*, he stopped short of outright committing himself to nominalism. At several crucial points he devoted space to discussing nominalists' commitments – refusing to posit numbers at all, refusing to posit numbers that do not number any collection of physical objects

---

[3] An exception is Goodman and Quine 1947, but since it is a joint paper, the more explicit expressions of nominalism there may indicate Goodman's influence rather than a change of heart on Quine's part.

(see p. 96 below), having a distaste for classes and properties (see pp. 105–107 below) – and treated them sympathetically. He remarked that opponents of abstract objects might view the failure of the unrestricted principle of class abstraction, and Gödel's incompleteness proof, as victories (see p. 138 below). A few years later, he was to cite incompleteness and the class paradoxes as "motivations for nominalism" (Quine 2008b [1946], 18–19). Still, back in the early 1940s, he also claimed that we must prioritize robust examination of the apparently realist foundations of mathematics over our "prior ontological dogma" (see p. 105 below).

There appears to be some echo of Carnap on the last page of this book, where some role is still assigned to "pseudo-statements" (see p. 138 below). But Quine's use of the label was misleading. The statements in question are not metaphysical. Nor are they dismissed as useless. They are the statements of classical mathematics, and the reason that they fall short of being statements is that, although they are useful, there are no abstract objects for them to be true (or false) about.

In *The Significance of the New Logic* and other nominalistically inclined writings of the period, Quine gave no explicit argument in favor of nominalism but wrote, in his Harvard nominalism lecture, "I'll put my cards on the table now and avow my prejudices: I should like to be able to accept nominalism" (Quine 2008b [1946], 9). These days, Quine's austere ontology is often attributed to an adherence to the maxim "no entity without identity." But worries about identification were less central to Quine's opposition to abstract posits in the early 1940s. It is true he notes that the identification criteria for classes are very clear, while the answer to the question "Under what condition do two matrices determine the same attribute?" (see p. 106 below) is obscure. But the early Quine remained dissatisfied with classes, despite their clear criteria of identity. He complained that they, "being abstract objects, are less clear and familiar than we might wish" (see p. 106 below). Later on in the book, he attempted to do away with them altogether by means of the virtual theory. At the time, his main objection to positing classes appears to have been their purported abstract nature, rather than their criteria of identity. In this respect his position at the time resembled classic nominalism more than his mature views on ontology. It was only around the time of "On What There Is" (1948) that concerns about identification began to outweigh nominalistic factors in Quine's estimation. Whereas in 1947 he had written off possibilia as incompatible with materialism (Quine 1947, 47), in 1948 his main argument against possibilia was that they lack clear criteria of identity (1948, 23). Generally, his reliance on criteria of identity appears to have grown as his conception of objects became more structuralist over the years, viewing posits increasingly as best explanations of intersections in our network of observations (Janssen-Lauret 2015, 155–157). By the early 1940s Quine's justifications for preferring one range of posits over another had not yet reached that level of sophistication. He articulated no argument stronger than our finding concrete posits more "clear and familiar" than abstract ones (see p. 106 below). Since the early Quine showed no inclination to doubt our right to talk about and assume the existence of physical objects like rivers (see pp. 80–81 below) or horses (see pp. 95–96 below), he may have been trying to dispense with the abstract in a quest for ontological parsimony. A sparse nominalistic language in which to formulate a unified science still seemed potentially within reach. Several of the moves made in this book make more sense when viewed through this modestly metaphysical, nominalistically inclined lens.

5 Ontology and Meta-Ontology

The Significance of the New Logic contains new material both on the topic of Quine's ontology – his answer to the question "What exists?" – as well as what has come to be called his "meta-ontology" – his account of how existence claims are attributed to speakers or theories – which Quine himself tended to call "ontological commitment," "ontic commitment," or "imputations of ontology." Quine was physicalistically inclined; his physicalism went hand in hand with his nominalistic sympathies. Although this book focuses on logic and its philosophy, his physicalism is visible in his expressions of four-dimensionalism about ordinary objects. Quine had first appealed to four-dimensionalism in 1939. Even then he had treated it as rather old hat, a position obviously familiar to his audience: "[t]he four-dimensional spatio-temporal view of nature is a device for facilitating logical analysis by rendering verbs tenseless" (Quine 1939a, 701). In *The Significance of the New Logic* he went beyond that familiar point – "Bucephalus is an extended portion of the spatio-temporal world [with] a spatial extension of several hectoliters and a temporal one of several years . . . far away from here" (see p. 95 below) – and developed an early version of the position of "Identity, Ostension, and Hypostasis" (Quine 1953a [1950]). He deployed four-dimensionalism in giving an account of the persistence of everyday objects. "Consider the river. It is an extended object, in time as well as in space . . . [it] remains the same river while it lasts; it remains the same identical totality of its various instantaneous states" (see p. 80 below). Such persistence conditions are used in this book to demystify apparent puzzles of change and identity over time. Later Quine saw them as contributing to a criterion of identity for rivers by, as he put it in the later, further developed version, "reading identity in place of river kinship" (Quine 1953a [1950], 66). In this book the notion of criteria of identity remains embryonic, not yet fully articulated.

Quine stressed that while nominalism is a constraining force on the nominalist's own ontology, it does not constrain a Quinean meta-ontology. Ontological commitments can be incurred to numbers or properties just as much as to rivers, horses, or particles; "there is" and "exists" mean the same whether the purported objects are concrete or abstract. This argument, the argument from the univocity of ontological vocabulary, is one of several arguments presented for the first time in this book that are clear precursors to arguments made famous by "On What There Is." In this book, as in that paper, Quine held that ontological vocabulary does not shift its meaning depending on what name or description it is concatenated with: "[t]hose who doubt (3) ['There is such a thing as the number 9^{9^9}'], as well as those who accept (3), understand the phrase 'there is such a thing as' in (3) in the same sense as in (1) ['There is such a thing as Bucephalus'] and (2) ['~ there is such a thing as Pegasus']" (see pp. 95–96 below). Here, as there, he claimed that it is not "exists" that has spatio-temporal connotations but certain terms purportedly designating certain objects: "[t]o deny that there is such a thing as Pegasus means that the object is not found in space and time, but ... only because, if there were such a thing as Pegasus, it would be a spatio-temporal object" (see p. 96 below).

The example of the non-existence of a disease – where diseases are taken to be abstract objects – is used in this book as well as in "Designation and Existence," but in support of different conclusions. In 1939, Quine had used the non-existence of the made-up disease hyperendemic fever to infer that "understanding of a term ... does not imply a designatum" (Quine 1939a, 703). In *The Significance of the New Logic*, by contrast, he used the example to invalidate the distinction between existence (for concrete objects) and subsistence (for abstract objects). He contended that the distinction is void because empirical facts can prove the existence or non-existence of a purported abstract object:

> introduce the expression "Paraná fever" as an abbreviation of the expression "the sickness that annihilated the majority of the inhabitants of Curitiba in the year 1903." The question ... whether there is such a sickness as an abstract object – is resolved only by means of the observation of nature ... Paraná fever does not exist – nor does it "subsist," even as an abstract object.

(see p. 96 below)

One of the well-known arguments in "On What There Is" appears to have been partly inspired by Quine's assistant, the young Brazilian Vicente Ferreira da Silva. Objecting to the vague supposition that there are different kinds of existence, or existence in a "plurality of worlds" (see p. 95 below), Quine cited his assistant's book as saying "different forms of existence ... are completely puerile" (Ferreira da Silva 1940, 33, quoted by Quine – see p. 95 below). Here, as in "On What There Is," Quine rebutted the potential reply that Pegasus exists as a mental entity. "The ideas of Bucephalus and Pegasus are not designated by the words 'Bucephalus' and 'Pegasus' in (1) and (2), but by other expressions: 'the idea of Bucephalus,' 'the idea of Pegasus'" (see p. 95 below).[4] All these new arguments in favor of a Quinean approach to ontological commitment may be connected to his novel conception, first put forward in this book, of logic as the science that applies to any domain of objects. Likewise, quantification may range over any domain of objects, concrete or abstract (see pp. 97–100 below). A logic-based approach to the ontological problem, Quinean ontological commitment treats all objects, concrete or abstract, equally, just like logic itself treats all objects equally.

Lastly, a significant meta-ontological shift taking place in the early 1940s was Quine's severing the link between names and ontology. In Quine's first foray into ontology in 1934, he had focused wholly on names as denoting terms. Without mentioning variables at all, he reached the conclusion that sentences do not name any special logical posits. Such posits would, implausibly, turn rules of derivation into law-like statements about certain objects: "[o]nce we postulate entities whereof sentences are symbols, the logical principles for manipulating sentences become principles concerning the entities – propositions – which the sentences denote" (1934b, 473). Logical rules are better understood as governing sentences themselves, not objects to which sentences refer, and therefore "the whole notion of sentences as names is superfluous" (1934b, 473). Although it speaks of names instead of variables, the paper prefigures several of Quine's later ontological and meta-ontological convictions. First, it shows him opposing positivist anti-metaphysics by taking existence questions seriously. Secondly, when we see him opting for the existence of sentences rather than propositions, his nominalistic and ontologically parsimonious tendencies are on display. Thirdly, it reveals that even at this early stage he explicitly connected the answers to ontological questions with the designating expressions of a true theory.

---

[4] Frege also makes this point in "Über Sinn und Bedeutung" (Frege 1892, 32), a paper that Quine cites as a notable influence on this book (see p. 83 n. iii below).

By the late 1930s Quine had begun to use the medieval term "categoremata" for expressions that designate objects and "syncategoremata" for terms that are meaningful without standing for something. Proper names are a typical example of the former; typical examples of the latter are such things as brackets, punctuation, and logical connectives. The medieval nominalism–realism debate was phrased in terms of the question whether predicates were syncategorematic or categorematic. In 1939, Quine had still thought that names were the expressions that revealed a theory's ontology. "To ask whether there is such an entity as roundness is thus not to question the meaningfulness of 'roundness'; it amounts rather to asking whether this word is a name or a syncategorematic expression" (Quine 1966 [1939], 197). He distinguished, then, between apparent names and names "in the semantic sense," that is, names with bearers. Only the latter stand for existents. Only they, not apparent names, are relevant to ontology: "the word 'Pegasus' is not a name in the semantic sense, i.e., ... it has no designatum" (Quine 1939a, 703). Although "Existence and Designation" contains the phrase "to be is to be the value of a variable," and puts it to ontological use, at the time Quine still spoke of genuine names being substituends for variables – the real word–world connection was still presumed to lie with names. By the late 1940s he had explicitly abjured any utility of proper names to ontology. By that point, he took only variables, not names, to be the paradigmatic categoremata: "The use of alleged names is no criterion, for we can repudiate their namehood at the drop of a hat unless the assumption of a corresponding entity can be spotted in the things we affirm in terms of bound variables" (Quine 1948, 32). When and why did Quine's change of heart occur?

We first find Quine stating that names are inessential in *Mathematical Logic*, on the grounds that they can always be converted into Russellian definite descriptions (Quine 1981a [1940], 151).[5] *The Significance of the New Logic* combines an expanded version of the *Mathematical Logic* argument with Quine's novel distinction between occurrences of names that are purely designative, serving only to single out their designata, and occurrences that are not purely designative. The latter do not merely talk about their designata (if they have them at all) but say something about an expression they occur in. "Giorgione is so-called because of his size" says something about the name "Giorgione" as well as about the artist Giorgione. "Pegasus does not exist" says something about the term "Pegasus" – namely, that it does not designate. It does not say something about the winged horse Pegasus – in particular, it does not attribute the special attribute of non-existence to him – because there is no such

---

[5] Quine's argument here is of dubious validity. For details, see Janssen-Lauret 2016, 597–601.

horse. Quine started out by distinguishing, as he had in 1939, between names in the semantic sense, which always designate, and terms that look like names but may or may not designate, which he called substantives (see p. 94 below). But he began to prepare the ground to admit only one kind of substantive: the pronoun. "It is not the mere use of a substantive, but its designative use, that commits us to the acceptance of an object designated by the substantive" (see p. 98 below). With that distinction in place, Quine was in a position to dispense with names for the purposes of ontology.

One key difference between occurrences that are purely designative and occurrences that are not is that the former do allow for existential generalization, but the latter do not. Apparent names can have non-designative occurrences; variables in existentially quantified claims cannot. So only bound variables in existential quantifications are truly categoremata; names are not. Quine then proceeded to introduce a convention for eliminating names altogether: convert them all into descriptions. Descriptions, in turn, are analysed in the Russellian way as quantifier phrases beginning with existential quantifiers. Thus they wear their ontological commitments on their sleeves. Some names already have a descriptive matrix associated with them, but, Quine argued, even if the names are primitive, they can easily be transformed into a descriptive matrix. We turn the name into a verb, such as "europizes" for "Europe," or "pegasizes" for "Pegasus." Quine had arrived at the more familiar formulation of ontological commitment: "All objects remain as before, but contact between objects and language is concentrated in the pronoun. The ontology to which a given use of language commits us simply includes the totality of objects within the range of the quantifier" (see p. 104 below).

But the *Significance of the New Logic* position is to an extent unstable. It has trouble accounting for certain parts of the logic of identity. Although it is a logical truth that everything is identical to itself, it is always logically possible for two things satisfying all and only the same predicates and descriptions to be, nevertheless, distinct. As Barcan Marcus pointed out, the equivalence expressed by means of two descriptions is weaker than that expressed by two names flanking the identity predicate. Although in natural language we might write "The author of Jane Eyre = the elder sister of Emily Brontë," its underlying logical form is really '$\exists x((Ax \land \forall y(Ay \to x = y)) \land \exists z(Sz \land \forall w(Sw \to z = w)) \land x = z)$'. Only variables appear next to the identity sign in that sentence. Names can also flank the identity sign – as in '$a = b$' – but descriptions themselves cannot. Barcan Marcus argued that this was because descriptive vocabulary and names have importantly distinct logical roles. Descriptive vocabulary employs predicates to ascribe characteristics. Even if certain predicates are uniquely satisfied, from a logical point of view, predicates have a semantic role that enables them to apply to more than one thing. By contrast, names have the special semantic role of referring directly to individuals; therefore they can only apply to one thing. Jointly with identity, names can be used to express sameness of thing. Descriptions only encode sameness of characteristics, which does not logically guarantee sameness of thing – even if in certain cases it is sufficient to infer sameness of thing (Barcan Marcus 1961, 310). Quine's 1940s' position is vulnerable to the objection that it leaves no role for the logical truth that indiscernibles can always be distinct.

Quine's mature position circumvented this objection by combining the dispensability of names with an idiosyncratic interpretation of the identity predicate. The later Quine replied to Barcan Marcus that, according to his view, the identity sign is not a logical predicate, expressing sameness of thing. It is a dummy predicate expressing, for each language, indiscernibility with respect to all the predicates of that language (Quine 1961).

6 Impure Designation, Quotation, Modality, and Extensionality

The historical context, and the early Quine's nominalistic leanings, also help us understand the connections drawn in this book between impure designation, quotation, modality, and analyticity. Although nowadays all of these are considered separate, mostly independent matters, in Quine's early work they are all deeply entwined. Much of the work on impure reference, analyticity, and modality is already familiar to us because it was published in "Notes on Existence and Necessity." It is also well known for its key influence on the debate between Quine and Carnap on semantics and analyticity. Quine's fledgling ideas sparked a large volume of correspondence between the two over the following year, all the more remarkable because Quine was kept very busy with his work for the US Navy (Creath 1990a, 294–377). But again there is also an ontological side to the story. Quine's fast-evolving thoughts on quotation, designation, modality, and analyticity are tied together by their links to his account of ontological commitment and his own ontology. In addition, there are under-explored historical connections, not only to *Principia* but also to Frege.

Despite Quine's Ph.D. and early publication record being focused on mathematical and philosophical logic, he had not had much exposure to Frege's work until the late 1930s, because it had not been widely available. We know that Quine must have looked at the *Grundgesetze* in the early 1930s, since he cites it briefly (1934b, 472). Still, Quine had not formed a full picture of Frege's importance to the field until he started adding historical notes to his *Mathematical Logic* manuscript. Even then, he only had limited access to Frege's writings. He could not find a copy of the *Begriffsschrift* in all of North America (1986a, 21). Nevertheless, during his stay in Brazil Quine still appears to have been much struck by Frege. His assistant, Vicente Ferreira da Silva, had clearly noticed, as he gave Quine a portrait of Frege as a present. Years later Quine still reminisced about the sad loss of that picture on his flight home (Quine 1986a, 24). Frege's influence is also palpable in *The Significance of the New Logic*. Where "Notes on Existence and Necessity" starts off with some brief philosophical remarks on identity and Leibniz's law, in the Portuguese original the material is framed in explicitly Fregean terms instead. There is a footnote attributing the "essential content" (see p. 83 n. iii below) of the sections on impure designation and modality to "Über Sinn und Bedeutung" (Frege 1892). Quine's efforts can be seen as an attempt to preserve Frege's insights compatibly with his own nominalist ontological sympathies.

Chapter III starts off on a pro-metaphysical, anti-positivist note with a rebuttal of early Wittgenstein's treatment of identity. The philosophy of logic of Wittgenstein's *Tractatus* (1922 [1921]), according to which all logical truths were mere tautologies and all philosophy a critique of language, had been enthusiastically endorsed by the philosophers of the Vienna Circle – especially by its "right" wing, headed by Schlick and Waismann – who assigned mathematics to the realm of the tautologous, too (Uebel 2017, 705–708). The early Wittgenstein had held that statements of identity are either empty or nonsensical, claiming we could not sensibly say that two things are the same, and only rather pointlessly say that one thing is one and the same. Quine swiftly dismissed him as "not distinguishing carefully between objects and their names" (see p. 81 below), countering that it is perfectly sensible and not at all pointless to concatenate two distinct names of the same thing with the identity sign. Demystifying metaphysical disputes by carefully separating word and designatum is a crucial theme of these discussions, and also a principle central to Quine's views on ontology and meta-ontology. We saw above that he disavowed ontological commitment in cases where apparent names do not occur designatively. His answer to a host of confusions about metaphysical topics was to distinguish clearly between occurrences of substantives that are designative and those that are either non-designative or not purely designative.

In this book, Quine can be seen to be grasping toward an extensionalist theory. His preference was for a science stated wholly in extensional terms, on the model of the extensional theory of mathematics (see p. 94 below). Quine developed an analogy between statements of ontology, where the validity of existential generalization indicates the assumption of an entity, and extensional statements, where quantification into a certain context yields sensible results and substitutivity of co-referential names is truth-preserving. As Frege had pointed out, Leibniz's law fails in contexts where we attribute propositional attitudes; we cannot freely substitute co-referential expressions for each other in those cases. Frege concluded that, in such contexts, what is referred to is not what the referent would have been in extensional contexts but rather the expression's sense. Abstract Fregean senses were unattractive posits to Quine, given his nominalistic leanings. He undertook to explain matters using only the less controversial posits of physical objects and human language. Although he was pleased with the suggestions he made in this book (Quine 1996, 7), they are often made rather tentatively (see pp. 85–86 below). Some were later embraced enthusiastically, some were adapted to account for later development of his views.

While the ontological motivation was significant for Quine, there is one probable additional influence, namely *Principia Mathematica*'s referential transparency. Although it is not discussed in this book, *Principia*'s solution to substitution failures is closer to Quine's than Frege's. Whitehead and Russell had called an occurrence "referentially transparent" just in case nothing is said of it, but by means of it something is said of something else (1964 [1910], Appendix C). Quine was later to embrace their terminology, although by that point he applied it to contexts rather than occurrences (Quine 1953b, 142). Like Quine in this book, and unlike Frege, Russell and Whitehead used a characterization that implies that the difference lies in whether the occurrence in question is wholly in the object language, being used only to denote or connote, or whether it in any way relies upon either the form of the expression itself or the form of the sentence in which it occurs. Like Quine's, Russell and Whitehead's characterization leaves room for cases that rely on the reference as well as the form of an expression, although Quine is the only one among them who presents a worked-out version of such a case. Quine's version of the doctrine in this book suggests explicitly what *Principia* hints at: that non-purely designative occurrences – or in middle-Quine parlance, opaque ones – have an element of quotation to them.

The simplest such case is the straightforward quotation context, such as "'Leibniz' has exactly seven letters." Here the opposite of referential transparency is true: something is said of the name, and the name is not used to say something of something else. That is, it occurs non-designatively. The statement quoted above is equally true whether the name stands for anything or not. Substitution of co-referential names fails: Leibniz was also called

Gottfried, but "'Gottfried' has exactly seven letters" is false. Existential generalization fails, too: "'Something' has exactly seven letters" is equally false. As we've seen, non-existence claims also contain non-designative occurrences of substantives. In "Pegasus does not exist," the substantive "Pegasus" is not used to say something of something else. But something is said of the substantive: that it does not name anything. Intersubstitutivity does not apply where there is no reference, and existential generalization fails spectacularly, yielding the nonsensical "There is something such that it does not exist."

The case of "Giorgione is so-called because of his size" is different. Here "Giorgione" is used designatively. It is used to truly say something of something else, namely of the painter Giorgio Barbarelli, known as "Giorgione," or "big George," because he was large. Everything true of Giorgione must, by Leibniz's law, remain true if we refer to him by his last name. But Barbarelli is not so-called because of his size. The first quoted sentence of this paragraph becomes false upon substitution of co-referential terms, and meaningless upon existential generalization on "Giorgione"; there is no sense to be made of "Something is so-called because of its size." The occurrence of "Giorgione" within the first quoted sentence has a dual role: something is said of it – that it applies by virtue of its referent's size – and by means of it something is also said of something else, because it singles out Giorgione. What is said of the painter in question is true not only because of what he is like but also because of the form of his name, since the Italian suffix "-one" connotes largeness. The occurrence is designative, but not purely designative. We need quotation to make clear what the point of the sentence is. When it is fully spelled out as "Giorgione was called 'Giorgione' because of his size," substitution of co-referential names and existential generalization once again yield sensible results. "Barbarelli was called 'Giorgione' because of his size" and "Someone was called 'Giorgione' because of his size" are both true.

Quotation contexts can also be brought in to account for propositional attitude ascriptions. Suppose Philip knows Marcus Tullius Cicero only as "Cicero," and is unaware of the English version of his *nomen gentile*. Then, substituting "Tully" for "Cicero" in "Philip believes that Cicero denounced Catiline" yields a falsehood – even though Quine optimistically entertained "no doubt" at all that Philip does believe that of Cicero (see p. 85 below). Existential generalization is also problematic: "there is something such that Philip is unaware that it denounced Catiline" is not obviously a true statement about Marcus Tullius Cicero. How are we to interpret the that-clause in the first quoted sentence of this paragraph? Frege had held that it refers to a sense, an abstract propositional object. But Quine preferred to avoid abstract objects, and would rather continue on the path that had worked so well for him in explaining the Giorgione case: appealing to both the form of the expressions and their designata. "Philip believes that Cicero denounced Catiline" likewise says something of "Cicero denounced Catiline" as well as of Cicero and Catiline. Quine speculated that the real logical form of "Philip believes that Cicero denounced Catiline" might be "Philip believes the sentence 'Cicero denounced Catiline.'" He was later to endorse this line wholeheartedly (Quine 1970, 14).

Lastly, Quine extended the quotation-context analysis to include modality. He tentatively put forward the suggestion that even modality might be quotational, if defined in terms of analyticity. In that case "□p" might be rendered as an instance of the schema "x is analytic," where "x" is replaced with a quotation-name of the sentence substituted for "p" in "□p" (see pp. 89–91 below). Modal statements, then, would simply be claims about sentences, too. But by invoking analyticity, Quine had gone beyond comfortably physicalistic talk of expressions and their spatio-temporal designata. It had become necessary to talk about meaning. As his account of meaning underwent a sea-change between this book and his mature period, this part of the account did, too. While Quine held firm to his quotation analysis of propositional attitudes, his account of modality eventually expanded to make some limited sense of essence (Janssen-Lauret 2017, 261–262). The quotation analysis of 1944 blocks all quantification into modal contexts, and Quine continued to maintain that such quantification made no sense in 1951 (1951, 22). Under the influence of Barcan Marcus (Barcan 1947, Barcan Marcus 1961, Barcan Marcus 1967), Quine grudgingly began to admit that such quantification was coherent. Even essence, he eventually conceded, was not a wholly incoherent notion, merely an inconstant one, varying with the context of enquiry (Quine 1960, 199, Quine 1976 [1972], 52). So the analysis of modal sentences was modified more than any of the other quotation-based analyses presented in this book owing to shifts in Quine's semantic views.

The topic of meaning, and especially analyticity, was one Quine had been dancing around since the beginning of *The Significance of the New Logic*. We can see from his letters of the following year that part of his struggle was his re-evaluation of Carnap's views. There are clear signs that he was further separating himself from his teacher in this book. In the Introduction, Quine had claimed to have "expressed some doubt that . . . conventionalism has any meaning at all" (see p. 14 below) in "Truth by Convention" – a rather stronger statement than he had actually made in 1936. Again, there are also ontological concerns – which Carnap would not have countenanced – driving Quine's fast-evolving attitudes toward analyticity. Even between writing the book and translating himself, Quine's convictions appear to have grown stronger. In the original book, he had said:

> what the *meaning* of an expression is – what kind of object – is not yet clear; but it is clear that, given a notion of meaning, we can explain the notion of *synonymity* easily as the relation between expressions that have the same meaning. Conversely also, given the relation of synonymity, it would be easy to derive the notion of meaning in the following way: the meaning of an expression is the class of all the expressions synonymous with it. Perhaps this second direction of construction is the more promising one.
>
> (see p. 89 below)

By "Notes on Existence and Necessity," the "Perhaps" had become a "No doubt." The quotation also shows Quine clearly expressing unease about construing meanings as a special kind of object. His idea that presupposing synonymity as primitive and explicating "meaning" in terms of it might provide an alternative to taking meaning as primitive, presumed explicable by positing meanings, is also likely to be explained by his opposition to positing abstract objects.

Part of the growing rift between Quine and Carnap on analyticity was forged by their diverging positions on extensionality. Here it was not just Quine who changed his mind, but Carnap, too. Having originally agreed with Quine that only extensional languages were acceptable, in 1938 Carnap had begun to dabble in intensional metalanguages, citing his principle of tolerance. Quine, having heard of this through Hempel, shot off a rather ill-advised letter telling Carnap "your principle of tolerance may finally lead you even to tolerate Hitler" (Quine 1990b, 241). Carnap was provoked enough to depart from his usual mild-mannered style in his reply, comparing the anti-intensional philosopher to "an entomologist who refuses to investigate fleas and lice because he dislikes them" (Carnap 1990, 245). Quine could not dissuade him from continuing down an increasingly intensional path, culminating in his advocating modal logic (Carnap 1947). In *The Significance of the New Logic*, Quine made his opposition to intensional constructions apparent, but was less clear on what his argument against them was. He stated that intensionality is not needed in mathematics, that intensional contexts are difficult to formulate "clearly and exactly" (see p. 93 below), and that they have the same defects as quotation contexts. Again it appears plausible that Quine's views were motivated by ontology. In their subsequent correspondence, Carnap dismissed Quine's syntactic objections as fallacious. In his replies it soon came out that Quine's real underlying reservations stemmed from his nominalistic sympathies. He objected to the idea that in modal contexts we quantify over concepts (Quine 1990b, 326) and, after some debate, admitted that Carnap's view was coherent, but maintained that it implied an ontology of abstract intensions (Quine 1990b,

371). In other words, intensional languages had ontological commitments that were an affront to his nominalist leanings. This point would subsequently make it into print a few years later, when Quine complained that "modal logic is committed to an ontology which repudiates material objects" (Quine 1947, 47).

In this book Quine laid the groundwork for his distinction between the theory of meaning and the theory of reference. In 1934, he had lacked that distinction, but appeared to be grasping around in the dark in search of it when he said: "the sentence as a whole is to be taken as a verbal combination which, though presumably conveying some manner of intelligence (I write with deliberate vagueness at this point), yet does not have that particular kind of meaning which consists in denoting or being a name of something" (Quine 1934b, 474). In 1939, he moved closer to the issue by deploying the medieval distinction between categoremata and syncategoremata, and making the distinction between understanding the meaning of a term and knowing its designatum. But in this book Quine added to the distinction between designation and meaning – "only [names] designate, whereas perhaps all words and other more complex unities capable of figuring in statements have meaning" – the idea that meaning should be explained in terms of synonymity, which in turn "calls for a definition or a criterion in psychological and linguistic terms." (See p. 89 below.) At this point he had not yet written off the theory of meaning as inherently confused, as he was to do later. But he was beginning to draw a distinction between extensional semantic relations such as designation and satisfaction, and what he viewed as the more nebulous, psychologically based type of meaning. In his first letter to Carnap upon his return from Brazil, he identified as the chief disagreement between them "your failure to keep meaning distinct from designatum," claiming that that distinction would "have obviated the seeming advantages ... of intensional contexts" (Quine 1990, 299). Again part of the motivation appears ontological, as well as epistemological and semantic. Quine was opposed to the intensional for ontological reasons. Talk of designation, truth-functions, and satisfaction may have been attractive to him because it is able to focus squarely on the two physicalistically acceptable levels of concrete designata and concrete utterances of statements, as long as we avoid impurely designative occurrences in which the two levels are confused.

7 Philosophy of Logic and Mathematics

Quine's evolving views on ontology, as well as his evolving views on meaning, are also key to understanding his account of the philosophy of logic and mathematics in this book. For some years, he had been torn between his great admiration for *Principia Mathematica*, which says that all arithmetic is just logic abbreviated, and his distrust of the abstract objects posited by mathematics and therefore, according to *Principia*, by logic. Quine was dissatisfied both with the realism of Russell and Whitehead about such objects and with the deflationary solutions proposed by the members of the Vienna Circle, who took an anti-metaphysical stance or, appealing to the *Tractatus*, maintained that logical and mathematical truths are mere tautologies.

As a result it may strike us as odd to find Quine writing in the Introduction to *The Significance of the New Logic* that logicism is true, and subsequently declaring in the final section of the book that mathematical theories are mere tools, consisting of pseudo-statements which are not truly true or false. These claims are among the philosophical loose ends the book contains – Quine did not pick them up again upon his return to philosophy. Over the course of the 1940s he changed his mind on the issue, and he had moved away from the lines of thought expressed in this book by the time the war had ended.[6] But they are instructive from an historical point of view, because they point to the influences that other philosophers, especially Tarski, had on Quine at the time and reveal a gradual shift in his philosophical allegiance away from Carnap. When Quine began his Ph.D. work in 1930, he might have supposed, for a hopeful year or so, that a kind of formalism would allow him to endorse the mathematical logic of *Principia* without its abstract ontology. Such a potential strategy is described in this book as identifying logical (and, assuming *Principia* is correct, mathematical) truth with provability (see p. 15 below). But Gödel's 1931 result established that such a formalist strategy is doomed to fail. In this book Quine presupposed (as he had in 1981a [1940], 1–7) that any specification of logical truth will have an element of the semantic to it. Logically true statements are those that remain true under any substitutions of other terms for their non-logical terms – as Quine put it, those in which only logical vocabulary occurs essentially. That characterization of logical truth still contains the term "true," in "remain true." Such uses of "true" or other semantic terms, e.g. "occurring essentially," cannot be reduced to pure syntax or paraphrased away. Appeals to the purely formal, conventional, or notational features of expressions are, as Gödel had shown, insufficient to determine logical or mathematical truth. The formalist line seemed dead in the water to Quine. Yet his nominalist leanings meant that he continued to resist the abstract ontological commitments

---

[6] Although there is some resemblance here to the views expressed in Quine's joint paper with Goodman from 1947, which presents "the sentences of mathematics merely as strings of marks without meaning," that paper justifies the intelligibility of mathematics primarily based on the "syntactical or metamathematical rules governing those marks" (Goodman and Quine 1947, 111). By contrast, this book invokes "pseudo-truth" and appeals to more semantic and world-based considerations, such as the utility of mathematics (see p. 138 below), i.e. the applications to natural science emphasized earlier on in the book (see pp. 15–16 below).

of the *Principia* system. In *The Significance of the New Logic* Quine deployed insights he derived from conversations with Tarski to forge a new kind of synthesis, if a rather uncomfortable one, between his dedication to mathematical logic and his desire for a parsimonious, concrete ontology. His appeal to the usefulness and pseudo-truth of mathematics can be viewed as a sort of instrumentalism about infinitistic mathematics.

In the Introduction to this book, Quine endorsed Tarski's conception of logic as "the common denominator of the special sciences" (see p. 13 below). Elaborating on this idea, Quine characterized logic as a completely general science whose truths apply to any domain of objects. As becomes apparent only much later in the book, such a characterization appears to render logic innocuous from a nominalistic point of view. If logic is the most general theory, compatible with the content of any special science (see p. 13 below), then it is equally compatible with theories that posit only a finite number of things. A tension between this conception of logic and that of *Principia* now comes into focus for us, although Quine waited until the end of the book to discuss it. The *Principia* system presupposes the Axiom of Infinity, and thus an infinite number of things in the universe. In 1941, of course, Tarski had vigorously maintained that that presupposition was intolerable. Quine had tended to agree with Tarski. Carnap, in his discussion notes, had attributed to Quine the idea that perhaps non-finitistic mathematics might stand to finitistic mathematics as observation sentences stand to theoretical physics (Carnap 2013 [1940–41], 150). A view with some similarities to that idea is sketched in the final section of *The Significance of the New Logic*. Quine proposed that classical mathematics could not strictly speaking be held true, given Gödel's proof, but ought to be treated as a useful tool, yielding "ideograms" that look and behave in most respects like statements (see pp. 137–138 below). His mature philosophy of mathematics was, of course, rather different, abandoning both the logicist and the nominalistic tendencies he expressed in this book. Quine's early 1940s philosophy of logic does have crucial similarities with his mature philosophy of logic, such as the conception of logical truths as those truths that remain true under all lexical substitutions (Quine 1970, xi). But he was to hold firm to the (Tarskian-inspired) philosophy of logic he put forward in *The Significance of the New Logic*, and this would lead Quine to abandon his logicist leanings.

Although Quine stated in the Introduction that logicism is true, he wavered on the question over the course of the book. Earlier on he described Russell's paradox, which involves sets or classes, as "purely logical" (see p. 12 below) and called '(y) (z) (w) ~ ((x) xz > w • ~ yz > w)' a logical truth (see p. 57 below). But toward the end of the book we see him slide from his former characterization of logic as the theory whose truths apply to any domain of objects to a characterization according to which logic is the theory without its own bespoke ontology. We might have expected to find him describing the theory of classes as something other than logic because logic does, but the theory of classes does not, apply to absolutely any domain of objects, since certain classes cannot belong to classes (see p. 113 below). Instead, Quine's argument is that the theory of classes comes with a vast, abstract ontology.

> The theory of classes, in contrast with logic in the strict sense, implies an ontology. It does not imply an exclusive ontology, as it imposes no restrictions on the type of objects remaining, the so-called "individuals"; but it implies a positive ontology of classes. This implication of an ontology of abstract objects is, although indispensable to classical mathematics, repugnant to many thinkers.
>
> *(see p. 111 below)*

The theory of classes, then, belongs not to logic, but to mathematics. But Quine's virtual theory of classes comes to his rescue, allowing logic in the strict sense to do a substantial part of the work generally assigned to the theory of classes, while still avoiding any special logical ontology. Only certain parts of mathematics can be tamed in this way. The virtual theory is not strong enough to legitimate all of classical mathematics.

The Significance of the New Logic ends with a description of Gödel's proof and Quine's estimation of its philosophical significance. Again, Quine stressed that the proof entailed that neither logical nor mathematical truth could be taken to consist in provability. "No formulation of the notion of theorem can cover all of the true statements that can be formulated even in this very restricted notation of elementary arithmetic, without also covering false statements. The same is true *a fortiori* for our logical notation, since it is capable of expressing arithmetic and much more" (see p. 137 below). He pointed out that even the potential infinite is affected by this problem. (Carnap's notes from the previous year reveal that both Quine and Tarski had qualms about the potential infinite and Carnap's reliance on a notion of possibility (Carnap 2013 [1940–41], 157).) Quine then described the upshot of Gödel's proof as a "victory for those who obstinately refuse to recognize abstract objects" (see p. 138 below), because, he claimed, it points to a conception of mathematics as a useful tool "without content in the full sense" (see p. 138 below).[7] Instead of a theory composed of true or false statements, mathematics draws "ideograms [that] behave as though they have meaning [because of our] use of the methods of the theory of quantification (whose meaning still remains unquestioned) in deriving theorems from the

---

[7] Greg Frost-Arnold points out that there is a close resemblance here to a view expressed by Tarski in 1941 (Carnap 2013 [1940–41], 153).

axioms we assume" (see p. 138 below). The book, then, ends on a note best described as a kind of instrumentalism about classical mathematics. Mathematics is justified by its usefulness, presumably the "fruitful applications to the natural sciences" he had invoked earlier in the book (see pp. 12–13 below). But the statements of classical mathematics, which presuppose infinite ranges of abstract objects, are not taken to truly (or falsely) describe anything of an abstract nature. As he grew out of his finitistic and nominalistic inclinations, Quine swore off the instrumentalist treatment of mathematics. Still, there are some points of contact with his mature philosophy. Although Quine's later indispensability arguments do admit the existence of abstract, mathematical posits, their justification still invokes their usefulness to the natural sciences – specifically, to physics. The mature Quine no longer abjured the literal truth of classical or infinitistic mathematics generally. Accordingly, his nominalistic leanings of the 1930s and 1940s had dropped away. Nevertheless, even in his later period he held firm to the idea that higher set theory, which has no applications, is merely recreational (Quine 1986b, 400).

Acknowledgments

I am grateful to the audience of the Glasgow conference "Quine: Structure and Understanding," and to Greg Frost-Arnold, Paul Gregory, Fraser MacBride, Douglas Quine, and Thomas Uebel. This research was supported by a CAPES postdoctoral grant.

References

Barcan, Ruth. 1947. The Identity of Individuals in a Strict Functional Calculus of Second Order. *The Journal of Symbolic Logic*. Vol. 12, No. 1, 12–15.

Barcan Marcus, Ruth. 1961. Modalities and Intensional Languages. *Synthese*. Vol. 13, No. 4, 302–322.

    1967. Essentialism in Modal Logic. *Noûs*. Vol. 1, No. 1, 90–96.

Ben-Menahem, Yemima. 2005. Black, White and Gray: Quine on Convention. *Synthese*. Vol. 146, No. 3, 245–282.

Carnap, Rudolf. 1947. *Meaning and Necessity*. University of Chicago Press.

    1990. Correspondence with Quine, in Creath (1990a).

    2013 (1940–41). Notes on Conversations with Quine and Tarski, in Frost-Arnold (2013).

Chisholm, Roderick. 1947. Review of *Os Estados Unidos e o Ressurgimento da Lógica*. *Philosophy and Phenomenological Research*. Vol. 7, No. 3, pp. 483–485.

Creath, Richard. 1990a. *Dear Carnap, Dear Van*. Oakland, CA: University of California Press.
1990b. "Introduction," in Creath 1990a, pp. 1–43.
da Costa, N. C. A. 1997. Review of Second Edition of *O Sentido da Nova Lógica*. *Journal of Symbolic Logic*. Vol. 62, No. 2, 688.
Ebbs, Gary. 2011. Carnap and Quine on Truth by Convention. *Mind*. Vol. 120, No. 478, 193–237.
Ferreira da Silva, Vicente. 1940. *Elementos de Lógica Matemática*. São Paulo: E Realizaçoes.
Frege, Gottlob. 1892. Über Sinn und Bedeutung. *Zeitschrift der Philosophie und Philosophischer Kritik*. n. s. Vol. 100, 25–50.
Frost-Arnold, Greg. 2011. Quine's Evolution from "Carnap's Disciple" to the Author of "Two Dogmas." *HOPOS: The Journal of the International Society for the History of the Philosophy of Science*. Vol. 1, 291–316.
2013. *Carnap, Tarski, and Quine at Harvard: Conversations on Logic, Mathematics and Science*. Chicago, IL: Open Court.
Gödel, Kurt. 1931. Über formal unentscheidbare Sätze der *Principia Mathematica* und verwandter Systeme I. *Monatshefte für Mathematik und Physik*. Vol. 39, 173–198.
Hylton, Peter. 2001. "The Defensible Province of Philosophy": Quine's 1934 Lectures on Carnap. In: Juliet Floyd and Sanford Shieh (eds.), *Future Pasts: The Analytic Tradition in Twentieth-Century Philosophy*. Oxford University Press.
2007. *Quine*. London: Routledge.
Goodman, Nelson and Willard Van Orman Quine. 1947. Steps Toward a Constructive Nominalism. *Journal of Symbolic Logic*. Vol. 12, No. 4, 105–122.
Janssen-Lauret, Frederique. 2015. Meta-Ontology, Naturalism, and the Quine–Barcan Marcus Debate. In: Janssen-Lauret and Kemp (2015, pp. 146–167).
2016. Committing to an Individual: Ontological Commitment, Reference, and Epistemology. *Synthese*. Vol. 193, No. 2, 583–604.
2017. The Quinean Roots of Lewis's Humeanism. *The Monist*. Vol. 100, No. 2, 249–265.
Janssen-Lauret, Frederique and Gary Kemp (eds.). 2015. *Quine and His Place in History*. Basingstoke: Palgrave Macmillan.
Kotarbinski, Tadeusz. 1966 (1929). *Gnoseology*. Oxford: Pergamon Press. Translation of *Elementy Teorii poznania, logiki formalnej i metodologii nauk*. Wroclaw: Zaklad Narodowy im. Ossolinskich, Wydawnictwo.
Lodge, Ann, Rolfe A. Leary, and Douglas B. Quine. 2015. Observations on the Contribution of W. V. Quine to Unified Science Theory. In: Janssen-Lauret and Kemp (2015, pp. 39–56).
Mancosu, P. 2005. Harvard 1940–41: Tarski, Carnap and Quine on a Finitistic Language of Mathematics for Science. *History and Philosophy of Logic*. Vol. 26, 327–357.
2008. Quine and Tarski on Nominalism. In: D. Zimmerman (ed.), *Oxford Studies in Metaphysics*. Oxford University Press, vol. IV.
Price, H. 2009. Metaphysics after Carnap: The Ghost Who Walks? In: D. J. Chalmers, D. Manley, and R. Wasserman (eds.), *Metametaphysics*. Oxford University Press, 320–346.
Quine, Willard Van Orman. 1934a. *A System of Logistic*. Cambridge, MA: Harvard University Press.

1934b. Ontological Remarks on the Propositional Calculus. *Mind*. Vol. 43, 472–476.
1936. Truth by Convention. In: O. Lee (ed.), *Philosophical Essays for A. N. Whitehead*. New York: Longmans.
1939a. Designation and Existence. *Journal of Philosophy*. Vol. 39, 701–709.
1939b. Relations and Reason. *Technology Review*. Vol. 41, 299–301, 324–327.
1941. *Elementary Logic*. Boston, MA: Ginn & Co.
1943. Notes on Existence and Necessity. *Journal of Philosophy*. Vol. 40, 113–127.
1944. *O Sentido da Nova Lógica*. São Paulo: Martins.
1947. The Problem of Interpreting Modal Logic. *Journal of Symbolic Logic*. Vol. 12, No. 2, 43–48.
1948. On What There Is. *Review of Metaphysics*. Vol. 2, 21–38.
1951. Two Dogmas of Empiricism. *Philosophical Review*. Vol. 60, 20–43.
1953a (1950). Identity, Ostension, and Hypostasis. In: *From a Logical Point of View*. Cambridge, MA: Harvard University Press.
1953b. Reference and Modality. In: *From a Logical Point of View*. Cambridge, MA: Harvard University Press.
1958. *El Sentido de la Nueva Lógica*, tr. Mario Bunge. Buenos Aires: Nueva Visión.
1960. *Word and Object*. Cambridge, MA: MIT Press.
1961. Reply to Professor Marcus. *Synthese*. Vol. 13, 343–347.
1963. *Set Theory and Its Logic*. Cambridge, MA: Harvard University Press.
1966 (1939). A Logistical Approach to the Ontological Problem. In: *The Ways of Paradox*. Cambridge, MA: Harvard University Press.
1970. *Philosophy of Logic*. Englewood Cliffs: Prentice-Hall.
1976 (1972). Vagaries of Definition. In: *The Ways of Paradox*. 2nd edn. Cambridge, MA: Harvard University Press.
1976. Whither Physical Objects? *Boston Studies in the Philosophy of Science*. Vol. 29, 497–504.
1981a (1940). *Mathematical Logic*. Cambridge, MA: Harvard University Press.
1981b (1966). Russell's Ontological Development. In: *Theories and Things*. Cambridge, MA: Harvard University Press.
1981c. Things and Their Place in Theories. In: *Theories and Things*. Cambridge, MA: Harvard University Press.
1986a. Autobiography. In: L. E. Hahn and P. A. Schilpp (eds.), *The Philosophy of W. V. Quine*. La Salle, IL: Open Court.
1986b. Reply to Charles Parsons. In: L. E. Hahn and P. A. Schilpp (eds.), *The Philosophy of W. V. Quine*. La Salle, IL: Open Court.
1990a (1934). Lectures on Carnap. In: Creath (1990a, pp. 47–103).
1990b (1932–70). Correspondence with Carnap. In: Creath (1990a, pp. 107–462).
1991. Two Dogmas in Retrospect. *Canadian Journal of Philosophy*. Vol. 21, No. 3, 265–274.
1996. *O Sentido da Nova Lógica*. 2nd edn. Universidade Federal do Paraná.
1997. Mission to Brazil. *Logique et Analyse*. Vol. 157, 5–8.
2003 (1946). Harvard Lectures on Hume. In: J. G. Buickerood (ed.), *Eighteenth-Century Thought*. New York: AMS Press, vol. I, pp. 171–254, reprinted in Quine (2008a).
2008a. *Confessions of a Confirmed Extensionalist*, ed. D. Føllesdal and D. B. Quine. Cambridge, MA: Harvard University Press.

2008b (1946). Nominalism. In: D. Zimmerman (ed.), *Oxford Studies in Metaphysics*. Oxford University Press, vol. IV, reprinted in Quine (2008a, pp. 7–23).

2016. *O Sentido da Nova Lógica*. 3rd edn. Universidade Federal do Paraná.

Schaffer, J. 2009. On What Grounds What. In: D. J. Chalmers, D. Manley, and R. Wasserman (eds.), *Metametaphysics*. Oxford University Press.

Stebbing, Susan. 1930. *A Modern Introduction to Logic*. London: Methuen.

Tahko, T. 2011. In Defence of Aristotelian Metaphysics. In: *Contemporary Aristotelian Metaphysics*. Cambridge University Press.

Tarski, Alfred. 1933. *Pojęcie prawdy w językach nauk dedukcyjnych*. Warsaw: Nakładem Towarzystwa Naukowego Warszawskiego.

1935. Der Wahrheitsbegriff in den formalisierten Sprachen, tr. L. Blaustein. *Studia Philosophica*. Vol. 1, pp. 261–405.

Uebel, Thomas. 2016. Vienna Circle. In: Edward N. Zalta (ed.), *The Stanford Encyclopedia of Philosophy*. Spring 2016 edn. https://plato.stanford.edu /archives/spr2016/entries/vienna-circle

2017. Wittgenstein and the Vienna Circle. In: H.-J. Glock and J. Hyman (eds.), *A Companion to Wittgenstein*. New York: John Wiley & Sons.

Whitehead, Alfred North and Bertrand Russell. 1964 (1910). *Principia Mathematica to *56*. Cambridge University Press.

Wittgenstein, Ludwig. 1921. Logisch-Philosophische Abhandlung. *Annalen der Naturphilosophie*. Vol. 14, 185–262.

1922 (1921). *Tractatus Logico-Philosophicus*. London: Kegan Paul.

The Significance of the New Logic

WILLARD VAN ORMAN QUINE

Contents

Preface to the First Edition

Understanding the philosophical and practical significance of modern logic is essential for justifying the in-depth study of the technical part of theoretical logic. But the inverse is also true: Some knowledge of logical techniques is necessary for learning the philosophical and practical implications of this theory. This book constitutes an introduction as much to the modern theoretical part of logic as to its general consequences.

The specific system of logic used in this work is the result of my efforts to balance three ideals: rigor in theoretical detail, convenience in practical applications, and simplicity of presentation. The last ideal was the principal objective. The system used is such that the reader will later be able to apply the techniques, but those who aim to delve more deeply into logical techniques will also be given useful suggestions for further reading. From the theoretical point of view, the kinds of rules adopted in this work help furnish a clear conception of the nature of modern logic, even if to the specialist it leaves something to be desired. Some important results, whose detailed proofs are referenced in the bibliography, are expounded without those proofs, so that space could instead be given over to their philosophical implications without turning the book into an advanced, difficult, and lengthy treatise.

The content of the book is in essence that of a series of lectures that I presented as Visiting Professor of the Free School of Sociology and Politics of São Paulo between June and September 1942, under the auspices of the Committee for Inter-American Artistic and Intellectual Relations. The logic presented here has certain similarities to that presented in my book *Mathematical Logic*, supplemented by the revisions proposed in my article "Element and Number." The discussion of its philosophical implications revolves around the ideas presented in my article "Designation and Existence," but goes much further. New material of an essentially philosophical nature, which makes up part of §§ 34–39 and 42, will also appear in English in the United States in the form of an article, "Notes on Necessity and Existence." § 1 and parts of §§ 7, 9, 10, and 18, are extracts from my book *Elementary Logic* (Ginn & Co.: Boston). In the Introduction and in § 8 there are some passages borrowed from *Mathematical Logic* (W. W. Norton & Co.: New York). I am grateful to the two aforementioned firms for permission to reproduce these excerpts, as well as to the editor of *Technology Review* for permission to use the material which is included in the final pages of the Introduction. Finally, some passages of the Introduction are extracts from a public lecture, "The United States and the Revival of Logic,"[1] delivered in São Paulo under the auspices of the União Cultural Brasil–Estados Unidos. The lecture will be published in the União Cultural Brasil–Estados Unidos' edited collection.[2]

I wish to express my gratitude to Cyro Berlinck, Director of the Free School of Sociology and Political Science of São Paulo, for having provided the necessary assistance in the preparation of the manuscript, and to Donald Pierson and Cyro Berlinck for kindly taking on the task of dealing with the details of the publication of the book after my departure. To Mrs. Dora Ferreira da Silva, my thanks for the great help and support that she provided in the preparation of the manuscript, and to Mrs. Laura Austregésilo for having produced the Portuguese version of § 31 and of part of the Introduction. I am grateful to Décio Almeida Prado and to Breno Silveira for their assistance in the correction of the Portuguese on certain pages. My greatest debt, however, is to Vicente Ferreira da Silva, who worked tirelessly at the imposing task of going over the Portuguese of the entire manuscript with me, and who, in addition, took it upon himself to edit the proofs.
São Paulo, September 8, 1942.

The Author

Preface to the Second Edition

I was amazed and delighted by Professor Tsuji's proposal to republish *O Sentido* after more than fifty years, and I am very grateful for his patient efforts to make it a reality.

Allow me to outline the origin of the book. Between 1941 and 1942, while the Nazis were invading Western Europe, I was teaching at Harvard but devoting my free time to preparing for a technical job in the Navy. Ideas about logic and the adjacent margins of philosophy still continued flowing, but I repressed them. In March of 1942, however, the opportunity arose for me to give a three-month course in São Paulo. This allowed me to put off taking up my commission as an officer in the Navy until my return. Thus when I went back to preparing the new lectures, everything that had been repressed came pouring out. The repressed ideas of the last year erupted and connected. My series of lectures virtually organized itself, with new angles and shortcuts that pleased me greatly as I surveyed them.

I wrote out the lectures in my halting Portuguese. I probably committed blatant errors. But people were kind and remained straight-faced. I mimeographed some parts so that the participants could study them. I then decided to leave all of the lectures in Brazil in the form of a book, which would have more impact than lectures to a small group in the classroom. Thus I embarked on the production of my fourth book, *O Sentido da Nova Lógica*. I looked upon this not only as a way of planting a seed on Brazilian soil, but also as my farewell to philosophy and abstract science for the foreseeable future, given the precarious situation the Western world was in.

The book is an introduction to modern logic, its techniques and its philosophy. An innovation from a technical point of view was the virtual theory of classes, which I explored extensively twenty-five years later in *Set Theory and Its Logic*. In the philosophical realm, some thoughts took form, and I decided to publish them without waiting for the book. To this end I found a stenographer and dictated an English translation from my own Portuguese. The work promptly appeared in the *Journal of Philosophy* as "Notes on Existence and Necessity."[3] It was all an insane rush, because I was running out of time.

Vicente Ferreira da Silva generously collaborated with me to turn the Portuguese of my lectures into the work we wanted to publish. When he improved the writing to the detriment of the thought, I intervened and we forged a third text which was acceptable on both counts. At least that was how I saw the process. I am startled now to be informed by Professor da Costa, through Professor Tsuji, that Vicente has a different view of the matter: that I "insisted on maintaining the grammatical structure of the book, as well as the neologisms that are found in it." Is it possible that he did not perceive that I was more apprehensive about distorted formulations of subtle points of logic? A lesson in prudence in the meeting of minds.

In any case, I agree with Professors Tsuji and da Costa's advice to maintain unaltered the text of the first edition, as foreign as it may sound. The language does justice to the history of the book.[a]

Willard Van Orman Quine
January 1995

---

[a] Parts of this preface were extracted from *The Time of My Life* (Quine 2000, 172–174), with the permission of M.I.T. Press.

Introduction

Within the last nine decades, logic has evolved to the point where it can be considered a completely new science. This evolution is generally thought to have begun with the still somewhat crude investigations of the mathematician George Boole, in the middle of the last century. Although these new developments were adumbrated by earlier publications, for example in some of Leibniz's works, the new logic only started its continuous development from Boole onward, through the work of Frege and Schröder, both Germans, Charles Peirce, who was American, and Peano, who was Italian. It came to full maturity in 1911–12 with the publication, in three large volumes, of the monumental work *Principia Mathematica* by the Englishmen Whitehead and Russell.

Ancient logic stands to the new logic not so much as a scientific predecessor, but as a pre-scientific fragment of the same discipline. In the words of Whitehead: "In the modern development of Logic, the traditional Aristotelian Logic takes its place as a simplification of the problem presented by the subject. In this there is an analogy to arithmetic of primitive tribes compared to modern mathematics." [i]

Aristotle's formal logic, consisting primarily of the theory of the syllogism, survived the Middle Ages intact without undergoing any major changes or progressive development. Even in the second half of the eighteenth century, Kant could speak of formal logic as a science that had already been perfected, and completed, two thousand years earlier. Nevertheless, people habitually engaged in fruitful deductive arguments of a kind almost completely unrelated to the arguments studied in the existing logic. In particular, great advances in mathematics were made this way. Still, mathematicians, and people in general, engaged in reasoning freely without redressing the theoretical inadequacy of

---

[i] From the preface to my *System of Logistic*. [This appears as footnote 2 in the first edition; this is a typo, as no footnote 1 precedes it in that edition.]

the formal logic of the time, or, at least, without concerning themselves with any attempt to reform or extend this logic. Perhaps they had become accustomed to not thinking of logic when they were engaged in proper reasoning.

And why not continue that way? The need for a new examination of the techniques of deduction was made apparent principally by mathematics itself, as we will now see.

Mathematicians were so busy reasoning and making discoveries about numbers, functions, and other mathematical entities, that they did not have time to reason about reasoning itself. But mathematical progress reached a stage where the role of deductive methods had to come in for special scrutiny. This occurred principally with the arrival on the scene of the higher infinities.

At the end of the nineteenth century, the German mathematician Georg Cantor discovered that there are multiple degrees of infinity. It is possible for two classes to be infinite, even though one is larger than the other. It became necessary to accept transfinite numbers, in addition to the usual numbers, to measure the difference in size between some of these infinite classes. Cantor showed that the collection of transfinite numbers is also infinite, and of a higher level of infinity than the infinity which any of the transfinite numbers can be used to measure.

This theory has several peculiar consequences. For example, Cantor showed that there are just as many even numbers as there are integers, and that there are just as many integers as there are integers and fractions combined, but that there are more real numbers than there are integers. The usual type of mathematical reasoning, relying on "intuition" or on "good sense," fails in the study of the higher infinities. The faculty of the imagination becomes useless when one goes beyond finite numbers and classes, or, in any case, beyond the first degree of infinity. We must explore the ocean that Cantor discovered by navigating blindly, depending only on the rigorous use of valid rules of deduction, and accepting the consequences.[ii] After Cantor, the techniques of modern logic have continued to prove useful in this respect, for instance in their deployment by the German Löwenheim, the Norwegian Skolem, and the Austrian Gödel.

But why should we concern ourselves with this outlandish theory of transfinite numbers? Recall the March Hare in *Alice in Wonderland*. He explained to Alice that he was constantly drinking tea with his two friends because it was always 6 o'clock, his watch being broken; and that many places had been set around the table so that they could change places after each sitting. But when Alice asked him what they did when they had finished going around the table,

[ii] Cf. Whitehead, "On Cardinal Numbers," p. 367.

the Hare complained that the subject was becoming tiresome. Mathematicians who turn their backs on transfinite numbers behave exactly like the March Hare. We must concern ourselves with this theory for the sake of coherence. Cantor established his theory on the basis of principles already accepted and employed in the development of other parts of mathematics, and by means of methods of deduction equally well-entrenched and commonly employed. We cannot coherently repudiate the theory of transfinite numbers, as strange as it may be, without sacrificing at the same time familiar and useful parts of mathematics that share the same foundations.

Perhaps we could break free from parts of that theory without such sacrifice in the following way. Perhaps we could arrive at a subtle formulation of the fundamental principles of mathematics, and the methods of deduction, in such a way that they would be sufficient for familiar and useful mathematical theories, but not for the more outlandish parts of Cantorian theory. But we will see that, even apart from transfinite arithmetic, we must make the methods of deduction explicit and study them intensively.

An even more pressing motivation for such logical enquiries arose at the beginning of this century, with the discovery by the British logician Bertrand Russell that the principles of reasoning tacitly accepted and used in mathematics, and perhaps outside of it, could involve us in contradiction. This discovery precipitated a crisis. The principles of deductive logic had to be made explicit and carefully formulated, and even revised, for mathematics in general to be properly supported.

These contradictions or paradoxes are curious and entertaining. A characteristic contradiction, for example, involves the notion of *denotation* in the sense that the adjective 'human' denotes every human being, the adjective 'green' every green thing, the adjective 'long' every long thing, and so on. Let us use the term *heterological* for every adjective that does not denote itself. For example, the adjective 'long'[iii] is heterological, because it does not denote itself, that is, it is not long. The adjective '*inglês*' is heterological, because it is not English – it is Portuguese. The adjective 'monosyllabic' is heterological, because it is not monosyllabic, it is pentasyllabic. On the other hand, the adjective 'short' is not heterological, because it denotes itself – it is short. The adjective '*português*' is not heterological, because it is a Portuguese adjective. The adjective 'pentasyllabic' is not heterological, because it is pentasyllabic. Now, the paradox appears when we ask, with respect to the

---

[iii] I use single quotation marks, as is done here, to form a name of a word or other expression. The expression formed by the addition of single quotation marks is the name of the expression contained within those quotation marks.

adjective 'heterological' itself, if it is heterological. It is heterological if and only if it does not denote itself, that is, if and only if it is *not* heterological.

This paradox, which we owe to the German logician Kurt Grelling, is not a purely logical paradox, because it depends on the non-logical notions of adjective and denotation. But the original paradox of Russell, which is very much analogous to it, *is* purely logical. It is about the *class* whose members are exactly the classes that are not members of themselves. This class is a member of itself if and only if it is not (cf. § 44).

These paradoxes and other, more complex ones, are entertaining enough, but they result in very serious problems. Their repercussions in mathematics are still being felt today. And, as we have noted, the discovery of the paradoxes created a need for the current revival of logic.

Another motivation for this revival is the search for more perspicuous foundations for some of the dubious ideas used in mathematics. The arrival on the scene of the heterodox theory of transfinite numbers naturally led to an attempt to give a general definition of the notions of number, and infinity, on the basis of other more fundamental notions. Long before Cantor's transfinite numbers, there were other mathematical notions standing in need of clarification by means of definitions in terms of perspicuous notions. One of these notions was that of the *infinitesimal*, fundamental to the differential calculus since the time of Newton and Leibniz. It was an absurd notion: that of a positive number which is infinitely small, but nevertheless greater than zero. It was Weierstrass, in the past century, who eliminated this absurdity and found a solid foundation for the differential calculus, called the theory of limits. Yet another notion that stood in need of clarification was, naturally, the notion of imaginary number – the square root of negative one.

Mathematicians are entitled to make senseless pronouncements if they like, as their work provides many fruitful applications to the natural sciences regardless. But it would be interesting, at least from a philosophical point of view, to make sense of such notions, to understand the content of mathematics. Even mathematicians themselves may find this useful.

This program of reducing one mathematical notion to another, moving toward greater clarity, may seem independent of the development of the new logic. As it happened, however, analysis became dependent on the increasingly exact understanding and employment of the kind of auxiliary notions central to the very principles of logic: the notions of class and of relation, and those that correspond to the words 'if', 'then', 'not', 'and', 'is', 'all', 'some', and various others. The most surprising result was that which showed all mathematical notions to be reducible, not only to some of those same mathematical notions, but reducible entirely to auxiliary logical notions. Apart from this the discovery was also made that these logical notions are reducible, in turn, to just three: one corresponding to the phrase 'neither ... nor', another to the word 'is', and a third to the word 'all', supplemented by a system of pronouns. So, by these reductions, every single mathematical statement turns out to be a mere abbreviation of a purely logical statement written exclusively in terms of these three notions, with nothing more to be added.

To say that the theorem '2 + 2 = 4', when written out in this tiny vocabulary, would be several meters long, and that the binomial theorem would reach from the North to the South Pole, is not to take away from the theoretical importance of this reduction. Despite this, it remains the case that every mathematical law is an abbreviation of a logical law. Pure mathematics is reducible to logic.

The new logic has already become an integral component of mathematical theory, not only as a theoretical basis, in the way we have just discussed, but also as a practical instrument for research within various special branches of mathematics. A key example is found in the partial solution of the well-known mathematical problem known as the Continuum Problem which the logician Kurt Gödel achieved two years ago.

What, then, is logic? What is it about? In a certain sense, we may say that logic is about everything. *Not* in the sense that logic is a universal science, of which every other science forms part and from whose laws the laws of any special science can be inferred. Logic is not a universal science in that sense; however, it is a *general* science, in the sense that logical truths apply to any objects whatsoever. The logical truth, for example, that says that each object is identical to itself applies once and for all to all objects studied by any of the sciences.

We can therefore say, not that logic *includes* the other sciences, but that it is *included* in all the other sciences in such a way that it forms the common part of all the sciences. Whatever logic asserts is what can be asserted about the objects of any of the sciences. Logic is, as Tarski suggests, the common denominator of the special sciences.

The way I have characterized the province of logic leaves much to be desired with regard to precision and explicitness. In addition, it does not offer any real indication of the purpose of logic, nor of the kinds of laws and problems with which logicians concern themselves; examples like 'every object is identical to itself' are of course too simple and trivial to be representative.

Yet a distinction between logical truths and other true statements is easily made by referring once again to the "logical vocabulary" composed of the fundamental words 'is', 'not', 'and', 'or', 'if', 'not', 'some', 'all', etc., and reducible, as mentioned earlier, to just a few of these. A statement is *logically true* if the words of the logical vocabulary occur in the statement in such a way that the statement will remain true, independently of its other components. Thus, let us consider the classic example:

(1) If all humans are mortal, and Socrates is human, then Socrates is mortal.

This statement is true, and it is true independently of the components 'human', 'mortal', and 'Socrates'; no substitution of other words for these can make it false. Only 'if', 'all', 'is', 'and', and 'then', items of the logical vocabulary, occur *essentially* in the statement, that is, in such a way that the substitution of other expressions for these words (for example: 'none' instead of 'all', 'is not' for 'is', and 'or' for 'and'), can make the statement false. *A statement is logically true*, in sum, *if only words belonging to the logical vocabulary occur essentially in the statement.*

I want to emphasize that I have not, so far, proposed any philosophical thesis, nor any gnoseology[3] as it relates to logical truth. In particular I have not proposed any conventionalist gnoseology according to which logical truths are established by arbitrary conventions governing the use of language. We need only observe that a description analogous to my description of logical truth would also serve, for example, for chemical truth: A chemical truth is any statement in which only the chemical vocabulary occurs essentially, supposing this vocabulary to be stipulated beforehand. But no one would draw the conclusion that the truths of chemistry are established merely by arbitrary linguistic conventions. In general, having recourse to a list of words and to the semantic notion of *occurring essentially*, in order to demarcate the limits of any science, does not imply anything with respect to *why* the statements of the science are true. The only clear method that I know of *demarcating* that class of truths which have as a typical member the statement 'Socrates is either human or not human' is the method in which we say that only the logical vocabulary occurs essentially in those statements; but this is not to say 'Socrates is either human or not human *because* certain conventions were established to govern the use of the words "is", "or", and "not".' On the contrary, I have expressed some doubt that the thesis of conventionalism has any meaning at all.[iv]

My demarcation of logical truth depends on the notion of "occurring essentially," the definition of which in turn depends explicitly on the general distinction between truth and falsity. Therefore, even though this demarcation of logical truth seems to be concerned only with statements and the words that occur in them, it does not depend only on the *notational* features of the

---

[iv] In the essay "Truth by Convention."

statements, because truth in general is not such a feature. In general we cannot know if a statement is true, nor if some word occurs essentially or accidentally in it, by investigating only the statement and not the world out there.

But if we could formulate a criterion of *logical* truth only in terms of the notational features of the statements, we would have a description of logical truth that would not use the notion of *occurring essentially*, nor depend on the general notion of truth. The practical value of the sought-for criterion would be to guide us practically in the discovery and recognition of truths in the domain of logic.

Of course we could not hope for any criterion of, for example, chemical truth, in terms of notational features. But it seems that logical truth in particular must be susceptible to such a criterion, given that when in practice we recognize logical truth, we always recognize it by uniquely inspecting the statement itself and perhaps certain questions related to it.

The criterion in question would consist in a strict formulation of the concept of logical proof, obeying two conditions: (1) every logical truth, and no falsehood, would have a proof (even though in many cases the proof may not have been discovered yet), and (2) every proof, once discovered, could be *authenticated* mechanically, without going beyond the notational designs of the statements. The formulation would cover mathematical truth in general, given the reduction of mathematics to logic.

However, the Austrian logician Gödel proved in 1931 that this program is impossible, that (1) and (2) are incompatible (cf. § 54). He proved that there cannot exist a coherent systematization within which every true statement of mathematics, not even of elementary arithmetic, is provable. Given any systematization of logic, there will be logical truths, and even arithmetical truths, that are provably unprovable. This is a paradoxical result of crucial importance for the philosophy of mathematics, as it contradicts the idea that mathematical or logical truth itself consists in the possibility of its proof.

Of the notion of logical truth, all we have left is our earlier definition in terms of general truth. We cannot replace this definition with rules of proof. Nevertheless, the formulation of the rules of proof remains important, as it is still only by means of proof methods, even though they are incomplete, that logical or mathematical truths that are not yet obvious can be brought to light. To the extent that the new logical techniques are useful, their rigorous formulation is desirable.

Lastly, let us consider the role of logic in the natural sciences.

Logic has its practical use in inference from premises which are not logical truths to conclusions which are not logical truths. Logic countenances such inference when the conditional statement 'If ... then ... ', connecting premise with conclusion, is itself logically true (like (1) above); and it is in this way that logical truth links up with extra-logical concerns. Precisely the analogous account holds with regard to applications of mathematics generally; the tremendous utility of mathematical techniques in natural science turns simply on the importance of discerning mathematical truths of the form 'If ... then ... ' whose component parts are statements of natural science.[v]

Logic, unlike the numerical branches of mathematics, traditionally figured in the natural sciences only in a tacit and quite rudimentary way. It plays just as subordinate a role as arithmetic played in the era of Roman numerals. But following the schematization of logic in the spirit of modern mathematics, the role of logic in the sciences promises to be something altogether different.

Until now, where number was less relevant mathematical techniques have usually been lacking. Thus it is that the progress of the natural sciences has always depended upon the discernment of measurable quantities of one sort or another. Measurement, in physics or in any other science, consists in correlating the subject matter of that science with the series of real numbers. These correlations are desirable because, once they are established, all of the well-developed theory of numerical mathematics is at hand as a tool for further reasoning.

But no science can rest entirely on measurement, and many scientific investigations are out of reach of this method. To those scientific problems for which measurement is not relevant, the techniques furnished by the numerical parts of mathematics are useless. We must either turn to the less familiar, underdeveloped parts of mathematics that deal with non-numerical matters – relations, for example – or use only common sense.

Among the non-numerical branches of mathematical theory that have proved useful to the natural sciences, perhaps the best known is group theory. When we consider a set of movements or other operations, group theory provides a systematic technique for treating the effects of the application of these operations one after the other. However, such non-numerical techniques only very rarely turn out helpful to the scientist.

It is on this point that the scientist could make very good use of the new mathematical logic. To the scientist longing for non-quantitative techniques, mathematical logic offers help in two ways: it provides explicit techniques for manipulating the simplest ingredients of language, and provides a clear and systematic basis on which to construct future theories to help with the demands of the special sciences that arise regularly.

[v] From my book *Mathematical Logic*, p. 7.

The principal interest of the new logic is therefore theoretical. This science, encompassing the roots of mathematics, constitutes the means for investigating the nature of mathematics in general. Moreover, the philosophical significance of the new logical discoveries is not limited to the philosophy of mathematics; it touches, as we shall see, upon central questions of philosophy – questions about necessity and possibility, and even questions of an ontological nature such as 'What is there?' and 'What is real?'.

I

The Theory of Composition

§ 1 Statements and Their Truth Values

Logic, in its modern form, is conveniently divided into two parts: the theory of deduction and the theory of classes. This is a fundamental distinction with considerable importance, as we shall see later, even for philosophy (§§ 44, 54).

The theory of deduction is divided in turn into two other parts: the theory of composition and the theory of quantification. The nature of these parts will be discussed later on. The theory of classes has parts that stand in need of further study – notably, the theory of identity (Chapter III), the algebra of classes (§ 47), and elementary arithmetic (§§ 52, 54).

The tripartite division into the theories of composition, quantification, and classes imposes a corresponding division upon the minimal logical vocabulary we discussed earlier on. The word 'not' belongs to the theory of composition, the word 'all' and its auxiliary system of pronouns to the theory of quantification, and the word 'is' to the theory of classes.

For the present, however, we shall leave aside the theories of quantification and of classes. To prepare the ground for a technical treatment of the first part of logic, which is about the compositional structure of statements, let us consider what a statement is. Statements are *sentences*, but not every sentence is a statement. Statements comprise just those sentences which are true and those which are false. These two properties of statements, truth and falsehood, are called the *truth values* of statements. Thus we say that the truth value of a statement is truth or falsehood according as the statement is true or false.

The sentences 'What time is it?', 'Close the door', 'That I were still a boy', *etcetera*, being neither true nor false, are not statements. Only *declarative* sentences are statements. Moreover, not all declarative sentences are statements. The declarative sentence 'I am ill' is in itself neither true nor false, because it can be truly uttered by one person and falsely by another. In the same way, 'He is ill' is in itself neither true nor false, because what the word 'he' refers to changes with the context. The sentence 'John is ill' is also in itself neither true nor false; the designatum of the name 'John' depends on the context, since there are many people with that name. The same is true of sentences that make essential use of words such as 'here' and 'there', given that each such sentence can be simultaneously truly uttered by one speaker and falsely by another. All declarative sentences of this kind must be further specified so that their truth value does not depend on the context, or the speaker, before they can count as statements with uniform truth values.

Logical analysis is made easier when we add the requirement that a statement's truth value remain the same independently of *time*. This can be done by removing tense from all our verbs, and using explicit chronological descriptions when we want to make temporal distinctions. For example, the sentence 'Brazil will become independent', affirmed on January 1, 1820, corresponds to the statement 'Brazil becomes independent after January 1, 1820'. This statement, where the word 'becomes' is understood tenselessly, is true once and for all, independently of the date of utterance.[5]

Although such refinements are important as a theoretical basis, it will be convenient in the practical construction of examples to use as statements such sentences as 'Brazil will become independent', or even 'I am ill'. But we must think of all such sentences as expanded into a genuine statement. The formal techniques of analysis depend on the supposition that a statement is a sentence which is true or false independently of context, speaker, and place and time of utterance.

§ 2 Conjunction and Denial. Truth Tables

The theory of composition deals with the different ways of *joining* statements *together* to form *compound* statements. One of the modes of composition, called *conjunction* by logicians, consists in joining two statements by the word 'and' – or, in the notation of mathematical logic, by the dot '•':

John is ill • Joe is away.

A *conjunctive* statement, thus formed, is true if both component statements are true; in all other cases it is false. To know the *truth value* of a conjunction, we just need to know the truth values of its components.

1st component	2nd component	Conjunction
T	T	T
F	T	F
T	F	F
F	F	F

Conjunction combines two or more statements at a time, while *denial*, to which we must now turn, is a method of elaborating a single statement in order to form another. Its truth table is as follows:

Component	Denial
T	F
F	T

In mathematical logic, the denial of a statement is formed by prefixing a *tilde* to the statement. Thus, '~ John is ill' means that John is not ill.

When conjunction and denial are applied in iteration to form a complex statement, for example:

(1)   ~ (John is ill • Joe is away)

we can always calculate the import of the result by using the truth tables given above. We can systematically determine which truth values of the ultimate components would make the compound statement true, and which truth values of the ultimate components would make it false. This is done as follows (using 'p' and 'q', for brevity's sake, in place of 'John is ill' and 'Joe is away'):

p	q	p • q	~ (p • q)
T	T	T	F
F	T	F	T
T	F	F	T
F	F	F	T

Underneath the simple components we write columns that exhaust the combinations of truth values. Then below the conjunction we indicate its truth value for each of the four cases, and finally we do the same below the denial. The last column is formed from the penultimate one, following the truth table for denial.

The truth table is:

p	q	~ (p • q)
T	T	F
F	T	T
T	F	T
F	F	T

leaving out the penultimate column, 'p • q', which is only an intermediate step in the derivation of the last column. The truth table makes the compound perfectly clear, provided the simple components are already understood. The compound merely denies the joint truth of the components, 'John is ill' and 'Joe is away'.

This truth table derivation can obviously be extended indefinitely for ever more complex combinations of conjunction and denial, even though the example used here is extremely simple. Another, equally simple, example is the following:

(2)   (~ John is ill) • Joe is away.

p	q	~p	(~p) • q
T	T	F	F
F	T	T	T
T	F	F	F
F	F	T	F

Here, as before, the intermediate column is not part of the final table.[i]

§ 3 Parentheses

Although (1) above is true in all cases except where 'John is ill' and 'Joe is away' are both true, (2) is true in only one case: where 'John is ill' is false and 'Joe is away' is true. We see illustrated here the importance of parentheses, whose use is the only thing that visibly distinguishes (1) from (2). While (1) corresponds to the words:

It is not the case that John is ill and Joe is away,

(2) corresponds to the words:

John is not ill but Joe is away.

To avoid the excessive use of parentheses, let us interpret the ambiguous form:

(3)   ~ John is ill • Joe is away

---

[i] The explicit use of truth-value tables only appears in the literature from 1920 to 1921 onward (Łukasiewicz, Post, Wittgenstein). However, techniques substantially equivalent to truth tables were presented by Peirce in 1885 (vol. III, §§ 387–388) and were, in fact, implicit even in Boole's "general rule of development" (1854, pp. 75–76).

Table 1

p	q	r	p • q	(p • q) • r	q • r	p • (q • r)
T	T	T	T	T	T	T
F	T	T	F	F	T	F
T	F	T	F	F	F	F
F	F	T	F	F	F	F
T	T	F	T	F	F	F
F	T	F	F	F	F	F
T	F	F	F	F	F	F
F	F	F	F	F	F	F

in the manner of (2) instead of (1). The tilde is interpreted as always governing the shortest sentence compatible with the placement of the parentheses.

The use of parentheses is never necessary within iterated conjunctions. We do not need to distinguish the two conjunctions '(p • q) • r' and 'p • (q • r)'. Both can be written equally well as 'p • q • r'. This is apparent when we construct a comparative truth table, Table 1. Here, as before, we begin by exhausting the ways of assigning truth values to the simple components. But there are three simple components to consider instead of two, and for this reason there are eight combinations of truth values instead of four. After exhausting those eight combinations, we proceed to calculate all the subsequent columns on the basis of the previous columns using the simple truth table for conjunction. The result shows that '(p • q) • r' and 'p • (q • r)' are equivalent, both being true only in the unique case in which all three simple components are true. It is clear that the situation is similar for conjunctions of four, five, or more components; every iterated conjunction can be expressed without parentheses as 'p • q • r • s • ...', and can be thought of simply as the simultaneous conjunction of all of the simple components. The conjunction is true only in the unique case in which all of the simple components are true.

§ 4 Complex Truth Tables

As is already clear, the truth-table method lets us calculate, step by step, the logical import of any combination of conjunctions and denials, whatever its degree of complexity. For instance, the truth table for the compound

(1)   ~ (~ (p • ~ q • r) • ~ (p • ~ r) • q)

Table 2

p	q	r	~q	~r	p•~q•r	~(p•~q•r)	p•~r	~(p•~r)	long[6] conjunction	long denial
T	T	T	F	F	F	T	F	T	T	F
F	T	T	F	F	F	T	F	T	T	F
T	F	T	T	F	T	F	F	T	F	T
F	F	T	T	F	F	T	F	T	F	T
T	T	F	F	T	F	T	T	F	F	T
F	T	F	F	T	F	T	F	T	T	F
T	F	F	T	T	F	T	T	F	F	T
F	F	F	T	T	F	T	F	T	F	T

is Table 2.

Note how much easier it is to treat iterated conjunctions as simultaneous conjunctions, held to be true only in the case where all of their components are true.

Strictly speaking, its outcome is only the first three columns of Table 2 plus the last one: The seven intermediate columns are simply instruments of deriva-tion. This final table shows that (1) is true in all cases except in (a) the case in which all three simple components are true, (b) the case in which the first simple component is false and the other two are true, and (c) the case in which the second simple component is true and the other two false.

Such is the very simple technique for deriving the truth-value table for any statement constructed by means of conjunction and denial. Where there are more than three simple components, the table will have more than eight lines; in general it will have 2^n lines wherever there are n simple compo-nents. A convenient system for exhausting the combinations of truth values of components is the system illustrated above for cases of one, two, and three components. The general method appears in Table 3. The top half of the table for two components, 'p' and 'q', is formed by adding to the table for one component a second column that contains 'T' in both places. The lower half of the table for two components is formed likewise, using 'F' in place of 'T'. In the same way, the table for three components, 'p', 'q', and 'r', is formed, following the top half of the table, from the table for two components, to which is added a third column that contains 'T' in all places, and correspond-ingly with regard to the lower half. The table for four components is formed from the table for three components according to the same rule, and so forth. In general, it may be seen that 'T' and 'F' alternate *simply* in the first column,

Table 3

	p	q	r	s	
	T	T	T	T	...
	F	T	T	T	...
1					
	T	F	T	T	...
	F	F	T	T	...
2					
	T	T	F	T	...
	F	T	F	T	...
	T	F	F	T	...
	F	F	F	T	...
3					
	T	T	T	F	...
	.	.	.	.	
	.	.	.	.	
	.	.	.	.	
	.	.	.	.	

in *pairs* in the second column, in groups of *four* in the third column, in groups of *eight* in the fourth column, and so forth.

In practice we can of course save ourselves the effort of working out the intermediate columns, like in Table 2, by using a faster method. One such method, applied to the example considered above, is the following: to obtain the upper half of the final column, we observe that 'r' must be true, so we substitute 'T' for 'r' within (1), thus:

$$\sim (\sim (p \bullet \sim q \bullet T) \bullet \sim (p \bullet F) \bullet q)$$

Noting that '~T' becomes 'F', and that 'T' as a component of a conjunction has no effect and can be omitted, we obtain:

$$\sim (\sim (p \bullet \sim q) \bullet \sim (p \bullet F) \bullet q)$$

Taking into account that every conjunction in which 'F' appears as a component becomes 'F', and that '~F' can be replaced by 'T', we obtain:

$$\sim(\sim(p \bullet \sim q) \bullet T \bullet q)$$

and then:

(2) $\sim(\sim(p \bullet \sim q) \bullet q)$

The upper half of our final column will therefore be just the column for (2). To determine the first two places in this column, we substitute 'T' for 'q' in (2) and reduce the result by means of operations similar to those just illustrated. We thus obtain simply 'F'. To determine the two following places of the column, we substitute 'F' for 'q' in (2) and reduce the result, obtaining 'T'. Then, to determine the lower half of our final column, we substitute 'F' for 'r' in (1) and reduce the result, obtaining '$\sim(\sim p \bullet q)$'. The first two places of this lower half are obtained with the substitution of 'T' for 'q' in '$\sim(\sim p \bullet q)$'; the result is reduced to 'p' itself, thus becoming 'T' in the first place and 'F' in the second. The last two places are obtained with the substitution of 'F' for 'q' in '$\sim(\sim p \bullet q)$': the result is reduced to 'T'. With some practice this method is very quick and greatly reduces the need to write things down, and we will come across other methods for speeding things up later. But these are just refinements. The earlier method, with intermediate columns, may be thought of as the fundamental technique, because of its schematic and lucid character.[7]

§ 5 Compounds Derived from Truth Tables

Now that we have a general technique for deriving the truth table for any compound constructed by means of conjunction and denial, what about going the other way? Is there also a technique such that, given any truth table, we can construct a compound out of conjunction and denial corresponding to it? Or are conjunction and denial sufficient only for constructing compounds that correspond to some of the possible truth tables, but not all?

The answer is perhaps the most important principle of the theory of composition: *there is*, in fact, *a technique such that, given any truth table, we can construct a compound by means of conjunction and denial that corresponds to that table.*[ii]

The importance of this fact will become apparent later on. Meanwhile, let us see what this technique consists in.

[ii] Post was the first to prove this truth. The proof that follows is an adaptation and simplification of his.

Table 4

	p_1	p_2	p_3	$\ldots$	p_n	Compound
1st Case	T	T	T	$\ldots$	T	?
2nd Case	F	T	T	$\ldots$	T	?
3rd Case	T	F	T	$\ldots$	T	?
4th Case	F	F	T	$\ldots$	T	?
5th Case	T	T	F	$\ldots$	T	?
6th Case	F	T	F	$\ldots$	T	?
.	.	.	.	.	.	.
.	.	.	.	.	.	.
.	.	.	.	.	.	.
$(2^n-1)^{th}$ Case	T	F	F	$\ldots$	F	?
$(2^n)^{th}$ Case	F	F	F	$\ldots$	F	?

Take any truth table and it will have the general form given in Table 4. Now take the 2^n corresponding conjunctions that we form by writing the conjunction

'$p_1 \bullet p_2 \bullet p_3 \bullet \ldots \bullet p_n$'

and by inserting the tilde where 'F' appears on the corresponding line of Table 4.

1st Conjunction:	$p_1 \bullet$		$p_2 \bullet$		$p_3 \bullet$	$\ldots \bullet$	p_n	Abbreviated:	C_1
2nd Conjunction:	$\sim p_1 \bullet$		$p_2 \bullet$		$p_3 \bullet$	$\ldots \bullet$	p_n		C_2
3rd ''	$p_1 \bullet$		$\sim p_2 \bullet$		$p_3 \bullet$	$\ldots \bullet$	p_n		C_3
4th ''	$\sim p_1 \bullet$		$\sim p_2 \bullet$		$p_3 \bullet$	$\ldots \bullet$	p_n		C_4
5th ''	$p_1 \bullet$		$p_2 \bullet$		$\sim p_3 \bullet$	$\ldots \bullet$	p_n		C_5
6th ''	$\sim p_1 \bullet$		$p_2 \bullet$		$\sim p_3 \bullet$	$\ldots \bullet$	p_n		C_6
.	.		.		.	.	.		.
.	.		.		.	.	.		.
.	.		.		.	.	.		.
$(2^n-1)^{th}$ ''	$p_1 \bullet$		$\sim p_2 \bullet$		$\sim p_3 \bullet$	$\ldots \bullet$	$\sim p_n$		C_{2^n-1}
$(2^n)^{th}$ ''	$\sim p_1 \bullet$		$\sim p_2 \bullet$		$\sim p_3 \bullet$	$\ldots \bullet$	$\sim p_n$		C_{2^n}

It is clear that the first conjunction is true only when 'p', 'p_2', and 'p_3' are true, that is, only in the first case, and that the second conjunction is true only in the second case, and so forth.

As a consequence, the denial of the first conjunction, that is, '$\sim (p_1 \bullet \sim p_2 \bullet \ldots \bullet p_n)$', or, in short, '$\sim C_1$', is true in all cases *except* the first, and, in general, '$\sim C_i$' is true in all cases except the ith.

As a consequence, '$\sim C_1 \bullet \sim C_2$', being true only when '$\sim C_1$' and '$\sim C_2$' are true, is true in all cases except in the first and second. Likewise, in general, '$\sim C_i \bullet \sim C_j \bullet \sim C_k \bullet \ldots$' is true in all cases except in the ith, the jth, and the kth.

But with this we already have the solution to our problem. We already have a technique for construing a compound by means of conjunction and denial corresponding to any truth table whatsoever. Since we want the compound to be true in all cases except in the case indicated by 'F' in the table, the compound we need is simply '$\sim C_i \bullet \sim C_j \bullet \sim C_k \bullet \ldots$', the cases indicated by 'F' in the table being the ith, the jth, the kth, ... Here 'C_i', 'C_j', 'C_k', etc. are in turn constructed from 'p_1', 'p_2', ... 'p_n' by conjunction and denial.

Let us summarize the technique. Take any truth table. *In the table that exhibits the various combinations of truth values of 'p_1', ..., 'p_n', ignore the combinations that make the compound true. For each of the remaining lines of the table, write the corresponding conjunction '$p_1 \bullet p_2 \bullet \ldots \bullet p_n$', with the tilde inserted in each position where there is an 'F' on the line. Finally, deny each of these resulting conjunctions and form the conjunctions of these denials* (if there is more than one).

For example, consider once again Table 2 that we derived earlier (§ 4), but now imagine that the table is given and that the problem is to reconstruct a compound for the table. That is, consider the *inverse* problem to the one whose solution we found by means of the truth table. In this truth table the combinations that receive the value 'F' are:

p	q	r
T	T	T
F	T	T
F	T	F

The corresponding conjunctions are '$p \bullet q \bullet r$', '$\sim p \bullet q \bullet r$', and '$\sim p \bullet q \bullet \sim r$'. By denying and then conjoining the results, we obtain:

$$\sim (p \bullet q \bullet r) \bullet \sim (\sim p \bullet q \bullet r) \bullet \sim (\sim p \bullet q \bullet \sim r)$$

(Note that this result would be written '$\sim C_1 \bullet \sim C_2 \bullet \sim C_6$' in the notation of the general argument.)

The result thus obtained differs from the original compound from which we previously derived the table. But this is not surprising; many compounds correspond to the same truth table, just like many arithmetical expressions designate the same number – for example '3 + 5', '4 + 4', '6 + 2'. There is, in fact, aside from the two compounds in this example, a third that is simpler and that has the same truth table: it is '$\sim (\sim p \bullet q) \bullet \sim (q \bullet r)$', as may be verified by deriving the table for this compound in the usual way.

The technique that we have just arrived at for constructing a corresponding compound for any truth table covers all cases except the extreme case where there are no 'F's at all in the compound column. The technique does not apply

Table 5

p_1 p_2 p_3 $\ldots$ p_n	$\sim p_1$	$p_1 \bullet \sim p_1 \bullet p_2 \bullet p_3 \bullet \ldots \bullet p_n$	$\sim(p_1 \bullet \sim p_1 \bullet p_2 \bullet \ldots \bullet p_n)$
T T T $\ldots$ T	F	F	T
F T T $\ldots$ T	T	F	T
T F T $\ldots$ T	F	F	T
F F T $\ldots$ T	T	F	T
T T F $\ldots$ T	F	F	T
. . . .	.	.	.
. . . .	.	.	.
. . . .	.	.	.
T F F $\ldots$ F	F	F	T
F F F $\ldots$ F	T	F	T

here, as the first sentence of the formulation of the general technique requires that we consider only lines with the value 'F', of which there are none in this case. Still, given a table of this type, we can easily write a compound for it. One such compound is '$\sim(p \bullet \sim p)$', or, if we wish to use 'p_1', 'p_2', $\ldots$ 'p_n' explicitly, '$\sim(p_1 \bullet \sim p_1 \bullet p_2 \bullet p_3 \bullet \ldots \bullet p_n)$', as we see in Table 5.

The column below '$p_1 \bullet \sim p_1 \bullet p_2 \bullet p_3 \bullet \ldots \bullet p_n$' contains an 'F' in each of its positions, as every line of the table contains an 'F' either below 'p_1' or below '$\sim p_1$'. Thus the column below the final denial contains 'T' in all of its positions.

The compound derived from any truth table, according to the technique established here, has a formula that is very simple and easy to understand: simple, because there are no parentheses within parentheses, and easy to understand, because it makes visible all the combinations of truth values of the components that would make the compound false. Any statement can be mechanically converted into this more convenient form, called the *canonical form*. The process consists in deriving the truth-table values of the given statement and then deriving the canonical statement from this table. We already know that the canonical form thus derived is not in general the simplest form possible: but any general technique for reducing statements to forms of minimal complexity would itself be a very complicated technique, and this is a refinement that may be left aside.

From the existence of a general technique for constructing compounds corresponding to any truth table by means of conjunction and denial follows the very important result that the theory of 'and' and 'not' also covers all other modes of composition of the so-called *extensional* kind: that is, of the kind in which the truth value of the compound statement depends on nothing but the truth values of the components. Among the connectives of this kind is . . .

§ 6 'Or'

'Or' has two different senses. In the so-called *inclusive* sense, at least one of the components must be true for the compound to be true. In the other, *exclusive* sense, exactly one component must be true. The two senses have the following truth tables:

p	q	p or q (incl.)	p or q (excl.)
T	T	T	F
F	T	T	T
T	F	T	T
T	F	F	F

Both senses of 'p or q' can be translated in terms of conjunction and denial; because we have truth tables for both senses of 'or', and on the other hand we have our technique for constructing compounds by means of conjunction and denial that correspond to any truth tables whatsoever. Applied to the truth table for the exclusive sense of 'p or q', the technique yields, first of all, the conjunctions 'p • q' and '~ p • ~ q', then the denials '~ (p • q)' and '~ (~ p • ~ q)', and finally the conjunction of these, that is, '~ (p • q) • ~ (~ p • ~ q)'. Thus we mechanically obtain the translation of exclusive 'or' in terms of conjunction and denial. The translation of inclusive 'or' is even simpler. Applied to the truth table for the inclusive sense of 'p or q', the general technique gives us, first of all, the single conjunction '~ p • ~ q', and then, as a final result, its denial '~ (~ p • ~ q)'.

The inclusive sense of 'p or q' can be expressed univocally as 'p or q or both'; and the exclusive sense can be expressed univocally as 'p or q but not both'. When we come across 'p or q' by itself, we generally do not know which sense is meant. In many cases the choice is arbitrary, as either sense will do equally well. For example, consider the expression 'x $\leq$ y'[8] – in words 'x < y or x = y'. Does 'or' have the inclusive or the exclusive sense here? It doesn't matter! As our truth tables make clear, the only difference between the two senses lies in the first of the four cases – that is, the compound truth case, in which both components are true. But when it comes to the components 'x < y' and 'x = y', the compound truth case does not arise at all, neither in reality nor in the mind of the speaker.

I would like to emphasize this because it is a common error to think that examples such as 'x < y or x = y' are clear cases of the exclusive use of 'or', an error that results in a tendency to exaggerate the role of the exclusive sense of 'or' in everyday language. The sentences 'x < y' and 'x = y' are in themselves mutually exclusive, or incompatible. But this fact, far from establishing that the context 'x < y or x = y' employs 'or' in the exclusive sense, *robs* us of the only case that allows us to distinguish between the exclusive and inclusive sense. The only practically possible cases that remain are these three:

x < y	x = y
F	T
T	F
F	F

But in these cases, the exclusive and inclusive senses of 'or' behave identically.

This becomes equally evident when we translate the two senses of 'x < y or x = y' in terms of conjunction and denial. The inclusive sense is:

$$\sim (\sim x < y \bullet \sim x = y)$$

and the exclusive sense is:

$$\sim (x < y \bullet x = y) \bullet \sim(\sim x < y \bullet \sim x = y)$$

How can we tell which sense is intended? The only difference is in the first conjunct '$\sim (x < y \bullet x = y)$', added to the statement with the inclusive sense to produce a statement with the exclusive sense. But this additional conjunct is a known truth (given any x and y) that we can therefore freely insert or omit. To omit it is not to deny it; we never say everything that we know.

In summary: Given that the sentences 'x < y' and 'x = y' are already mutually exclusive by nature, it is immaterial whether we take 'or' as repeating this exclusion or not.

When it comes to establishing incontestable examples of the exclusive use of 'or', we must imagine circumstances in which the person who uses 'or' clearly and positively means to contradict the compound truth of the components, and to do so explicitly within the same statement. Such examples are rare, but they exist. An example given by Tarski supposes that a boy asks his father to take him to the beach and afterwards to the movies. The father responds in a tone of refusal: 'We'll *either* go to the beach *or* to the movies'. Here the exclusive use is clear; the father not only wants to promise, but to simultaneously promise and refuse.

It is very easy, however, to find cases in which the inclusive interpretation is mandatory. For example, when it is decreed that passports will be issued only to people who were either born in the country or have married natives, this does not mean that people who were born in the country and have married natives are denied passports.

Most uses of 'or' in ordinary language are of the type that admit only the inclusive interpretation, or of the 'x < y or x = y' type, which fits both interpretations. So it will be useful here, in order to avoid any ambiguity, to agree to take 'or' *always* in the inclusive sense from now on. The rare exceptions, like 'We'll *either* go to the beach *or* to the movies', said in a tone of refusal, can be thought of as completed explicitly by the addition of the words 'but not both'.

Often in mathematical logic a special sign is introduced in place of 'or' in the inclusive sense. But I see little advantage in such a multiplication of signs; we are not interested here in some kind of mystical kabbalah, nor in shorthand. What matters, theoretically and practically, is the reducibility of 'or' and other extensional connectives to conjunction and denial, as well as the techniques, some of which we have already discussed, that govern the use of these connectives.

§ 7 'If – Then'

Aside from 'not', 'and', and 'or', another connective that plays an important role in ordinary language is 'if p then q'. This compound is called the *conditional*, and its components are called, respectively, the *antecedent* and the *consequent*. Given that the conditional affirms its consequent only conditionally, the falsity of the consequent only falsifies the entire conditional where the antecedent is held true. Therefore, the only case in which a conditional is false is the case in which the antecedent is true and the consequent false. Thus we arrive at the following truth table:

p	q	if p then q
T	T	T
F	T	T
T	F	F
F	F	T

We know how to construct a compound of conjunction and denial according to this table: We form the conjunction 'p • ~ q' and deny it, obtaining '~ (p • ~ q)'. This is the *extensional conditional*. Every extensional conditional with a true consequent is true, and every one with a false antecedent is true. The result is that, for example, the conditionals:

> If lead is fusible, then the sea is salt,
> If lead floats on water, then the sea is salt,
> If lead floats on water, then the sea is sweet,

are all true. This fact might induce us to think that the extensional conditional does not conform to the ordinary usage of the conditional. We might think the ordinary conditional supposes a certain connection, perhaps causal, between the conditions described in the antecedent and the consequent, such that the three examples that we have just considered would be false. I don't think this is true. It seems to me that to declare these three examples false is no less of a departure from ordinary usage than to declare them true. What is foreign to ordinary usage is the examples themselves, not their truth. In practice we do not utter conditionals when the truth values of their components are already known. But this does not stop us from identifying 'if p then q' with '$\sim (p \cdot \sim q)$', because it is equally obvious that in practice we would not use a compound of the form '$\sim (p \cdot \sim q)$', any more than 'if p then q', when we already know what the truth values of the components are. The reason is obvious: instead of affirming '$\sim (p \cdot \sim q)$', or 'if p then q', we could provide more information in less space by only affirming 'q' or denying 'p'. The causal connection is part of the reason for affirming a statement of the form '$\sim (p \cdot \sim q)$', but not part of its content; the same applies to a spoken utterance of 'if p then q'. Therefore, I hold that '$\sim (p \cdot \sim q)$' provides a good translation of the words 'if p then q', and that the truth table under consideration is well suited to the conditional.

Now let us consider certain other uses of 'if – then', which must be analyzed differently. This connective is also used in expressing general laws, such as:

> If something interests me, then it bores George.

The intimate connection between interesting me and boring George is part of the content of this statement; it does not merely figure in its motivation. This example, however, which we can call the *general conditional*, is not in fact composed of two component statements; it is not a conditional in that sense. Its nature is exhibited more clearly in this formulation:

> Whatever may be selected, if it interests me then it bores George.

This statement has the effect of affirming an unlimited array of conditionals of the form:

> If —— interests me, then —— bores George.

Each of the separate conditionals, for example:

> If basketball interests me, then basketball bores George,

can still be understood in the sense proposed earlier:

> ~ (basketball interests me • ~ basketball bores George).

The connection between interesting me and boring George is expressed in this conditional not just by the connective 'if – then', but by being governed by the prefix 'whatever may be selected'. We will study this device later, in the theory of quantification.

Another use of 'if – then' that should be considered separately is the "contrary-to-fact use," in which the verb of the antecedent appears in the subjunctive; for example:

> If Belgium had approved the extension of the Maginot Line, then France would have been unbeatable.

It is obvious that the truth table for the conditional does not work here, nor the mode of translation '~(p • ~q)'. If the falsehood of the antecedent is enough to make such a conditional true, every "contrary-to-fact" conditional would be vacuous and useless, because their antecedents are already known to be false. It is easily verifiable that the contrary-to-fact conditional does not lend itself to any formulation by means of the truth table: it is not *extensional*. Therefore, when we speak of the indicative conditional, taking it in the extensional way represented by the truth table, we must remember that we are not talking about the contrary-to-fact conditional, whose linguistic form is easily distinguished from the extensional conditional.

Obviously, the contrary-to-fact conditional is less clear, and more dubious from the scientific point of view, than the regular conditional. This and other *intensional* modes of statement composition (that is, non-extensional modes of composition), will be shelved while we look at the theory of composition, but we will return later to the general question of intensional composition.

§ 8 Implication

A point that is worth dwelling on, before we abandon the subject of the conditional, is that I have not, so far, used the verb 'to imply'. In the literature there is an unfortunate confusion between 'if – then' and 'implies', so that we often see authors write 'p implies q' in place of 'if p then q' or '~ (p • ~ q)'. Implication is not a mode of composition of statements; it is a *relation* between statements, as, for example, love and hate are relations between persons. The verb 'implies', like the verbs 'loves' and 'hates', always goes between names, not statements. To say that Hitler hates Stalin, we put the word 'hates' between the two personal names, not between the two men; similarly, to say that a given statement implies another, we must put the word 'implies' between the names of the two statements, not between the statements. Although the words 'if – then' combine with statements, as in the following example:

If there are nine planets, then there are more than seven,

the word 'implies' is only inserted between substantives – names of statements – in the following manner:

'There are nine planets' implies 'there are more than seven planets'

or:

The tenth statement on the page implies the last.

Naturally, we cannot represent implication by means of '~ (p • ~ q)', nor by means of any truth table, because here we are not engaged in composing statements extensionally or in any other manner. When two statements *rhyme*, this does not depend on the truth values of the statements, yet this relation does not involve us in the intensional composition of statements either, and the same goes for implication.

What exactly is the relation of implication? That depends on how we interpret it. What we may call *logical implication*, for example, is the relation that holds between two statements in a given order, when the conditional formed from those statements in the same order is logically true. This is the relation by which, as I said before (in the Introduction), logic finds its practical applications. A notion of *physical* implication could similarly be defined based on the notion of physical truth, and so forth. Later on we shall be concerned with certain notions of implication that are even more restricted than that of logical implication.

§ 9 On Translation in General

There are other extensional connectives beside 'or' and 'if – then', but these are so obvious that they do not call for detailed investigation. One is the connective 'neither – nor': 'neither p nor q'. Clearly this connective is merely a different way of saying 'not p and not q', that is '~ p • ~ q'.

Another connective, 'but', can always be replaced by '•'; from a logical point of view, we cannot tell 'and' and 'but' apart. The difference is a only rhetorical one, as we can see by comparing these examples:

> John is sick but Joe is here,
> John is sick and Joe is away.

The difference here is rhetorical, not logical, because substituting 'but' for 'and' or vice-versa never has the effect of making a true statement false; its only effect is that of making the statement sound more or less natural.

We could extend our investigations to other connectives such as 'except', 'although', 'unless', so as to arrive at a rudimentary dictionary for guiding translations in terms of '~' and '•'. But, as we saw before in our discussion of 'or' and 'if – then', the dictionary could not consist of a mere list of one-to-one mappings, no more than a dictionary translating between two natural languages could.

It is also clear that the best results are obtained, when translating between two natural languages, when we do not depend in the first place on the mappings suggested by the dictionary, but instead seek to reconstruct the sentence or the whole paragraph within the context of the new language. The case of translation from a natural language into logical symbolism is just the same. However, even though we have to practice a great deal – practice Portuguese, for example – before we can think of a sentence directly in Portuguese, fortunately there is no such obstacle in thinking of a sentence in terms of '~' and '•'. These signs already correspond exactly to two words of the native language, such that it is a simple matter of paraphrasing a given sentence of the native language into another sentence pertaining to a restricted part of the same language.

It is in this spirit of "re-thinking" that we must undertake translations into logical signs. That this is necessary is apparent not only from our discussion of individual connectives, but also from the issue of grouping posed by complex contexts. In the compound:

> Neither will Philip be declassified, nor will the Ideal Club win first prize and the Excelsior Club second,

for example, the question arises whether the whole is to be construed as having the form 'neither p nor (q and r)' or the form '(neither p nor q) and r'. We can show that these two forms, symbolically '$\sim p \cdot \sim (q \cdot r)$' and '$(\sim p \cdot \sim q) \cdot r$', have different truth tables. But in fact there can be no doubt that the correct meaning is 'neither p nor (q and r)', seeing that the word 'win' occurs only once and governs the two subsequent clauses. Such are the non-systematic indications of grouping used in everyday language, in contrast to the schematic use of parentheses characteristic of logical language.

Often, in ordinary language, we cannot decide what the argument is except on the basis of the overall context, or on the basis of psychological judgments about the probable motives of our interlocutor. In the compound:

> The Ideal Club will win the prize and the Excelsior Club will remain in second place if Philip is declassified,

for example, there is no internal evidence for a decision between the two forms '(p and q) if r' and 'p and (q and r)', that is, between the two non-equivalent forms '~ (r • ~ (p • q))' and 'p • ~ (r • ~ q)'.

§ 10 Centripetal Translation

Even though translation into symbols must be accomplished by reconstructing the statement in the new language, we must not attempt this kind of translation all at once. Such attempts usually lead to errors when dealing with a complex statement such as this:

(1)   If the hill tribes remain rebellious or the colonists complain about further assaults, then the authority of the colonial governor will not be reduced, nor will the Junta abandon its control of the port, unless the Colonial Office fails to send new instructions.[9]

The most dependable technique is that of *centripetal translation*. The first step of this technique is to work out the outermost structure[10] of a given statement, and then impose that outer structure on the statement in our translation, before working our way inward. In the above example, it is easy to see that 'if p then q' is the outermost structure, that is, that 'if – then' is the main connective of the compound, although we are dealing with a typical problem of the determination of grouping here. Translating the compound 'if p then q' as '~ (p • ~ q)', we have:

(2)   ~ (the hill tribes will remain rebellious or the colonists will complain about further assaults • ~ (the authority of the colonial governor will not be reduced, nor will the Junta abandon its control of the port, unless the Colonial Office fails to send new instructions)).

The second step of the technique of centripetal translation is to pick out the longest compound, figure out its outermost structure, and then translate that compound in accordance with that structure. In the example, we take the component 'the authority ... new instructions' and decide (perhaps with some hesitation about the question of grouping) that its outermost structure is that of 'p unless q'. Note also that the main connective, 'unless', has the force of 'if' (at least in the given concrete context) such that 'p unless q' can be understood as 'p if q', that is, as 'if q then p', or '~ (q • ~ p)'.[11] So the component under consideration is translated:

> ~ (the Colonial Office fails to send new instructions • ~ (the authority of the colonial governor will not be reduced, nor will the Junta abandon its control of the port)).

When we substitute this translation for 'the authority ... new instructions' in (2), we see an occurrence of the combination '~ ~' which, as we can see from its truth table, is superfluous:

$$
\begin{array}{ccc}
p & \sim p & \sim\sim p \\
T & F & T \\
F & T & F
\end{array}
$$

To avoid having to refer frequently to the equivalence between '~ ~ p' and 'p', it is convenient to regard the notation '~ ~ p' as non-existent, taking the mode of denying a denial to be simply that of erasing the tilde instead of duplicating it. Thus we arrive at:

(3)   ~ (the hill tribes will remain rebellious or the colonists will complain about further assaults • the Colonial Office fails to send new instructions • ~ (the authority of the colonial governor will not be reduced, nor will the Junta abandon its control of the port)).

The next step in the technique of centripetal translation is, just like the previous step, to take the longest component and translate it in accordance with its outer structure. Continue in this way until only simple components remain. In the example, we take the component 'the authority ... the port' and note that it has the form 'neither p nor q', that is, '~ p • ~ q'. The resulting translation of this component is:

> ~ the authority of the colonial governor will be reduced • ~ the Junta will abandon control of the port.

Substituting this component, we transform (3) into:

(4)   ~ (the hill tribes will remain rebellious or the colonists will complain about further assaults • the Colonial Office fails to send new instructions • ~ (~ the authority of the colonial governor will be reduced • ~ the Junta will abandon its control of the port)).

Then we note that the component 'the hill tribes ... assaults' has the form of 'p or q', which reduces to '~ (~ p • ~ q)'. Finally we note that the component 'the ... instructions' has the form 'not p', that is, '~p'. Introducing these translations into (4), we obtain the final result:

(5)   ~ (~ (~ the hill tribes will remain rebellious • ~ the colonists will complain about further assaults) • ~ the Colonial Office sends new instructions • ~ (~ the authority of the colonial governor will be reduced • ~ the Junta will abandon its control of the port)).

The form exemplified is:

'~ (~ (~ p • ~ q) • ~ r • ~ (~ s • ~ t))'.

§ 11 Compositional Equivalence

Translation in terms of '~' and '•' has the effect of revealing and resolving ambiguities, either with regard to the sense of some of our natural-language connectives, or with regard to issues of grouping. But the primary goal of such translation is to make statements susceptible to truth-table techniques, by means of which we can determine that certain statements are equivalent to others or follow logically from others.

Translation itself immediately reveals certain equivalences, transforming different statements of natural language into the same statement in terms of '~' and '•'. For example, both of the following statements:

> If this lake flows northward and that valley does not go into the mountains, then we are in the basin of the Amazon,

> If this lake flows northward, then either that valley goes into the mountains, or we are in the basin of the Amazon,

translate, according to the technique of centripetal translation that we studied above, into the single statement:

> ~ (this lake flows northward • ~ that valley goes into the mountains • ~ we are in the basin of the Amazon).

But other equivalences remain to be determined following translation in terms of '~' and '•', given that, as we noted above (§ 5), different compounds of '~' and '•' may have the same truth-value table. The technique for determining such equivalences consists simply in constructing a truth table on the basis of the simple components of the two compounds that we want to compare, and then deriving the corresponding columns for the two compounds and checking

Table 6

p	q	r	$\sim (p \bullet \sim (q \bullet r))$	$\sim (p \bullet \sim q) \bullet \sim (p \bullet \sim r)$
T	T	T	T	T
F	T	T	T	T
T	F	T	F	F
F	F	T	T	T
T	T	F	F	F
F	T	F	T	T
T	F	F	F	F
F	F	F	T	T

whether these columns are the same. For example, to prove the equivalence of the statements:

If the drought continues, there will be famine and migration,

If the drought continues there will be famine, and if the drought continues there will be migration,

we translate the statements in terms of '~' and '•' in the following manner:

~ (the drought continues • ~ (there will be famine • there will be migration))

~ (the drought continues • ~ there will be famine) • ~ (the drought continues • ~ there will be migration)

and then, using 'p', 'q', and 'r', for brevity's sake, in place of 'the drought continues', 'there will be famine', and 'there will be migration', we construct Table 6 using our familiar techniques (§ 4).

Let us scrutinize the expression 'simple components', which we have just used in the formulation of the technique for determining equivalence, to see if it is sufficiently exact. We are not concerned here with absolute simplicity: the "simple" components can have any degree of complexity in relation to, for example, the quantificational structures we will consider later on. The "simple" components of a given statement are merely the statements, which are not conjunctions or denials, that we combine by means of conjunction and denial to form the given statement.

The relation of equivalence which is verified by comparing truth tables is, clearly, the relation between two statements constructed in such a way, by means of conjunction and denial, that their truth values coincide independently of the truth values of the simple components. This is the relation of *being exactly alike in truth value in virtue of their compositional structure alone.* This relation can, for this reason, be called *compositional equivalence.* More generally, we may call *logically equivalent* all statements that have the same truth value in virtue of their logical structure, that is, in virtue of their structure with regard to logical vocabulary. Thus compositional equivalence constitutes the kind of logical equivalence which pertains only to the two particles '~' and '•' of our logical vocabulary.

As the truth table above showed, any two statements of the form

(1) $\sim (p \bullet \sim (q \bullet r)), \quad \sim (p \bullet \sim q) \bullet \sim (p \bullet \sim r)$

are compositionally equivalent. Other examples would be, as we have effectively already noted (§§ 3, 10), all pairs of the forms:

$$(p \bullet q) \bullet r, \quad p \bullet (q \bullet r),$$
$$\sim \sim p, \quad p;$$

Therefore, let us conventionally absorb these equivalences in the notation itself, abandoning the use of '~ ~' and the use of parentheses within iterated conjunctions. Other examples of compositional equivalence occur in all pairs of the following forms:

(2) $p \bullet q, \quad q \bullet p,$

(3) $p \bullet p, \quad p,$

(4) $p \bullet \sim (q \bullet \sim p), \quad p,$

(5) $p \bullet \sim p, \quad q \bullet \sim q,$

as may be verified by constructing pairs of truth tables in the manner just illustrated.

In practice, we often verify equivalences by successive transformations rather than by the truth-table method. For example, since we know any two statements that have one of the forms (1)–(5) are equivalent, we can establish the equivalence of any two statements of the form

(6) $p \bullet \sim (q \bullet \sim q), \quad p$

in the following manner: '$p \bullet \sim (q \bullet \sim q)$' is equivalent, by (5), to '$p \bullet \sim (p \bullet \sim p)$', which is equivalent, by (4), to 'p'.

Likewise we can establish the equivalence of any two statements of the form:

(7) $p \bullet q \bullet \sim q, \quad r \bullet \sim r$

in the following manner: '$p \bullet q \bullet \sim q$' is equivalent, by (5), to '$p \bullet p \bullet \sim p$', which is equivalent, by (3), to '$p \bullet \sim p$', which is equivalent, by (5), to '$r \bullet \sim r$'.

Such transformations on the basis of (1)–(5) suffice, in fact, to establish any compositional equivalence. Nevertheless, derivations become shorter if we use not only (1)–(5), but also, in a cumulative manner, any other pairs already derived. Thus, on the basis of (1)–(5) with (6), we may obtain:

(8)   p • ~ (p • q),   p • ~ q

in the following manner: 'p • ~ (p • q)' (which is the denial of '~ (p • ~ (p • q))', given the abolition of '~ ~') is equivalent, by (1), to '~ (~ (p • ~ p) • ~ (p • ~ q))', which is equivalent, by (2), to '~ (~ (p • ~ q) • ~ (p • ~ p))', which is equivalent, by (6), to 'p • ~ q'.

Likewise we may obtain:

(9)   ~ (p • q) • ~ (p • ~ q),   ~ p

in the following manner: '~ (p • q) • ~ (p • ~ q)' is equivalent, by (1), to '~ (p • ~ (~ q • q)', which is equivalent by (2), to '~ (p • ~ (q • ~ q))', which is equivalent, by (6), to '~ p'.

In practice, having such background knowledge of forms stored away for our use can help us work out cases of compositional equivalence, and can be particularly useful when trying to reduce a statement to its simplest equivalent (cf. § 5). But it is a dispensable luxury, because the prior truth-table criterion already suffices for deciding any compositional equivalence. In addition, the truth-table criterion has the fundamental advantage of being purely mechanical, while any attempt to establish the equivalence we want by means of transformation requires, in general, a non-systematic search.

§ 12 Compositional Implication

Compositional implication is the relation between a statement and any statement that follows from it in virtue of nothing but their compositional structures. One compound compositionally implies another when the two are constructed by means of conjunction and denial such that no change in the truth values of the simple components can simultaneously make the first compound true and the second one false. In consequence, compositional implication, like compositional equivalence, is determined by pairs of truth tables. So in determining implication, the column that corresponds to the second compound does not need to be completed in places where the column that corresponds to the first compound contains 'F'. For example, in order to verify that the statement:

If John doesn't come, Joe and Philip will come

Table 7

p	q	r	~ (~p • ~ (q • r))	~ (~ p • ~ r)
T	T	T	T	T
F	T	T	T	T
T	F	T	T	T
F	F	T	F	–
T	T	F	T	T
F	T	F	F	–
T	F	F	T	T
F	F	F	F	–

compositionally implies the statement:

John or Philip will come,

we translate the statements in terms of '~' and '•', in the following manner:

~ (~ John will come • ~ (Joe will come • Philip will come)),

~ (~ John will come • ~ Philip will come).

and then, using 'p', 'q', and 'r', for brevity's sake, in place of the three simple components, we construct Table 7, and we know that the second compound has the value 'T' in all cases in which the first compound has the value 'T'. We are saved the work of deriving the truth value of the second compound in other cases, given that the implication has already been established.

To say that the second compound has the value 'T' in all cases in which the first one has the value 'T' is to say that the first has the value 'F' in all cases in which the second has the value 'F'. For this reason, an alternative method that is equally fit for purpose is to construct the entire column of the second compound and afterwards construct just one part of the column of the first compound, considering only the cases in which the second compound has the value 'F'. This method is recommended when, as in the above example, the second compound is simpler than the first. The fact is that if we had used this method in the given example, we would have had to calculate the truth value of the first component in only two cases.

Other simple examples of compositional implication, testable by means of truth tables, are the following: 'p • q' implies 'p', '~ p' implies '~ (p • q)', 'p • ~ (p • q)' implies '~ q'; these letters may be replaced by any statement.

In addition, each example of equivalence (§ 11) yields two examples of implication, since, obviously, equivalence is simply reciprocal implication. This is why the theory of equivalence can be thought of as part of the theory of implication. But inversely, the theory of implication can also be thought of as part of the theory of equivalence, because, as is easily seen, one statement implies another if, and only if, the first is equivalent to the conjunction of the two.

§ 13 Compositional Truth

If we call *logically* true every truth in which only the logical vocabulary occurs essentially (cf. Introduction), we can now, more specifically, call all truths *compositionally* true in which only the compositional part of the logical vocabulary occurs essentially, that is, only the symbols for conjunction and denial. In other words, just as a statement is called logically true if it is true in virtue of its logical structure alone, it is called, more specifically, compositionally true if it is true in virtue of its compositional structure alone.

Although there is no general mechanical criterion for logical truth, the type of logical truth that we call compositional truth does admit of a mechanical criterion, and a very simple one: We have only to construct a truth table for the statement and note whether the final column contains 'T' in all places. For example, to demonstrate the compositional truth of the sentence:

If John and Joe come, then John will come,

we translate it into logical notation as follows:

~ (John will come • Joe will come • ~ John will come)

and construct its truth table:

p	q	~ (p • q • ~ p)
T	T	T
F	T	T
T	F	T
F	F	T

Compositional implication admits of a formulation based on compositional truth, which is analogous to the formulation of logical implication offered earlier (§ 8) based on logical truth. It is easily seen that one statement compositionally implies another if and only if the conditional that has the first statement as antecedent, and the second as consequent, is compositionally true. Thus the example of compositional truth cited above corresponds directly to the implication, as stated earlier (§ 12), between 'p • q' and 'p'. Although the theory of compositional implication (and consequently also that of compositional equivalence) can be considered in this way as a part of the theory of compositional truth, the inverse is equally correct; because, as is easily verified, a statement is compositionally true if and only if it is compositionally implied by its denial. In fact, the theories of compositional truth, of compositional implication, and of compositional equivalence, are merely aspects of a single theory, the theory of composition.

We noted in the study of equivalence (§ 11) how the truth-table method can be replaced or supplemented by a method of successive transformation. This method can be generalized to allow for checking compositional implications and compositional truths. The general method is to start with a certain list of initial statements and enlarge this list, step by step, in such a way that each added statement is either the result of the transformation, on the basis of a known equivalence, of a statement already on the list, or is inferred from a statement already on the list or from a conjunction of these on the basis of a known implication. The conjunction of the initial statements of the list, omitting those that are compositionally true, implies each of the derived statements on the list: and if all of the initial statements are compositionally true, the derived ones are as well. This serial method serves, therefore, for the derivation of implications as well as of compositional truths. It is nevertheless a dispensable method, as was the serial method for generating equivalences (§ 11): the simple truth-table techniques are sufficient.

§ 14 Reduction to One Primitive. Miscellaneous Remarks

Conjunction and denial can be reduced to a single connective, that of *joint denial*, having the logical sign '↓'. The compound 'p ↓ q' has the sense of 'neither p nor q', and is characterized by the truth table:

p	q	p ↓ q
T	T	F
F	T	F
T	F	F
F	F	T

The denial '~ p' and the conjunction 'p • q' can be expressed on the basis of joint denial as 'p ↓ p' and '(p ↓ p) ↓ (q ↓ q)', as we see by deriving the truth tables for these compounds on the basis of the truth table given for 'p ↓ q'.

Another reduction, equally possible, has as its basis *alternative denial*, 'p | q', characterized by the truth table:

p	q	p | q
T	T	F
F	T	T
T	F	T
F	F	T

We can express '~ p' and 'p • q' as 'p| p' and '(p| q)| (p| q)'.[iii]

One of the theoretical advantages of such a reduction is that it simplifies the strict formulation of the notion of compositional truth. If we use only '↓' instead of '•' and '~', the result is that *a statement is compositionally true if and only if it belongs to every class x which satisfies the following condition: x has as its members exactly those statements that are not immediate components*[iv] *of any joint denial that belongs to x.* Although we may have to read this formulation several times before we understand it, and to think about it some more before we are sure that it is exactly right, it is, nevertheless, a much simpler formulation than an equally exact formulation would be that explicitly deals with truth tables and the use of the letters 'T' and 'F'.

Another formulation of compositional truth, this time based upon the use of '|' instead of '~' and '•', is this: *a statement is compositionally true if, and only if, it belongs to a series of statements each of which either has the form:*

$$(p| (q| r)) | ((s| (s| s)) | ((s| q) | ((p| s) | (p| s))))$$

or is such that the result of writing it in the last blank of '( )| (( )| ( ))', *and of writing a given previous statement of the series in the first blank, and any given statement whatsoever in the other blank, is one of the previous statements in the series.* This formulation is interesting for incorporating a deductive method of generating compositional truths on a restricted basis, and using a simple rule of deduction. It is a culmination, in terms of economy and precision, of the type of theory exemplified earlier in the development of equivalences by successive transformation (§ 11). The proof that this formulation covers all compositional truths is complicated.[v]

[iii] These reductions, of joint denial as well as of alternative denial, were discovered by Sheffer (1913). Both were already known to Peirce, but his notes were not published until 1933 (vol. IV, §§ 12, 264).

[iv] The *immediate components* of a joint denial S (or of a conjunction S, etc.) are those statements whose joint denial (or conjunction, etc.) is S.

[v] The literature contains various proofs of this kind, but they all relate to different choices of axiomatic foundations and rules of deduction. The first one was Post's (1921), and the shortest and simplest is perhaps mine (1938). The discovery that the axiomatic foundation and the rule used here are equivalent to provably adequate axiomatic foundations and rules was made by Łukasiewicz (1920) [ed. correction of '(1929)' in Quine's original text], based on results in Nicod (1918).

When we are interested in logic as an instrument and not as an object of theoretical investigation, it is much easier and more useful to explicitly formulate compositional truth, implication, and equivalence on the basis of truth tables. It is also much easier to preserve '•' and '~': Compounds written using '↓' (or likewise '|') would reach inconvenient lengths.

The practical applications of the techniques of the theory of composition are realized, in large part, within the theory of "quantification" that we will study next. As we will see, the "quantificational" techniques make essential use of compositional techniques. In the natural sciences or in daily life, it is rare that our investigation of the logical implications between statements rests only on purely compositional structures, without any input from quantificational structures. Nevertheless, from time to time we encounter statements of a considerable degree of purely compositional complexity, as in the example of the hill tribes and the colonists (§ 10), and in these cases, whether in the search for a simpler equivalent form, or in the search for implications between the given compound and others, the pure techniques of the theory of composition are applicable.

The North American engineer C. E. Shannon uses these techniques advantageously to resolve certain problems in the design and simplification of electrical circuits. If a circuit passes through contacts A and B, the condition under which the circuit is closed is the conjunction 'A is closed • B is closed' in the case where A and B are placed in series, and it is '~ (~ A is closed • ~ B is closed)' in the case in which A and B are placed in parallel. This results in a certain correspondence between the design of a complex electrical network and the design of a complex compound in the theory of composition, such that the behavior of the network can be calculated, up to a certain point, by means of compositional techniques. The problem of simplifying the network, while retaining the same effects, is transformed into the logical problem of reducing a compound to its simplest equivalent.[vi]

[vi] See, aside from Shannon's article, my "Relations and Reason."

II

Theory of Quantification

§ 15 The Quantifier

The most important step in the development of modern logic occurred when Frege, in 1879, devised his theory of quantification. The theory governs the use of prefixes '(x)', '(y)', etc. called *quantifiers*. We apply these to expressions that have the form of statements, except that they have letters 'x', 'y', etc. instead of names of things. The result, called a *quantification*, is true if and only if the expression that follows the prefix remains true no matter which thing is taken as the designatum of the letter 'x' (or 'y', etc.). The prefix '(x)' can be read 'whatever x may be' or, equivalently, 'every object x is such that', and analogously for '(y)', etc. Thus '(x) x exists' means 'Whatever x may be, x exists', that is, 'Every object x is such that x exists'; 'Everything exists' for short. Analogously, '(y) y = y' means 'Whatever y may be, y = y', that is, 'Everything is such that y = y' or 'Everything is identical to itself'.

So we can see that quantification corresponds, indirectly, to the natural-language use of the word 'all', or, better yet, 'every' or 'everything'. The correspondence is indirect because 'everything' behaves syntactically like a substantive, while quantification does not yield a corresponding substantive. This lack of syntactic correspondence is an advantage of the procedure of quantification theory, because the substantive form of the expression 'every' or 'everything' is a deceptive feature of natural language. We can see this by means of the example:

(1)   Everything is either human or something other than human.

Although the statement:

       Bucephalus is either human or something other than human.

can be thought of as an abbreviation of:

Either Bucephalus is human or Bucephalus is something other than human,

(1) cannot in the same way be thought of as an abbreviation of:

(2)   Either everything is human or everything is something other than human.

The compound (2) is false, because it is composed of two false statements joined by 'either . . . or', but (1) is obviously true. The notation of quantification theory distinguishes (1) from (2), as (1) is written as follows:

(3)   (x) (either x is human or x is something other than human),

or, translating 'either p or q' as the expression '$\sim (\sim p \bullet \sim q)$':

(4)   (x) $\sim$ ($\sim$ x is human $\bullet$ $\sim$ x is something other than human),

while (2) is written:

(5)   (x) x is human or (x) is something other than human,

that is:

(6) $\sim$ ($\sim$ (x) x is human $\bullet$ $\sim$ (x) x is something other than human).

(The quantifier, like the tilde, should be taken as governing the shortest possible phrase compatible with the placement of the parentheses. So in (5) and (6), the first '(x)' governs only 'x is human'.)

Another example: even though the statements 'The new pier is not combustible' and 'The new pier is incombustible' are mere verbal variations of one another, it is not clear that the statement 'Everything is not combustible' is a mere verbal variation of the false statement 'Everything is incombustible', that is, '(x) x is incombustible', or:

(7)   (x) $\sim$ x is combustible.

The statement 'Everything is not combustible' can also be taken in the sense of 'Not everything is combustible', that is:

(8) $\sim$ (x) x is combustible,

the denial of the false quantified statement '(x) x is combustible'.

The only difference between the truths (3), (4), and (8), on the one hand, and the falsehoods (5), (6), and (7), on the other, is a difference in grouping, or in the placement of the quantifier. An advantage of quantifier notation is that it makes explicit what is hidden, or expressed only non-systematically, in natural language.

Another example that illustrates the deceptive character of natural language is this: although the statement 'Bucephalus is identical to Bucephalus' is just another way of stating the truth 'Bucephalus is identical to himself', the statement 'Everything is identical to everything' is false, and far from equivalent to the truth 'Everything is identical to itself'. The expression 'everything' does not behave like an ordinary substantive.

Another pseudo-substantive of natural language, exactly analogous to 'everything', is 'something'; yet another is 'nothing'. These expressions, just like 'everything', can be translated using only the quantifier notation, together with that of denial. For example, the false quantified statement (7) can be read as 'Nothing is combustible'. So its denial:

(9) $\sim (x) \sim x$ is combustible

can be read as 'Something is combustible' or 'Some things are combustible'. As the simple prefix '(x)' has the sense of 'every object x is such that', we can deduce from the examples just given that the complex prefixes '$(x) \sim$' and '$\sim (x) \sim$' effectively mean 'no object x is such that' and 'some object x is such that'. But note that '$(x) \sim$' and '$\sim (x) \sim$' are not units in their own right. Each of the individual signs applies to the context that follows it, such that (9) is the denial of (7), and (7) is the quantification of '$\sim x$ is combustible', and the latter is the denial of 'x is combustible'.

The use of the word 'every' together with a less general term than 'thing', as, for example, in 'every human being', is also translated by means of a quantifier, with the aid of denial and conjunction. The statement 'Every human being is mortal', which says that nothing is human and yet is not mortal, is written:

$(x) \sim (x$ is human $\bullet \sim x$ is mortal$)$.

Here we have a quantified conditional – exactly the structure that we anticipated earlier (§ 7) and called the general conditional. The example we considered was 'If something interests me, then it bores George', that is, 'Everything that interests me, bores George', that is:

$(x) \sim (x$ interests me $\bullet \sim$ bores George$)$.

The analogous use of 'none' and 'some' is also easily translated. The statement 'No bird has fur' is written:

$(x) \sim (x$ is a bird $\bullet \sim x$ has fur$)$,

and its denial, 'Some birds have fur', is written:

$\sim (x) \sim (x$ is a bird $\bullet x$ has fur$)$.

§ 16 Logical Pronouns

I will call the letters 'x', 'y', etc. auxiliaries to the quantificational notation, *logical pronouns*. Their pronominal character becomes obvious when we observe that '(x) x exists', '(y) y = y', etc. can be read as 'Everything is such that *it* exists', 'Everything is such that *it* is identical to *it*', etc. We can see that while the quantifier '(x)', (or '(y)', etc.) corresponds to the words 'everything is such that', the logical pronoun 'x' (or 'y', etc.), when it occurs after a quantifier, corresponds to the pronoun 'it'. In other examples, naturally, the pronoun could be 'he' or 'she' instead of 'it', but there is always a pronoun referring back to the word 'everything' which is part of the verbal idiom corresponding to the quantifier. Note that the common conception of pronouns as, above all, place-holders for names, is mistaken. In these examples the pronoun serves a function that names cannot fulfill, because such contexts do not merely discuss a certain nameable object. In fact, as we have just seen, it is only an unfortunate accident of language that the expression 'everything', the grammatical antecedent of the pronoun, has a substantive form. Far from being based on names, pronouns are, from a logical point of view, much more fundamental than names, as will become increasingly clear in what follows (especially in § 41).

The reason we need a variety of letters 'x', 'y', etc. as logical pronouns, instead of just one, becomes apparent when we try to translate into symbols the statement 'Every person understands some language'. Following the method of centripetal translation, our first step is translation into this form:

(x) ~ (x is a person • ~ x understands some language).

Now the inner part, 'x understands some language', must be translated using another letter, like this:

~ (y) ~ (y is a language • x understands y).

The entire statement becomes:

(1)   (x) ~ (x is a person • (y) ~ (y is a language • x understands y)).

The choice of different letters corresponds to the use in natural language of the expressions 'the former' and 'the latter', or to 'first', 'second', 'third', to avoid confusion between the references of different pronouns. Statement (1) corresponds literally to the words:

> Whatever you may select, *it* is such that it is not the case that *it* is a person and that whatever you may next select is such that it is not the case that *the latter* is a language and that *the former* understands *the latter*.

Another example of the need for distinct logical pronouns is the false statement 'Everything is identical to everything', mentioned earlier (§ 15). Two steps of centripetal translation reduce this to '(x) (y) x = y', which contrasts with the true statement '(x) x = x', or '(y) y = y'.

It is obvious that the use of letters as logical pronouns is modeled on the use of letters as "variables" in algebra. In fact, logical pronouns are usually called variables, and I'm avoiding this term only to emphasize that here we are not concerned with special objects that undergo a process of variation. But the notion of variation does not really apply to the so-called variables of algebra, as these are in the final analysis mere logical pronouns. The theory of quantifica-tion thus clarifies the general notion of a variable that is so fundamental to mathematics. When presented with a typical page of a mathematics book, a basic exercise is to make explicit all of the quantifications in such a way that each "variable" assumes the role of a logical pronoun referring back to some quantifier. An argument that begins with the words 'Let x be a prime number', for example, becomes a general conditional of the form:

(x) ~ (x is a prime number • ~ ...)

where we fill in the blank with the main argument, which may be several paragraphs long.[i]

§ 17 Matrices and Schemata

Expressions of the type 'x = y', 'y = y', 'x is combustible', '~ x is combustible', etc., to which we commonly apply quantifiers, are called *matrices*. Although they have the form of statements, matrices are not, in general, statements. They are neither true nor false because they contain *free* pronouns, that is, pronouns which lack a quantifier to which they refer back. The matrix 'x is combustible' is neither true nor false, just as its verbal equivalent '*it* is combustible' is neither true nor false without some grammatical antecedent for the pronoun 'it'. Nevertheless, for the sake of convenience we will think of statements as matrices too, taking the former as a limiting case of the latter. So the notion of a matrix is a more general one than that of a statement. Generally speaking a matrix is *either* a statement *or* can be turned into a (true or false) statement by applying one or more quantifiers.

There is a fundamental difference between matrices and expressions such as '~ (p • ~ q)', used in the theory of composition, which contain occurrences of

---

[i] The pronominal character of the variable was pointed out by Peano in 1897 (p. 26).

the letters 'p', 'q', etc. These expressions, called *schemata*, are no more than diagrams, whose purpose is to facilitate discussion of the general forms of statements. From a formal point of view, the fundamental difference is this: every matrix can occur as part of a statement, if the wider context is one in which a quantifier is applied to it. Schemata, however, can never occur in this way. Matrices, when they are not statements, are fragments of statements, but schemata are only diagrams of statements.

This difference obviously depends on the fact that the quantifiers contain only pronouns such as 'x', 'y', etc., and never schematic letters such as 'p', 'q', etc. This is not, however, an arbitrary difference. One might think that the matrices and the schemata are essentially analogous, the only difference being that the schemata exhibit 'p', 'q', etc., which represent component statements, while the matrices exhibit 'x', 'y', etc., which represent component names. We turn the schema '~ (p • q)' into a statement when we replace the letters with statements, and we turn the matrix 'x = y' or 'x is combustible' into a statement when we replace the letters with names, such as 'Rio', 'capital of Brazil', 'Pier 13 of Porto Alegre'. Now, it is exactly for this reason that the following contrast arises: pronouns 'x', 'y', etc. *take* any *names of objects* as *substituends* and thus *stand for* or *talk about* any of the objects named, while the schematic letters 'p', 'q', etc. *take* only *non-names* as *substituends* and thus do not *stand for* or *talk about* any object, concrete or abstract. Thus we can prefix to a matrix the quantifier '(x)', with the sense 'whatever x may be', or 'every object x is such that', but we cannot prefix the quantifier '(p)' to a matrix with any kind of comparable sense. To hold that '(p)' can have the sense of 'every statement p is such that' is simply confused. '(p)' would be analogous, not to '(x)' taken in the correct sense of 'every object x such that', but to something with a completely different sense, namely 'every name x is such that'.

We already noted that there is a definite partial analogy between schemata and matrices: Schemata are turned into statements by replacing the letters with statements, while matrices are turned into statements by replacing letters with names. This means we might easily think that the matrix has the same diagrammatic character that we have attributed to the schema. But matrices also have the capacity to occur as part of quantified statements, while schemata do not.

Another, more subtle point worth dwelling on is that we cannot simply say that a quantification[12] beginning with '(x)' is true whenever the matrix that follows '(x)' is true for any substitution of names for 'x'. This is because there are objects without names. We know, for example, that given any notation there are certain real numbers that cannot be given any kind of name, neither a simple name nor a name in the form of a complex description, within that notation. Therefore, it is possible for a quantification '(x) . . . ', that is, 'Every object x such that . . . ', to be false even though every substitution of names for 'x' makes the matrix true. This brings home the point that the use of quantifiers is a method that allows for discourse about *objects* in general, be they abstract or concrete, not a method that merely allows for discourse about the substitution of names or sentences for letters.

§ 18 A Complex Example of Translation

Our earlier discussion of the translation of ordinary-language statements into logical notation (§ 9–10) is equally pertinent when there are quantificational structures to take into account in addition to compositional structures. Translation now becomes an even more complicated undertaking. Working through an especially complicated example will perhaps suffice to clarify the general issue. Take the statement:

(1)   Until a radio salesman has sold a radio to a person who does not like radios, he is not a master of his trade.

Reference to time plays an important role in this example, and this we must make explicit.

(2)   Every moment at which a radio salesman is a master of his trade follows a period during which he sells a radio to someone who does not like radios at the beginning of this period.

Following the principle of centripetal translation, we look for the outermost structure of (2), which is perhaps best rendered as 'every radio salesman is such that . . . ', that is, '(x) ~ (x is a radio salesman • ~ . . .)'. Thus, (2) transforms into:

(3)   (x) ~ (x is a radio salesman • ~ every moment at which x is a master of his trade follows a period during which x sells a radio to a person who does not like radios at the beginning of this period).

The phrase 'every . . . of this period' which occurs in (3) has the structure 'every moment at which . . . is such that . . . ', that is, '(y) ~ (y is a moment • at y . . . • ~ . . .)'. Thus (3) becomes:

(4)   (x) ~ (x is a radio salesman • ~ (y) ~ (y is a moment • x is a master of his trade at y • ~ y follows a period during which x sells a radio to a person who does not like radios at the beginning of this period)).

The phrase 'y follows . . . of this period' has the form 'some period is such that . . . ', that is, '~ (z) ~ (z is a period • . . .)'. Thus (4) becomes:

(5)   (x) ~ (x is a radio salesman • ~ (y) ~ (y is a moment • x is a master of his trade at y • (z) ~ (z is a period • y follows z • x sells a radio during z to a person who does not like radios at the beginning of z))).

The clause 'x sells . . . of z' has the form 'some radio is such that . . . ', so that (5) becomes:

(6)   (x) ~ (x is a radio salesman • ~ (y) ~ (y is a moment • x is a master of his trade at y • (z) ~ (z is a period • y follows z • ~ (w) ~ (w is a radio • x sells w during z to a person who does not like radios at the beginning of z)))).

The clause 'x sells w . . . of z' has the form 'some person is such that . . . ', so that (6) becomes:

(7)   (x) ~ (x is a radio salesman • ~ (y) ~ (y is a moment • x is a master of his trade at y • (z) ~ (z is a period • y follows z • ~ (w) ~ (w is a radio • ~ (v) ~ (v is a person • x sells w to v during x • ~ v likes radios at the beginning of z))))).

How far to take our analysis depends, naturally, on what our aims are. Usually the goal is to uncover enough of the quantificational and compositional structure to show that the given statement is, for example, logically true (which (7) is not) or related to other given statements by logical implication or equivalence.

What the outermost structure is for each step is to some extent an arbitrary choice. Such was the situation in the last three steps above. We might have taken the phrase 'y follows . . . this period' in (4) as having the structure 'some radio is such that . . . ' or equally 'some person is such that . . . ', leaving the structure 'some period is such that . . . ' until later. The results of these alternative forms of analysis would be different from (7) but still equivalent to it. Certain choices, however, would be incorrect. For example, we cannot analyze (2) as:

(x) ~ (x is a moment • at x a radio salesman is . . . • ~ x follows a period during which he . . .), removing 'he' from its grammatical complement 'a salesman'. The quantified phrase which is about the salesman must have sufficiently wide scope to include both referential expressions.

§ 19 Vacuous Quantification

When we speak of the quantification of a matrix, we need not suppose that the pronoun occurring in the quantifier must always occur free in the matrix. We may think of any matrix without an 'x' – for example, 'Socrates is mortal' – as containing 'x' vacuously, like so:

(1)   Socrates is mortal • x = x.

The quantification:

(2)   (x) Socrates is mortal,

that is:

(3)   (x) (Socrates is mortal • x = x),

is true or false depending on whether 'Socrates is mortal' is true or false. Thus, 'x = x' being filled in for every object x, the conjunction (1) as a whole will either be satisfied by everything or by nothing, depending on whether its other component is true or false. In general, therefore, when 'x' does not occur free in a given matrix, the result of applying the quantifier '(x)' to the matrix can be treated as the matrix itself, and the quantifier then becomes vacuous. We may even conveniently drop the quantifier, and think of the matrix as a quantification in its own right in relation to 'x'.

Earlier on we sacrificed a little of the simplicity of our "grammar" of tildes and parentheses to simplify the techniques of the theory of composition by taking the use of '~ ~' and the use of parentheses in conjunctions as ungrammatical. Now we can sacrifice a little of the simplicity of our quantificational grammar to simplify the technique of the theory of quantification in an analogous way: by taking every expression of type (2), that is, every use of the quantifier as the prefix to a matrix in which the pronoun in question is not free, as ungrammatical.

The minor increase in grammatical complexity that the tilde[13] underwent was that the notation of denial no longer consisted in prefixing a tilde in all cases, but became the erasure of a tilde in cases where a denial was denied. Now the minor increase in grammatical complexity that the quantifier is to undergo is that the notation of quantification no longer always consists in prefixing a quantifier. To quantify a matrix which contains a free occurrence of the pronoun of the quantifier, we add the quantifier as a prefix; but to quantify a matrix which does not contain a free occurrence of the pronoun of the quantifier, we keep the matrix unaltered, and do not add a quantifier.

§ 20 Quantificational Truth and Validity

Quantificational truth is a kind of logical truth that is more inclusive than compositional truth. A statement is quantificationally true when it is of a form constructed by means of conjunction, denial, and quantification that remains true under any change of its other components. In short, a statement is quantificationally true when only compositional and quantificational notations occur essentially in it. For example, the statement:

> If something affects everything, then it affects itself.

that is:

> (y) ~ (y affects everything • ~ y affects y),

that is:

(1)   (y) ~ ((x) y affects x • ~ y affects y),

is quantificationally true, as we can replace the verb 'affects' with any other verb without ever producing a false statement.

A generalization of the notion of quantificational truth, which is useful for a systematic treatment of quantificational truths, is the notion of *quantificational validity*. I will call *quantificationally valid*, or (in this chapter) *valid* for short, every matrix that is quantificationally true or can become quantificationally true by prefixing quantifiers. Thus, for example, matrix (1) is valid, since it is a quantificationally true statement. Also, the matrix:

(2)   ~ ((x) y affects x • ~ y affects y)

is valid, given that the application of '(y)' converts it into the quantificational truth (1). Note that matrix (2), though valid, is neither true nor false, because it is not a statement. The category of valid matrices is therefore more inclusive than that of quantificational truths; quantificational truths are just those valid matrices that are statements, that is, that do not contain free pronouns.

Every matrix of the form:

(A)   ~ ((x) fx • ~ fy)

is valid, as 'fx' can be replaced with any matrix, and 'fy' with a matrix that differs from the first one only in containing 'y' as a free pronoun wherever the first matrix contains 'x' as a free pronoun. Matrix (2) is one of the valid matrices of the form (A). Another one is:

(3)   ~ ((x) z affects x • ~ z affects y).

While applying the quantifier '(y)' is enough to transform matrix (2) into a logical truth, we need to apply two quantifiers, '(y)' and '(z)' in that order, to transform matrix (3) into a logical truth:

(4)   (y) (z) ~ ((x) z affects x • ~ z affects y).

Other valid matrices of the form (A) may need even more than two initial qualifiers to turn them into logical truths, for example, the matrix:

(5)   ~ ((x) xz > w • ~ yz > w)

needs the quantifiers '(y)', '(z)', '(w)' to be transformed into the logical truth:

(6)   (y) (z) (w) ~ ((x) xz > w • ~ yz > w).

But all matrices of form (A) are equally valid, independently of the number of free pronouns, as all statements of type (1), (4), and (6) are obviously logical truths.

Naturally, there is an unlimited variety of other forms of valid matrices in addition to (A). The systematic study of these forms is a central task of the theory of quantification. Valid matrices of the special form (A) (and also those that use other pronouns in place of 'x' and 'y') constitute a convenient starting-point for the serial derivation of other valid matrices. The purpose of such derivation of valid matrices is, in the end, to derive quantificational truths, since quantificational truths are valid matrices without free pronouns. It happens that it is easier to derive valid matrices in general than to derive only those which lack free pronouns.

Before we go on, we must reflect on the use of the ideograms 'fx' and 'fy' in (A), supplementary to the earlier schematic use of 'p', 'q', etc. It is clear that when we think of a matrix as occupying the place of 'fx', that matrix need not contain 'x' as a free pronoun. In cases where it does not, we must think, not of '(x) fx', but of the same matrix without the additional prefix '(x)' (cf. § 19). In short, '(x) fx' always represents the quantification of the expression represented by 'fx', but not always an expression that begins with '(x)'. It is a situation analogous to that of '~ p', which always represents the denial of the expression represented by 'p', but not always an expression that begins with '~' (given that the denial can consist in the erasure of a previous tilde).

§ 21 Compositional Implication as a Proof Tool

The notion of compositional truth is easily generalized to the notion of the *compositional validity* of matrices, analogous to the notion of quantificational validity. Just as the statement:

$$\sim \text{(John will come} \bullet \text{Joe will come} \bullet \sim \text{John will come)}$$

is compositionally true, the matrix:

$$\sim \text{(x will come} \bullet \text{y will come} \bullet \sim \text{x will come)}$$

can be called compositionally valid. The definition is as follows: A matrix is compositionally valid when it is constructed out of its simple components (in the same sense of 'simple' that we used in the theory of composition; cf. § 11) just as a compositionally true statement is constructed out of its simple components. That is, a matrix is called compositionally valid if the result of replacing its simple components with statements is always compositionally true.

Compositional implication and compositional equivalence can be generalized in the same way for application to matrices in general. In fact, we can define these generalized relations on the basis of compositional validity, analogous to the way in which the compositional implication and equivalence of statements were formulated before on the basis of compositional truth. One matrix implies another compositionally if the conditional formed by the respective matrices is compositionally valid, and the compositional equivalence of matrices is their reciprocal implication. Thus the matrix 'x will come • y will come' compositionally implies the matrix 'x will come', and is compositionally equivalent to the matrix 'y will come • x will come'.

It is clear that in practice we do not have to substitute component matrices for statements to determine the validity, implication, or equivalence of matrices. We can use the truth-table technique, applying it directly to matrices and to their components as if they were statements. The truth-table test that shows the statement 'John will come • Joe will come' implies 'Joe will come', for example, would proceed mechanically in the same way if we had, instead of 'John will come' and 'Joe will come', 'x will come' and 'y will come'. But of course, when we apply truth-tables directly to matrices in this way, we must bear in mind that we are using a mechanical method of calculation, and that the letters 'T' and 'F' in the truth-tables no longer directly signify the truth values of the components and compounds under consideration, given that in general matrices do not have truth values. What the letters 'T' and 'F' truly indicate in such applications is not the values of the matrices, but the values of the statements which they take as substituends.

We will continue (in this chapter) to take the word 'valid', when used by itself, in the sense of quantificational validity. Compositional validity is, obviously, a kind of quantificational validity, but it is a type to which we will rarely have to refer. The notions that we will use most frequently are those of compositional implication and compositional equivalence between matrices.

Compositional implication between matrices amounts to a tool for proving validity for new matrices on the basis of given valid matrices, because it is obvious that every compositional matrix implied by a valid matrix, or by a conjunction of valid matrices, must also be valid.

This is how we can prove, for example, on the basis of valid matrices of the form (A), the (quantificational) validity of every matrix of the form:

(B) $\sim ((x)\ fx \bullet (x) \sim fx)$.

For if we take the schematic expression 'fx' to be such that any matrix can take its place, we can check by means of Table 8 that '$\sim ((x)\ fx \bullet \sim fx)$' is compositionally implied by the conjunction of two valid matrices of the form (A), e.g. '$\sim ((x)\ fx \bullet (x) \sim fy)$' and $\sim ((x) \sim fx \bullet fy)$'.

From the validity of matrices of the form (B), it follows, for example, that the statements:

(1)   It is not the case that everything and yet nothing is perishable,

(2)   If everything is perishable, then something is perishable,

Table 8

(x) fx	(x) ~ fx	fy	~((x) fx • ~ fy) • ~ ((x) ~ fx • fy)	~ ((x) fx • (x) ~ fx)
T	T	T	F	F
F	T	T	-	T
T	F	T	-	T
F	F	T	-	T
T	T	F	F	F
F	T	F	-	T
T	F	F	-	T
F	F	F	-	T

are quantificationally true, as their translation is the same, namely:

~ ((x) x is perishable • (x) ~ x is perishable),

which has the form (B) and is therefore valid, that is, quantificationally true (since it is a statement).

§ 22 Other Rules of Proof

In the compositional equivalence between matrices, we have a second relation for the derivation of new valid matrices on the basis of given valid matrices. Indeed, when we replace any part of a valid matrix with another matrix compositionally equivalent to that part, it is obvious that the result must also be valid. For example, if a valid matrix has a part of the form 'p • q', changing this part to 'q • p' does not affect the validity of the context.

To affirm that everything meets two given conditions at the same time is to affirm that everything meets the first condition and also that everything meets the second. In general, therefore, the forms '(x) (fx • gx)' and '(x) fx • (x) gx' are interchangeable. Substituting '(x) (fx • gx)' for '(x) fx • (x) gx', or vice-versa, within any valid matrix, will obviously preserve validity, and thus we have here a third method for deriving new valid matrices on the basis of given valid matrices. (Instead of the 'x' in our example, we could of course use any other pronoun.)

An example of the use of the three rules of proof considered so far is the proof that every matrix of the form:

(C)   ~ ((x) ~ (fx • gx) • (x) fx • ~ (x) gx)

is valid. Taking 'fx' and 'gx' as replaceable by any matrices, we observe that the matrix:

(1)   ~ ((x) fx • (x) gx • ~ (x) gx),

since it is compositionally valid, is compositionally implied by matrices of the form (A) or of any other form, for when we constructed the truth table we encountered no 'F's in the column below (1). Thus (1) has already been "proven" according to the first of our rules of proof. (The same is true for any compositionally valid matrix.) Now, applying our third rule to (1), which is about the distribution of quantifiers, we conclude that the matrix:

(2)   ~ ((x) (fx • gx) • ~ (x) gx)

is valid. Then we note, by means of our truth tables, that 'fx • gx' and '~ (fx • ~ gx) • fx' are compositionally equivalent. We therefore conclude from (2) that:

(3)   ~ ((x) (~ (fx • ~ gx) • fx) • ~ (x) gx)

is valid, according to our second rule. Finally, the step from (3) to (C) consists
in the use of the third rule.

From the validity of matrices of the form (C), it follows that the statements:

(4)   If every created object is perishable, and every object is created, then
           everything is perishable,

(5)   If no spirit is perishable, and everything is spirit, then nothing is
           perishable,

(6)   If everything is matter or spirit, and nothing is matter, then everything
           is spirit,

(7)   If only spirits are created, and there are no spirits, then nothing is created,

are quantificationally true, given that their translations are, respectively:

(8)   ~ ((x) ~ (x is created • ~ x is perishable) • (x) x is created • ~ (x) x is
           perishable),

(9)   ~ ((x) ~ (x is spirit • x is perishable) • (x) x is spirit • ~ (x) ~ x is
           perishable),

(10)   ~ ((x) ~ (~ x is matter • ~ x is spirit) • (x) ~ x is matter • ~ (x) x is spirit),

(11)   ~ ((x) ~ (~ x is spirit • x is created) • (x) ~ x is spirit • ~ (x) ~ x is created).

It follows equally that the statements:

(12)   If everything is created and nothing is perishable, then some created
           object is not perishable,

(13)   If every created object is perishable, and some object is not perishable,
           then some object is not created,

are quantificationally true, given that they also translate into (8) (setting aside
the question of the order of the three components of the conjunction). Variants
of (9)–(11) are constructible in an analogous way.

We have to introduce one more rule of proof. This rule is based on the fact
that the quantification of any valid matrix, in relation to any pronoun, is a
valid matrix. For example, take a matrix whose free pronouns are 'x', 'y', and
'z'. The result of its quantification in relation to any of its non-free pronouns,
let us say 'w', is the valid matrix itself without any alteration (cf. § 19). The
result of its quantification in relation to any of its free pronouns, say, 'z', is the
matrix formed from the original matrix by prefixing '(z)'. The matrix thus

formed is valid for the same reason as the original matrix, because both can be converted into a quantification of the form '(x) (y) (z) fxyz' by the application of quantifiers.

One of the proofs carried out with the help of this fourth rule is the proof that every matrix of the form:

(D) $\sim (\sim (x) \sim (fx \cdot gx) \cdot (x) \sim fx)$

is valid. Imagining matrices in the positions of the schematic expressions 'fx' and 'gx', we begin the deduction of (D), like that of (C), by introducing a compositionally valid matrix:

$$\sim (\sim fx \cdot fx \cdot gx).$$

From this, by means of our new rule, we obtain:

(14) $(x) (\sim fx \cdot fx \cdot gx).$

But, given (C), we also know that the matrix:

(15) $\sim ((x) \sim (\sim fx \cdot fx \cdot gx) \cdot (x) \cdot \sim fx \cdot \sim (x) \cdot \sim (fx \cdot gx))$

is valid. The conjunction of (14) and (15) compositionally implies (D).

From the validity of matrices of the form (D), it follows, for example, that the statements:

(16)   If some fish fly, there are fish,

(17)   If not only birds fly, not everything is a bird,

are quantificationally true, given that they translate as:

(18) $\sim (\sim (x) \sim (x \text{ is a fish} \cdot x \text{ flies}) \cdot (x) \sim x \text{ is a fish}),$

(19) $\sim (\sim (x) \sim (\sim x \text{ is a bird} \cdot x \text{ flies}) \cdot (x) x \text{ is a bird}).$

Likewise with regard to the variant formulations of (18) and (19):

(20)   If fish do not exist, no fish flies,

(21)   If everything is a bird, only birds fly.

§ 23 General Observations on Proof Techniques

In summary, our technique for proving validity consists in beginning with matrices of the form (A) and deriving other matrices by iterated application of four operations:

(i) *inference of what is compositionally implied,*
(ii) *interchangeability of compositional equivalence,*
(iii) *interchangeability of clauses of the forms* '(x) (fx • gx)' *and* '(x) fx • (x) gx',
(iv) *quantification.*

In the course of carrying out such proofs we have accumulated a collection of valid matrices to draw upon in subsequent proofs. For example, we have already used (C) in this way in the penultimate step of the proof of (D). Instead, we could have inserted three more steps in our proof of (D) in order to give an explicit definition of case (15) of (C) directly on the basis of (A), since these three steps would be exactly analogous to the steps that led us originally to (C). We can also see that referring to (C), or to the other intermediate results in the process of proving validity, simply serves to avoid having to do the same thing multiple times.

The proof method here described determines a class of valid matrices, including matrices of the form (A) and all matrices derivable from them by iterated applications of our four operations (i)–(iv). We know that this class exhausts the valid matrices. The proof of this fact is, essentially, due to Gödel (1930). His argument, which is subtle and complicated, applies to a systematization of the theory of quantification different from mine, but it would be easy to establish the equivalence of the two systematizations.

The definition of quantificational truth is based on the general notion of truth. A quantificational truth is a statement in which only the notations of conjunction, denial, and quantification occur essentially, and the notion of occurring essentially is in turn based on the general notion of truth. Now, however, we have an equivalent formulation of quantificational truth that does not use the general notion of truth. A quantificational truth is a statement that can be derived from matrices of type (A) by means of the operations (i)–(iv).

In addition to this theoretical advantage, the present formulation is useful from a practical point of view as a technique for establishing any quantificational truth or, more generally, any valid matrix. Note, however, that this proof method is not as satisfactory as the type of technique exemplified by truth tables in the theory of composition. The truth tables decide mechanically if any statement is compositionally true or not. However, to establish that a given statement is quantificationally true, we must try to derive it on the basis of (A) and (i)–(iv). Once we have found such a derivation, we can authenticate it by means of mechanical inspection, but the search for the derivation is a non-systematic, non-mechanical process. What we have is, in short, just a mechanical method of authentication for proofs of quantificational truth, and not a mechanical criterion for quantificational truth itself. Indeed, we know that such a criterion is impossible. The proof of this fact is due to Church (1936).

When we pass from quantificational truth to logical or mathematical truths in the broader sense, we find that even a general method of mechanically authenticable proof becomes impossible; this is Gödel's result, which I mentioned in the Introduction. (Cf. also § 54.)

§ 24 Quantificational Implication

Just as we say that a statement is *compositionally implied* by another statement when the former follows from the latter purely in virtue of the structures of the two statements with respect to conjunction and denial, we now say that a statement is *quantificationally implied* when it follows from another in virtue of the structure of the two statements with respect to conjunction, denial, and quantification.

Just as compositional implication relates statements whose conditional is compositionally true, quantificational implication relates statements whose conditional is quantificationally true. The quantificational truth of (2) in § 21, for example, means that the statement 'Everything is perishable' quantificationally implies the statement 'Some object is perishable'. For each of the examples (4)–(7), (12), (13), (16), (17), (20) and (21) (§ 22) of quantificational truth there is a corresponding example of quantificational implication.

Previously we adopted the useful convention of treating compositional implication as a relation that holds not just between statements, but between matrices in general. The same holds with regard to quantificational implication, and it is formulated in an analogous fashion: one matrix quantificationally implies another whenever the conditional formed from the respective matrices is (quantificationally) valid. Thus, for example, the validity of the conditional matrix (2) of § 20 means that the matrix 'y affects everything' implies the matrix 'y affects y', even though the matrices are not statements.

In the same way, more generally, quantificational implication holds between each pair of matrices of the form:

(1)   (x) fx,   fy,

given the validity of every matrix of the form 'If (x) fx then fy', that is, of the form (A). In accord with (B)–(D),[ii] likewise, we note that quantificational implication holds between every pair of matrices of any of the following three forms:

[ii] Principles (A)–(D) and others are listed together, for the convenience of the reader, at the end of this book.

(2)   (x) fx,   ~ (x) ~ fx,

(3)   (x) ~ (fx • ~ gx) • (x) fx,   (x) gx,

(4)   ~ (x) ~ (fx • gx),   ~ (x) ~ fx,

no matter whether they are statements.

The forms of validity (A)–(D) also make room for other forms of implication aside from (1)–(4). The form (C), for example, encompasses not only the conditional with '(x) ~ (fx • ~ gx) • (x) fx' as its antecedent and '(x) gx' as its consequent, but also the conditional with '(x) ~ (fx • ~ gx)' as its antecedent and '~ ((x) fx • ~ (x) gx)' as its consequent. Thus, because matrices of form (C) are valid, quantificational implication not only holds between all pairs of form (3), but also between all pairs of the form:

(5)   (x) ~ (fx • ~ gx),   ~ ((x) fx • ~ (x) gx),

that is:

       (x) (if fx then gx),   if (x) fx then (x) gx.

For example, 'Every created object is perishable' quantificationally implies 'If every object is created then every object is perishable'.

But (C) also encompasses the conditional whose antecedent is '(x) ~ (fx • gx) • ~ (x) gx' and whose consequent is '~ (x) fx' (if we vary or set aside the order of the conjunction); and, likewise, the conditional whose antecedent is '(x) fx • ~ (x) gx' and whose consequent is '~ (x) ~ (fx • ~ gx)'; and, likewise, the conditional whose antecedent is '~ (x) gx' and whose consequent is '~ ((x) ~ (fx • ~ gx) • (x) fx)'; and, likewise, the conditional whose antecedent is '(x) fx' and whose consequent is '~ ((x) ~ (fx • ~ gx) • ~ (x) gx)'. We thus have four more forms of implication, in addition to (3) and (5), also based on (C). In the same way, we have three more forms of implication, in addition to (1), (2), and (4), based on (A), (B), and (D);

       ~fy,   ~ (x) fx.
   (x) ~ fx,   ~ (x) fx.
   (x) ~ fx,   (x) ~ (fx • gx).

§ 25 Quantificational Equivalence

Although quantificational implication plays a central role in the applications of logic (cf. Introduction), it does not carry any additional techniques in its wake. Each case of quantificational implication, since it consists in the validity of the conditional, can be proved according to our complete proof method for validity. The same is true for *quantificational equivalence*, when we define it as reciprocal quantificational implication, because each proof of quantificational equivalence consists in proving implications going both ways, that is, in proving the validity of the two conditionals.

For example, any two matrices of the form:

(1) $\sim (p \bullet \sim (x)\, fx)$ $(x) \sim (p \bullet \sim fx)$

where we may replace 'fx' with any matrix, and 'p' with any matrix in which 'x' is not free, are quantificationally equivalent. To establish this fact we must prove the validity of all the conditional matrices of the following two forms:

(E) $\sim (\sim (p \bullet \sim (x)\, fx \bullet \sim (x) \sim (p \bullet \sim fx))$
(E') $\sim ((x) \sim (p \bullet \sim fx) \bullet p \bullet \sim (x)\, fx).$

But this second form is already accounted for directly by (C). To establish (E), we observe that the two forms:

(2) $\sim (\sim (x) \sim (\sim fx \bullet p) \bullet (x)\, fx)$

(3) $\sim (\sim (x) \sim (p \bullet \sim fx) \bullet \sim p)$

are accounted for by (D). We then obtain:

(4) $\sim (\sim (x) \sim (p \bullet \sim fx) \bullet (x)\, fx)$

from (2) by (ii), and finally we obtain (E) from (3) and (4) by (i).

The equivalence thus established shows that the following type of conditional:

> If p, then, whatever x may be, fx,

is interchangeable with the quantification:

> Whatever x may be, if p, then fx,

where 'x' does not occur free in the antecedent.

We have already seen another example of quantificational equivalence, namely the pair:

> $(x)\,(fx \bullet gx),$ $(x)\, fx \bullet (x)\, gx.$

This was the reason that we adopted the deductive operation (iii). Based on (1), it may be helpful to adopt another analogous deductive operation:

(v)   *interchangeability of sentences of the forms* '$\sim (p \bullet \sim (x)\, fx)$' *and* '$(x) \sim (p \bullet \sim fx)$'

But this additional operation is there merely for the sake of convenience, and it is theoretically dispensable. We can show[iii] that, once we have established quantificational equivalence based on (A) and (i)–(iv), every proof that proceeds by interchanging such equivalent sentences can be accounted for using (A) and (i)–(iv).

As an illustration of the application of (v), note that the complex statement (7) of § 18 contains three parts of the form '~ (p • ~ (x) fx)', and that the transformation of these parts into '(x) ~ (p • ~ fx)' serves to reduce (7) to the simple statement:

> (x) (y) ~ (x is a radio salesman • y is a moment • x is a master of his trade at y • (z) (w) (v) ~ (z is a period • y follows z • w is a radio • v is a person • x sells w to v during z • ~ v likes radios at the beginning of z)).

§ 26 Alphabetic Variance. Commutativity of Quantifiers

A useful way to write proofs of validity is illustrated below. The letters 'a', 'b', 'F', etc., within formulas, serve as abbreviations of the formulas listed in the left margin as '(a)', '(b)', '(F)', etc.

(F)   ~ ((x) (y) fxy • ~ (y) (x) fxy).

Proof:

(a)	~ ((y) fxy • ~ fxy)	(A)
(b)	~ ((x) a • ~ c)	(C)
(c)	~ ((x) (y) fxy • ~ (x) fxy)	From (a) and (b) by (i) and (iv).
(d)	~ ((y) c • ~ F)	(C)
(F)	From (c) and (d) by (i) and (iv).	

The derivation of (c) consists in passing from (a) to '(x) a' by means of (iv), and conjoining the latter with (b) compositionally implies (c). The last step of the proof is similar.

Note that the last 'y' in (a) is free, as the first clause '(y) fxy' governs only the quantifier '(y)' in (a). We could have used 'z' in place of the last 'y' in (a) and in the later steps without changing the significance of the context. We can obtain (1) below, a variant of (F), by a series of steps analogous to (a)–(d):

(1)   ~ ((x) (y) fxy • ~ (z) (x) fxz)

[iii] By an argument similar to the one found in *Mathematical Logic*, § 18.

We can also derive another variant:

(2)   ~ ((x) (y) fxy • ~ (z) (w) fwz)

as follows:

(a)	~ ((x) fxz • ~ fwz)	(A)
(b)	~ ((w) a • ~ c)	(C)
(c)	~ ((x) fxz • ~ (w) fwz)	From (a) and (b) by (i) and (iv).
(d)	~ ((z) c • ~ e)	(C)
(e)	~ ((z) (x) fxz • ~ (z) (w) fwz)	From (c) and (d) by (i) and (iv).
(2)	From (1) and (e) by (i).	

The only difference between (F), (1), and (2) is in the different choice of letters that function as pronouns. Adding one more deductive operation, in addition to (i)–(iv), is useful, namely:

(vi)   *alphabetic variance of pronouns*

We can formulate the rule regarding the alphabetic variance of pronouns as follows: *If two matrices differ only in that the first exhibits a certain free pronoun in exactly those places where the second matrix exhibits a certain other free pronoun, and if we apply quantifiers containing the respective pronouns in question to the respective matrices, then the result of substituting one of these quantifications for another, within any valid matrix, will be valid.*

But (vi) is, like (v), theoretically dispensable, because it can always be replaced with an argument of the theory expounded above, more or less in the way just exemplified in the proof of (2) on the basis of (1).

One part of the content of this rule of alphabetic variance was already implicit in our way of using (A). For we understand by matrices of the form (A) not only matrices constructed by the substitution of 'fx' and 'fy' in the schema (A) itself, but also matrices constructed by substitution in the variants:

~ ((x) fx • ~ fz)   ~ ((y) fy • ~ fz)

etc., of (A). We retain the same attitude with regard to (B), (C), etc., since we know that variants of (B), (C), etc., with other choices of letters, would be derivable from the corresponding variants of (A). The only aspect in which the explicit use of (vi) overrides this implicit original use is in the partial change of a letter – as, for example, in passing from (F) to (1), we change 'y' in the second quantification but not in the first.

We now go on to institute one more deductive operation. The validity of matrices of the form (F) means that each matrix of the form '(x) (y) fxy' quantificationally implies the corresponding matrix of the form '(y) (x) fxy'. Every quantification of a quantification implies the result of the commutation of the two initial quantifiers. In fact, we have here an equivalence, given that the inverse implication of '(x) (y) fxy' for '(y) (x) fxy' is simply another case of the same principle of commutativity that we have just affirmed. In short, the order of adjacent quantifiers does not matter. Adding one more item to our list of deductive operations may be useful in practice:

(vii)   *commutativity of adjacent quantifiers*

The addition of this operation is dispensable, however, as it is in the case of (v) and (vi).

    It is important to note that the order of the quantifiers can be essential when they are separated by a tilde. The matrix of the form '(x) ~ (y) fxy' is not equivalent, in general, to the corresponding matrix of the form '(y) ~ (x) fxy'. For example, (3) of § 19 being true, the statement:

(y) ~ (x) (y is human • x = x)

is false, while:

(x) ~ (y) (y is human • x = x)

is true.

    Likewise, a matrix of the form '(x) ~ (y) fxy' is not equivalent, in general, to any matrices of the forms '~ (x) ~ (y) ~ fxy' or '~ (y) ~ (x) ~ fxy'. For example, if we suppose that the only objects that exist are positive whole numbers, we see that:

(x) ~ (y) (x is divisible by y)

is true, meaning that no number is divisible by all numbers; but

~ (x) ~ (y) ~ (x is divisible by y)

is false, meaning that some number is not divisible by any number; and

~ (y) ~ (x) ~ (x is divisible by y)

is false, meaning that some number is not a factor of any number.

    Between two of these three forms, however, there is an implication: '~ (y) ~ (x) ~ fxy' implies '(x) ~ (y) fxy'. This is established in the following proof of validity:

(G)   ~ (~ (y) ~ (x) ~ fxy • ~ (x) ~ (y) fxy)

Proof:

(a)	~ ((y) fxy • ~ fxy)	(A)
(b)	~ (~ fxy • (y) fxy)	From (a) by (ii).
(c)	~ ((x) b • (x) ~ fxy • ~ (x) ~ (y) fxy)	(C)
(d)	~ (~ (x) ~ (y) fxy • (x) ~ fxy)	From (b) and (c) by (i) and (iv).
(e)	~ (~ (x) ~ (y) fxy • ~ (y) ~ (x) ~ fxy)	From (d) by (iv) and (v).
(G)	From (e) by (i).	

What we have just established with (G) is that any matrix of the type:

> There is some object y such that there is no object x such that . . .

implies the corresponding matrix of the type:

> There is no object x such that every object y is such that . . .

When we replace 'fxy' in (G) with a denied matrix, the two complex prefixes '~ (y) ~ (x) ~' and '(x) ~ (y)' become '~ (y) ~ (x)' and '(x) ~ (y) ~'. It follows that any matrix of the type:

> There is some object y such that, whatever x may be . . .

implies the corresponding matrix of the type:

> Whatever x may be, there is some object y such that . . .

even though in general the inverse implication does not hold.

§ 27 The Syllogism

There is a type of reasoning, well known since Aristotle under the name of the *syllogism*, which is exemplified by the argument:

(1)   No β is γ and every α is β; therefore, no α is γ,

with any terms being substitutable for 'α', 'β', and 'γ', as for example 'philosopher', 'human', 'infallible'. This reasoning depends on the fact that the conjunction 'No β is γ and every α is β' implies 'No α is γ'. To establish this implication within the theory of quantification, we must prove the validity of the corresponding conditional:

(2)   If no β is γ and every α is β, then no α is γ.

Writing 'fx ', 'gz', and 'hx' in place of 'x is α', 'x is β', 'x is γ', we arrive at the following symbolic form:

(H) $\sim ((x) \sim (gx \bullet hx) \bullet (x) \sim (fx \bullet \sim gx) \bullet \sim (x) \sim (fx \bullet hx)).$

Proof:
(a) $\sim (\sim (gx \bullet hx) \bullet \sim (fx \bullet \sim gx) \bullet (fx \bullet hx))^{14}$

By (i).
(b) $\sim ((x) a \bullet \sim c)$ (C)
(c) $\sim ((x) (\sim (gx \bullet hx) \bullet \sim (fx \bullet \sim gx)) \bullet \sim (x) \sim (fx \bullet hx))$

From (a) and (b) by (i) and (iv).
(H)   From (c) by (iii).

(H) is a formulation not only of the conditional (2), but also of a great variety of conditionals with other natural-language forms. (2) is the version that results when we use the clause '$(x) \sim (fx \bullet hx)$' as the consequent of the conditional. But when we use '$\sim (x) \sim (fx \bullet \sim gx)$' or '$\sim (x) \sim (gx \bullet hx)$' in this role, the following alternative versions of (H) result:

(3)   If no β is γ and some α is γ, then some α is not β,

(4)   If every α is β and some α is γ, then some β is γ.

If we take 'hx' in the sense of 'x is not γ' in place of 'x is γ', we obtain the following versions in place of (2)–(4):

If every β is γ and every α is β, then every α is γ,

If every β is γ and some α is not γ, then some α is not β,

If every α is β and some α is not γ, then some β is not γ.

Assigning to 'gx' the sense of 'x is not β', we obtain more variants, and, assigning to 'fx' the sense of 'x is not α', we obtain yet other variants. We see thus that (1) is only one among various forms of arguments, quite different in their natural-language formulations, all accounted for equally by (H).

    Fifteen of these forms were distinguished, classified, named, and studied in the traditional theory of the syllogism.
    Another nine forms, not covered by (H), were also studied under the name of the syllogism. One of these is:

(5)   Every β is γ and every β is α; therefore, some γ is α.

The conditional corresponding to (5), written using 'fx', 'gx', and 'hx', is:

(6) $\sim ((x) \sim (gx \bullet \sim hx) \bullet (x) \sim (gx \bullet \sim fx) \bullet (x) \sim (fx \bullet hx)).$

The other eight forms are variants of (5) also covered by (6), just as the five earlier forms were covered by (H).

However, the conditionals of form (6) are not, in general, quantificationally valid. It is easy, in fact, to deduce false conclusions from true premises according to (5). Take 'α' to mean 'horned', for example, and 'β' to mean 'unicorn', and 'γ' to mean 'hypomorph'. The statement 'Every β is γ', that is '(x) ~ (x is β • ~ x is γ) ', is true. But, as unicorns do not not exist, the conjunction 'x is β • ~ x is γ' is not satisfied by any object x. The statement 'Every β is α' is shown to be true in the same way. And yet, the statement 'Some α is γ' is false.

It is clear, in general, that the form of argument (5) is legitimate only under the supplemental hypothesis 'There is a β' – a hypothesis that fails in the case of 'There is a unicorn'. The conditional whose quantificational validity is to be established has for its antecedent the triple conjunction 'every β is γ, every β is α, and there is a β'. That is, what we must prove is not (6), but the following instead:

(I)   ~ ((x) ~ (gx • ~hx) • (x) ~ (gx • ~fx) • ~ (x) ~ gx • (x) ~ (fx • hx)).

Proof:

(a)   ~ (~ (gx • ~ hx) • ~ (gx • ~ fx) • ~ (fx • hx) • gx)   By (i).

(b)   ~ ((x) a • ~ c)   (C)

(c)   ~ ((x) (~ (gx • ~hx) • ~ (gx • ~ fx) • ~ (fx • hx)) • ~ (x) ~ gx)
                                                      From (a) and (b) by (i) and (iv).

(d)   ~ ((x) ~ (gx • ~ hx) • (x) ~ (gx • ~ fx) • (x) ~ (fx • hx) • ~ (x) ~ gx)
                                                      From (c) by (iii) (twice).

(I)   From (d) by (i).

§ 28 Inferences Involving Names

In traditional logic, statements of the type 'Socrates is human' were usually treated as having the form 'Every α is β' – perhaps with the formulation 'Everything that is identical to Socrates is human'. 'Socrates is not infallible' was considered analogously as having the form 'No α is γ'. The argument:

(7)   No human is infallible and Socrates is human; therefore, Socrates is not infallible

would thus be taken as having form (1) of § 27. It would be equally possible to treat 'Socrates is human' as having the form 'Some α is β', in the manner of 'Some object identical to Socrates is human', and to treat 'Socrates is infallible', analogously, as having the form 'Some α is not γ'. (7), in that case, does not have the form (1), but one of the various other syllogistic forms.

Both methods of interpretation are, from the point of view of the theory of quantification, artificial. The two interpretations of 'Socrates is human' translate into symbols as follows:

(8)   (x) ~ (x = Socrates • ~ x is human),

(9)   ~ (x) ~ (x = Socrates • x is human).

Evidently, 'Socrates is human' is less similar to (8) or (9) than to the clause 'x is human' which forms part of (8) and (9). It would be more natural to think of (7) as having the form:

(10)   No β is γ, and y is β; therefore, y is not γ

than as having the form of (1). Thus interpreted, inference (7) is based upon the quantificational implication of the matrix 'y is not infallible' by the matrix 'No human is infallible and y is human'. The valid conditional in question can be written using 'g' and 'h' as follows:

(11)   ~ ((x) ~ (gx • hx) • gy • hy).

But this is just a case of (A).

Under the given interpretation of 'gx' and 'hx', (11) corresponds to the words:

(12)   If no human is infallible, and y is human, then y is not infallible;

but what we need in order to establish that the statement 'No human is infallible and Socrates is human' implies 'Socrates is not infallible', is, first of all, the conditional:

(13)   If no human is infallible, and Socrates is human, then Socrates is not infallible.

However, the established validity of (12) (that is, of (11)) means that the statement '(y)12' is quantificationally true, and the conditional statement (13) in turn is one of the cases covered by the general conditional '(y)12'.

The procedure illustrated above is a useful method for proving statements that contain names, as in (13), without having to introduce the consideration of names within the theory of quantification. They can be proved in the theory of quantification using a free pronoun ('y', above) in place of the name, establishing in what follows the validity of a matrix (like (11) or (12) above) in place of the truth of the desired statement ((13) above). The supplementary step that leads us to the statement we want (in the example, the step from '(y)12' to (13)) consists in deriving a singular case from a quantification. The principle that governs the latter step is called the principle of *application*, and can be thought of as lying outside the pure theory of quantification. Certain considerations related to this principle will appear later (§§ 39–41).

§ 29 Deduction on the Basis of Premises

Consider the premises:

(1)   Every person who enters the building, without being accompanied by a member of the firm, is questioned by the guard.

(2)   Some of Fiorecchio's subordinates entered the building without being accompanied by any other person.

(3)   The guard did not question any of Fiorecchio's subordinates.

and the conclusion:

(4)   One of Fiorecchio's subordinates is a member of the firm.

Translating these statements into symbols, with 'fx', 'gxy', 'hx', 'jx', and 'kx' in place of 'x is a person who enters the building', 'x accompanies y', 'x is a member of the firm', 'the guard questions x', and 'x is Fiorecchio's subordinate', (1)–(4) become:

(5) $(y) \sim ((x) \sim (hy \cdot gxy) \cdot fy \cdot \sim jy)$,

(6) $\sim (y) \sim (fy \cdot ky \cdot (x) \sim (\sim kx \cdot gxy))$,

(7) $(y) \sim (jy \cdot ky)$,

(8) $\sim (x) \sim (hx \cdot kx)$.

We must prove the conditional whose antecedent is the conjunction of (5)–(7) and whose consequent is (8). Using the numerals '5', '6', '7', '8' as abbreviations of statements we called (5), (6), (7), and (8), the conditional to be proved is:

(9) $\sim (5 \cdot 6 \cdot 7 \cdot \sim 8)$.

It is easy, however, to follow an alternative method. Instead of proving (9) simply on the basis of logic, we prove (8) on the basis of logic together with premises (5)–(7).

Proof:

(a)	~ (7 • 5 • ~ 8)^{15}	(H)
(b)	(y) ~ ((x) ~ (hx • gxy) • fy • ky)	From (7), (5), and (a) by (i).
(c)	(y) ~ (fy • ky • (x) ~ (hx • gxy))	From (b) by (ii).
(d)	~ (~ e • c • 6)	(H)

(e)   ~ (y) ~ (~ (x) ~ (hx • gxy) • (x) ~ (~ kx • gxy))

From (6), (c), and (d) by (i).

(f)   ~ ((x) ~ (~ kx • gxy) • ~ 8 • ~ (x) ~ (~ hx • gxy))

(H)

(g)   ~ (~ 8 • ~ (x) ~ (hx • gxy) • (x) ~ (~kx • gxy))

From (f) by (ii).

(h)   ~ (~ 8 • e)

From (g) by (iv) and (v).

(8)   From (e) and (h) by (i).

We can express (b) in words as:

(10)   No person who enters the building, without being accompanied by a member of the firm, is Fiorecchio's subordinate.

This statement is a syllogistic consequence of (3) and (1), and the syllogistic argument finds its quantificational expression in the first two lines of the proof.
We can express (e) in words as:

(11)   Some person who is accompanied by a member of the firm is accompanied only by Fiorecchio's subordinates.

This statement is a syllogistic consequence of (10) and (2), and the syllogistic argument is quantificationally expressed in lines (c)–(e). The argument from (11) to (4), which is carried out in the last four lines of the proof above, does not belong to the part of the theory of quantification that corresponds to the theory of the syllogism.

In this proof, premises (5)–(7) are invoked in a form analogous to the way in which forms whose validity is established were cited in earlier proofs. There are, however, certain differences. We are accustomed to invoke the forms (A)–(I) in order to establish the validity of any matrix that is an instance of those forms. For example, to establish (a), we invoke (H), even though (a) exhibits 'j' and 'k' where (H) exhibits 'g' and 'h'. By contrast, invoking the premises (5)–(7) serves only to introduce those specific premises; no substitution of the parts 'fy', 'gxy', etc. is permissible here. The premises (5)–(7) were assumed only under certain interpretations of these parts, and would become false under other interpretations.

Another restriction that we must impose on the use of premises is the following: operation (iv) must not be used so as to introduce a quantifier corresponding to a pronoun which is free in a premise. It would be wrong, for example, to argue that 'fy' implies '(x) fx', on the basis of the following proof of the conclusion '(x) fx' from the premise 'fy':

| (a) | (y) fy | From the premise by (iv). |
| | (x) fx | From (a) by (vi). |

In fact, 'fy' does not in general imply '(x)fx'. When, for example, we give 'fy' (and 'fx') the meaning 'y is human' (and 'x is human'), the implication fails. The conditional matrix '~ (fy • ~ (x)fx)' is not valid, because its quantification '(y) ~ (fy • ~ (x)fx)' is false. To show that this quantification is false, we merely have to designate an object y that does not satisfy '~ (fy • ~ (x) fx)'. Socrates is such an object, since the conjunction 'Socrates is human • ~ (x) x is human' is true.

Nevertheless, when we obey these two restrictions, the method of deduction on the basis of premises is perfectly acceptable. When we derive a conclusion on the basis of given premises together with any valid matrices, using the operations (i), (ii), etc., according to the two restrictions just considered, we may conclude that the conjunction of the premises quantificationally implies the conclusion. (The justification of the method will be omitted here.) That is, we can conclude that the conditional formed by the premises and the conclusion is valid. The proof of (8) on the basis of (5)–(7), above, establishes that the conjunction of (5)–(7) quantificationally implies (8), and that the conditional (9) is valid, whatever the matrices represented by 'fx', 'gxy', etc. may be.

Because (9) is provable directly on the basis of (A) by means of (i)–(iv), the current method of deduction on the basis of premises is simply a convenience, and is theoretically dispensable.

§ 30 Monadic Theory of Quantification

Among the schemata that depict the forms of matrices, we call *monadic* those that exhibit only 'x' as a pronoun, and do not exhibit any free pronoun. Let us stipulate, in addition, that the quantifier '(x)', in a monadic schema, never occurs[16] within its own scope as in '(x) (... (x) fx ...)'. The schemata (B), (C), (D), (E), (H), and (I) are typical monadic schemata. It is also clear that various non-monadic schemata, in the sense here described, can be turned into monadic ones by means of (v) and (vi).

There can be no mechanical criterion for deciding in general if the matrices depicted by a given schema are valid. There is, however, a mechanical criterion that achieves this goal for monadic schemata.[iv] Here we will only present and illustrate that criterion, without justifying it.

Take any monadic schema, whose schematic letters are 'f', 'g', 'h', ..., 'p', 'q', 'r', ... We subject each of the quantifications in this schema to the following quadruple process of transformation:

(a) If the quantification, let us say '(x) (...)', lacks any of the letters 'f', 'g', 'h', ..., let us say 'h', we provide the missing letter by transforming '(x) (...)' into '(x) (... • ~ (hx • ~ hx))' (which is a transformation by (ii)).

(b) We transform the entire text governed by the quantifier (a transformation by (ii)) into canonical form (§ 5), always arranging the letters 'f', 'g', ... in alphabetical order.

(c) We distribute the quantifier according to (iii).

(d) If the resulting quantifiers contain any of the letters 'p', 'q' or 'r', ... (which represent matrices that do not contain 'x' as a free pronoun), we move the letter outside of the quantification by (v).

After repeating the process above in relation to all of the quantifications concerned, validity can be proved just by determining whether the result is compositionally implied by:

(1) $\sim$ ((x) $\sim$ (fx • gx • hx • ...) • (x) $\sim$ ($\sim$ fx • gx • hx • ...) • (x) $\sim$ (fx • $\sim$ gx • hx • ...) • (x) $\sim$ ($\sim$ fx • $\sim$ gx • hx ...) • (x) $\sim$ (fx • gx • $\sim$ hx • ...) • ...).

Let us apply this method to principle (H) of the syllogism. Subjecting the first quantification of (H), that is, '(x) $\sim$ (gx • hx)', to the transformation (a), we obtain:

(2)   (x) $\sim$ (gx • hx • $\sim$ (fx • $\sim$ fx)).

Transforming the part '$\sim$ (gx • hx • $\sim$ (fx • $\sim$ fx))' of (2) into canonical form, according to (b), we convert (2) into:

(x) ($\sim$ (fx • gx • hx) • $\sim$ ($\sim$ fx • gx • hx)).

Distributing '(x)', according to (c), we obtain:

(x) $\sim$ (fx • gx • hx) • (x) $\sim$ ($\sim$ fx • gx • hx).

The other quantifications of (H) become, by the same process, respectively:

(x) $\sim$ (fx • $\sim$ gx • hx) • (x) $\sim$ ($\sim$ fx • $\sim$ gx • $\sim$ hx),
(x) $\sim$ (fx • gx • hx) • (x) $\sim$ ($\sim$ fx • $\sim$ gx • $\sim$ hx).

[iv] This fact was discovered by Löwenheim. The criterion that will be formulated here differs from that of Löwenheim with regard to the details.

Thus (H) becomes:

(3) $\sim((x)\sim(fx \bullet gx \bullet hx) \bullet (x) \sim (\sim fx \bullet gx \bullet hx) \bullet (x) \sim (fx \bullet \sim gx \bullet hx) \bullet (x) \sim$
       $(fx \bullet \sim gx \bullet \sim hx) \bullet \sim ((x) \sim (fx \bullet gx \bullet hx) \bullet (x) \sim (fx \bullet \sim gx \bullet hx)))$.

It remains to be determined whether (1) (which is determined only for the case of the three letters 'f', 'g', 'h') compositionally implies (3). We can answer in the affirmative without considering (1), since formula (3) has the compositionally valid form '$\sim (p \bullet q \bullet r \bullet s \bullet \sim (p \bullet r))$'.

We will now see how the method applies to (E) and (B). In (E), the first quantification '(x)fx' is already at hand, and does not require any of the operations (a)–(d). The other quantification, '(x) $\sim$ (p $\bullet \sim$ fx)', becomes '$\sim$ (p $\bullet \sim$ (x) fx)' according to (d), in such a way that (E) transforms into:

       $\sim (\sim (p \bullet \sim (x) fx) \bullet p \bullet \sim (x) fx)$,

whose compositional validity is clear. With regard to (B), both quantifications '(x) fx' and '(x) $\sim$ fx' are already at hand, in such a way that we have only to determine whether (B) is compositionally implied by (1). As (B) is not compositionally valid,[v] we must explicitly consider (1). But (1), determined by the case of a single letter 'f', is identical to (B), and thus implies (B) compositionally.

Although the monadic part of the theory of quantification is an especially simple part, it is an important part which includes, in particular, syllogistic logic. It is for this reason that the existence of a mechanical criterion of validity, adequate to this part of the theory, is of interest. In the general theory of quantification, however, we must always be content with methods that depend on the non-systematic search for proofs.

§ 31 The Practical Aspect[17]

An understanding of the techniques of the theory of quantification can be useful in a way that is directly connected to practical life. One field where these techniques have proved useful is that of insurance. Writing the clauses of an insurance contract is, at times, a complicated matter. The regulations involved in the employees' pension plan of a large corporation can take up more than a dozen closely printed pages. Now suppose that the plan has finally been written out in a series of about fifty long paragraphs, covering all of the special

---

[v] More exactly: matrices of the form (B) are not compositionally valid. The application here of the terminology of validity and of implication directly to the schemata is inexact but convenient.

combinations of important circumstances that may arise on the part of the employees. What reason have we to judge that all of this could not have been equivalently formulated in half the space and with half the work, only by recombining and reclassifying the employees' circumstances by means of different rules? If such a simplification exists, common-sense thinking will never reveal it, unless by chance, because the pension plan is too complicated to be considered *in toto*. We can, however, schematize the clauses in terms of the notation of the theory of quantification, afterwards systematically transforming the set of clauses into the simplest equivalent, and finally translating the result back into everyday language.

The usefulness of the theory of quantification as applied to insurance is not limited to the simplification of contracts. The theory has also shown itself useful in testing the consistency of a set of clauses, in determining the implications of a contract for one or another random set of circumstances, in detecting clear differences between two connected contracts, in short, in every place where there are apparent advantages in manipulating the terms of a contract with mathematical facility.

This field of application is already being explored by the Prudential Insurance Company, due to the efforts of Mr. Edmund C. Berkeley of that firm. It seems that the systematic analysis of quantificational reasoning will someday show itself useful in the same way in various sciences. The development of a systematic arithmetic enhanced the practical manipulation of the most complex numerical concepts, and the theory of quantification promises to be an analogous extension with respect to the concepts implicit in everyday language.

Up to the present, however, the greatest value of the theory remains in the theoretical area, residing principally in the theoretical clarification of what constitutes logical truth and the relation of "following logically," that is, the relation of implication.

III

Identity and Existence

§ 32 Identity

We have already encountered the notation of identity, 'x=y', several times in our examples, but we have yet to study identity explicitly as a logical idea. Identity is a notion so simple and fundamental that it is difficult to explain it more clearly, except by merely translating it into synonymous terms. To say that x and y are identical is to say that they are the same thing. Every object is identical to itself and to nothing else.

Even though identity is such an elementary notion, nevertheless it has been the object of persistent confusion. One of these confusions is found in the dictum of one of the most ancient philosophers, Heraclitus: "We cannot bathe in the same river twice." As the waters renew themselves continuously, reasoned Heraclitus, there would be another river at the moment of the second bath. Another form of the same difficulty is found in the question of how we can say that a person preserves the same body, given that the material constitution of the body is continuously changing. In general, the difficulty is one of conceiving how an object that changes remains identical to itself. The origin of this difficulty resides less in the idea of identity itself, and more in the treatment of time.

Consider the river. It is an extended object, in time as well as in space. It is the totality of its various instantaneous states, as well as of the sections of various lengths between its source and its delta. The river is not the totality of certain drops of water; each drop shares the spatial extension of the river only within a portion of the temporal duration of the drop and of the river. Now, the river, whatever changes it may undergo, as much in relation to its material constitution as in relation to other factors, remains the same river while it lasts; it remains the same identical totality of its various instantaneous states. By analogy, the same is true of the human body. It is only the various instantaneous

80

states that compose the whole river, or the whole body. Each differs from all the others. Still, each of these instantaneous states is also identical to *itself.*

Another type of confusion about identity is seen in the observation of Wittgenstein: to say of an object that it is identical to itself is empty, and to say that it is identical to another object is a mistake.[18] We must, however, distinguish not between two cases, but among three, exemplified by the statements 'Cicero = Cicero', 'Cicero = Catiline', and 'Cicero = Tully'. Of these three statements, the first is empty and the second false; but the third is neither empty nor false. The third is informative, as it combines two different names, and is also true, given that the two names are names of the same object. Wittgenstein, not distinguishing carefully between objects and their names, thinks that every true affirmation of identity must contain the sign '=' and repeat same name on either side of it, as in 'Cicero = Cicero'; but Wittgenstein does not recognize that '=' should only appear between names of the same object, and that in cases where identity statements are useful, those names will be two different ones. Cicero is identical to Tully, even though the name 'Cicero' is different from the name 'Tully'; likewise the Nile is longer than the Paranaiba, even though the name 'Nile' is shorter than the name 'Paranaiba'.[19]

The same confusion between the identity of objects and the identity of their names is found in the minds of many mathematicians. They believe that an equation, for example '5 + 3 = 2 + 6', relates two numbers that are equal in some sense, but still not identical, since the expressions '5 + 3' and '2 + 6' are different from one another. Whitehead, in his book *Universal Algebra*, made the same claim regarding the law 'x + y = y + x'.

This confusion between sign and object sometimes leads to the idea that identity is a relation between the signs themselves, and not between objects. Leibniz, for example, wrote: "Two terms are the *same* (*eadem*) if one can be substituted by the other without impairing the truth of the context (*salva veritate*)."[i] It is clear that the terms are not the same; it is the objects indicated by the terms that are the same. We use the names of objects to affirm the identity of objects, just as we use them to affirm any other relation between objects. The affirmation of the identity of the objects is true if the terms used in the affirmation are connected by a certain other relation, that of designating the same object.

---

[i] Cf. Lewis, *Survey*, p. 373. [Lewis actually translates Leibniz rather differently, as saying: "Two terms are the same (*eadem*) if one can be substituted by the other without altering the truth of any statement (*salva veritate*)" (eds.)]

§ 33 Principles of Identity

One of the fundamental principles of identity is part of what was formulated rather confusedly in the quotation from Leibniz. It is the principle of *substitutivity of identity*, according to which (approximately speaking) given a true statement of identity, one of its two terms may be substituted for the other in any true statement and the result will be true. A more exact formulation of the principle is that every matrix of the form:

(J) $\sim (x = y \cdot fx \cdot \sim fy)$

becomes true when initial quantifiers are applied. In short, every such matrix is valid. It is not quantificationally valid in the sense that the result of such application of quantifiers is quantificationally true, but valid in the sense that any result of such application of quantifiers is true (in fact, logically true). We can introduce the terms 'identically valid' and 'identically true' to correspond to the present extension of logic beyond the theory of quantification.

This formulation of the principle of substitutivity is inexact with regard to the expression 'every matrix of the form (J)'. We must take this expression in the following sense: every matrix formed from (J) by replacing 'fx' and 'fy' with matrices such that the second matrix differs from the first only in containing free occurrences of 'y' in place of some free occurrences of 'x'. Note, by contrast, that in the matrices 'of the form (A)', the matrix that replaces 'fy' must contain 'y' in place of all of the free occurrences of 'x' in the matrix that replaces 'fx'.[ii]

Aside from (J), the only other fundamental principle is that of *self-identity*:

(K) $(x)\ x = x.$

That is, the matrix '$x = x$' is valid, and the statement '$(x)\ x = x$' is true. The quantifier is written at some distance to the left so that we can consider only the matrix when we refer to (K) in the course of later proofs. This treatment of the initial quantifiers of the theorems will be the usual one.

Other principles are easy to derive. One of them, the principle of the *transitivity* of identity, affirms that, whatever x, y, and z may be, if x = y and y = z, then x = z. That is,

(L) $(x)\ (y)\ (z) \sim (x = y \cdot y = z \cdot \sim x = z).$

[ii] In a more rigorous and detailed study than the present one, the contrast noted above would be stated more explicitly and systematically. Cf. my books *Elementary Logic*, § 45, and *Mathematical Logic*, §§ 15, 30.

Proof:

(a) $\sim (y = z \bullet x = y \bullet \sim x = z)$ (J)

(L)   From (a) by (i).

The following principle of the *symmetry* of identity states that in a statement of identity, order is immaterial:

(M) $(x)\,(y) \sim (x = y \bullet \sim y = x)$.

Proof:

(a) $\sim(x = y \bullet x = x \bullet \sim y = x)$ (J)

(M)   From (a) and (K) by (i).

The following principle affirms that every object is identical to some object.

(N) $(x) \sim (y) \sim x = y$.

Proof:

(a) $\sim ((y) \sim x = y \bullet x = x)$ (A)

(N)   From (a) and (K) by (i).

§ 34 Occurrences That Are Not Purely Designative[iii]

The formulation (J) of the principle of substitutivity contains pronouns as the terms of the identity; but let us examine some more the less technical version, given earlier, according to which the names contained within a true statement of identity are interchangeable without impairing the truth of any context. It is easy to find cases contrary to this principle.[20] For example, the statements:

(1)   Giorgione = Barbarelli,

(2)   Giorgione was so-called because of his size.

are true; however, replacement of the name 'Giorgione' by the name 'Barbarelli' turns (2) into the falsehood:

(3)   Barbarelli was so-called because of his size.

Furthermore, the statements:

(4)   Cicero = Tully,

(5)   'Cicero' contains six letters

[iii] The essential contents of § 34 and § 36 are due to Frege (1892).

are true, but replacement of the first name by the second turns (5) false. Yet the basis of the principle of substitutivity appears quite solid; whatever can be said about the person Cicero (or Giorgione) should be equally true of the person Tully (or Barbarelli), this being the same person.

In the case of (5), this paradox resolves itself immediately. The fact is that (5) is not a statement about the person Cicero, but simply about the word 'Cicero'. The principle of substitutivity should not be extended to contexts in which the name to be supplanted occurs without referring simply to the object.

The relation of name to the object whose name it is, is called *designation*; the name 'Cicero', for example, designates the man Cicero. An occurrence of the name in which the name refers simply to the object designated, I shall call *purely designative*. Failure of substitutivity reveals merely that the occurrence to be supplanted is not purely designative, and that the statement depends not only upon the object but on the form of the name. For it is clear that whatever can be affirmed about the *object* remains true when we refer to the object by any other name.

An expression that consists of another expression between single quotes constitutes a name of that other expression; and it is clear in general that the occurrence of that other expression or any part of it, within the context of quotes, is not designative. In particular the occurrence of the personal name within the context of quotes in (5) is not designative, nor subject to the substitutivity principle. The personal name occurs there merely as a fragment of a longer name which contains, beside this fragment, the two quotation marks. To make a substitution upon a personal name, within such a context, would be no more justifiable than to make a substitution upon the term 'cat' within the context 'cattle'.

The example (2) is a little more subtle, for it is a statement about a man and not merely about his name. It was the man, not his name, that was called so and so; and it was the man, not his name, who was large.[21] Nevertheless, the failure of substitutivity shows that the occurrence of the personal name in (2) is not purely[22] designative. It is easy in fact to translate (2) into another statement which contains two occurrences of the name, one purely designative and the other not:

(6)   Giorgione was called 'Giorgione' because of his size.

The first occurrence is purely designative. Substitution on the basis of (1) converts (6) into another statement equally true:

> Barbarelli was called 'Giorgione' because of his size.

The second occurrence of the personal name is no more designative than any other occurrence within a context of quotes.

To get an example of another common type of statement in which names do not occur designatively, consider any person who is called Philip and satisfies the condition:

(7)   Philip is unaware that Tully denounced Catiline,

or perhaps the condition:

(8)   Philip believes that Tegucigalpa is in Nicaragua.

Substitution on the basis of (4) transforms (7) into the statement:

(9)   Philip is unaware that Cicero denounced Catiline,

no doubt false. Substitution on the basis of the true identity:

Tegucigalpa = Capital of Honduras

transforms the truth (8) likewise into the falsehood:

(10)   Philip believes that the capital of Honduras is in Nicaragua.

We see, therefore, that the occurrences of the names 'Tully' and 'Tegucigalpa' in (7)–(8) are not purely designative.

In this there is a fundamental contrast between (7), or (8), and:

Crassus heard Tully denounce Catiline.

This statement affirms a relation between three persons, and the persons remain so related independently of the names applied to them. But (7) cannot be considered simply as affirming a relation between three persons, nor (8) a relation between person, city, and country – at least, not so long as we interpret our words in such a way as to admit (7) and (8) as true and (9) and (10) as false.

Some readers may wish to construe unawareness and belief as relations between persons and statements, thus writing (7) and (8) in the manner:

Philip is unaware of 'Tully denounced Catiline',

Philip believes 'Tegucigalpa is in Nicaragua',

the purpose being to put within a context of single quotes every not purely designative occurrence of a name. It is not necessary, however, to force an analogy thus between cases of the type (7)–(8) and those of the type (5)–(6). It is unnecessary to insist that every indesignative occurrence of a name forms part of the name of an expression. What is important is to insist that the contexts 'is unaware that … ' and 'believes that … ' are, like the context of single quotes, contexts in which names do not occur purely designatively. The same is true of the contexts 'knows that … ', 'says that … ', 'doubts that … ', 'is surprised that … ', etc.

§ 35 Positions Where Pronouns Cannot Go[23]

It becomes even clearer that the occurrence of the name 'Giorgione' in (2) is not purely designative when we try to use a pronoun in place of this occurrence, for example in the manner:

(11)   ~ (x) ~ x was so-called because of his size,

that is:

(12)   There exists someone (or more generally: something) that was so-called because of its size.

This combination of words can make sense only within a broader context, where the word 'so' refers back to a word used earlier on. Considered without any wider context, as a variant or consequence of statement (2), the expression (12) (or (11)) lacks meaning. It makes no sense to say of an object simply that it is "so-called." Would this object be the person Giorgione, that is, Barbarelli? Then the affirmation that this object is "so-called" would be true in form (2) of § 34 and at the same time false in form (3).

It is, in fact, natural that a meaningless result arises from using a pronoun in this way in the position of a non-designative occurrence of a name. The pronoun 'x' constitutes, in combination with the quantifier '(x)', a way for us to refer generally to all things. Although the things can be of any type, concrete or abstract, physical or mental, it is clear that nothing meaningful can result from the use of the pronoun in a position that is simply unsuited to the designation of anything. It makes no sense to use the pronoun in place of the syllable 'zil' in 'Brazil is large', in the manner of '~ (x) ~ Bra$x$ is large', that is, 'There exists an object such that Bra-it is large'; and the use of the pronoun in place of a not purely designative occurrence of a noun is analogous to this example, though less grotesque.

It makes good sense, however, to use the pronoun in the position of the purely designative occurrence of the name 'Giorgione' in (6). We can affirm, for example, that

(13)   ~ (x) ~ x was called 'Giorgione' because of his size,

that is,

> Someone (better: something) is called 'Giorgione' because of its size.

Now let us consider the result of the use of a pronoun in place of the non-designative occurrence of the personal name in (5). Let us look at the apparent statement:

(14) $\sim (x) \sim$ 'x' contains six letters

and its apparent verbal equivalent:

(15)   Some object is such that 'it' contains six letters.

Every expression formed by applying single quotes is the name of the expression between the single quotes; and, in particular, the expression that consists of the letter 'x' and two single quotes is the name of this letter itself. The expression:

(16)   'x' contains six letters

simply says:

> The penultimate letter of the (Brazilian) alphabet has six letters,

and is, for this reason, a false statement. In (14) the occurrence of the letter between quotes does not refer back to the quantifier, so it is just as irrelevant as an occurrence of the same letter within the context of 'box' or 'Mexico' would be. We see, therefore, that the use of the quantifier '(x)' in (14), prefixed to the denial of (16), simply violates the rule that vacuous quantifiers must be suppressed (§ 19).

Example (15) has a similar status to that of (14). The expression:

> 'it' contains six letters

is a false statement, becoming true only when we replace 'six 'with 'two'. The prefix 'some object is such that' in (15) is vacuous.

It is significantly less obvious, but also significantly more important to recognize, that the use of the pronoun in the positions of not purely designative occurrences of the names 'Tully' and 'Tegucigalpa' in (7) and (8) also leads to meaningless outcomes. Consider the case:

(17) $\sim (x) \sim$ Philip is unaware that x denounces Catiline,

in words:

> There exists someone (better: something) such that Phillip is unaware that it denounced Catiline.

Although grammatically correct, these expressions are meaningless, at least when we interpret our words in such a manner as to admit (7) as true and (9) as false. For is Tully, that is, Cicero, the person who Philip is unaware denounced Catiline? But such an affirmation would be true in form (7) and at the same time false in form (9).

Note that the expression:

(18)   Philip is unaware that ~ (x) ~ x denounced Catiline

differs from (17), and has clear meaning; it is a false statement affirming that Phillip is unaware that Catiline was denounced. The use that makes no sense is that in which, as in example (17), the expression of the form 'is unaware that . . . ', 'believes that . . . ', 'says that . . . ', etc. contains a pronoun that refers back to a quantifier used before that expression. This knowledge imposes on the use of the quantifiers and their verbal equivalents a restriction that may be restrictive, even unsettling, but is nevertheless inevitable.

§ 36 Meaning. Synonymy. Necessity[24]

To say that two names designate the same object is not to say that they are *synonymous*, that is, that they have the same meaning. To determine the synonymity of two names or other expressions it should be sufficient to understand the expressions; but to determine that two names designate the same object, it is commonly necessary to investigate the world. The names 'Evening Star' and 'Morning Star', for example, are not synonymous, having been applied each to a certain ball of matter according to a different criterion. But it appears from astronomical investigations that it is the same ball, the same planet, in both cases; that is, the names designate the same thing. The identity:

(1)   Evening Star = Morning Star

is a truth of astronomy, not following merely from the meanings of the words.

It results equally from astronomical researches, and not merely from the meanings of the words, that the object (the number, or degree of multiplicity) designated by the numeral '9' is the same as that designated by the complex name 'the number of planets'. The identity:

(2)   The number of planets = 9

is a truth (so far as we know at the moment) of astronomy. The names the 'number of planets' and '9' are not synonymous; they do not have the same meaning. This fact is emphasized by the possibility, ever present, that (2) be refuted by the discovery of another planet.

Another contrast between designation and meaning is that only certain very definite expressions designate (viz., the names of the objects designated), whereas perhaps all words and other more complex unities capable of figuring in statements have meaning.

Just what the *meaning* of an expression is – what kind of object – is not yet clear; but it is clear that, given a notion of meaning, we can explain the notion of *synonymity* easily as the relation between expressions that have the same meaning. Conversely also, given the relation of synonymity, it would be easy to derive the notion of meaning in the following way: the meaning of an expression is the class of all the expressions synonymous with it. Perhaps[25] this second direction of construction is the more promising one. The relation of synonymity, in turn, calls for a definition or a criterion in psychological and linguistic terms. Such a definition, which up to the present has perhaps never even been sketched, would be a fundamental contribution at once to philology and philosophy.

The relation of synonymity is presupposed, as we have seen, in the notion of meaning, which is used so abundantly in everyday discourse. The notion of synonymity figures implicitly also whenever we use the method of indirect quotations. In indirect quotation we do not insist on a literal repetition of the words of the person quoted, but we insist on a *synonymous* sentence; we require reproduction of the *meaning*. Such synonymity differs even from logical equivalence; and exactly what it is remains unspecified.

The relation of synonymity is presupposed also in the notion, so current in philosophical circles since Kant, of *analytic* statements. It is usual to describe an analytic statement as a statement that is true by virtue of the *meanings* of the words; or as a statement that follows logically from the meanings of the words. Given the notion of synonymy, and given also the notion of logical truth, we can define an analytic statement as any statement that is logically true or can be reduced to a logical truth by the substitution of expressions by synonymous expressions. The statement 'No bachelor is married', for example, is analytic, reducing to the truth 'No unmarried man is married' by replacing the expression 'bachelor' with the expression 'unmarried man'.[26]

Among the various possible senses of the vague adverb 'necessarily' we can single out one – the sense of *analytic* necessity – according to the following criterion: the result of applying 'necessarily' to a statement is true if the original statement is analytic, and in the contrary case this result is false.

The statement:[27]

(3)   Necessarily no bachelor[28] is married,

for example, is equivalent to:

(4)   'No bachelor is married' is analytic,

and is therefore true. The statement:

(5)   9 is necessarily greater than 7

is equivalent to

(6)   '9 > 7' is analytic

and is therefore true (if we recognize the reducibility of arithmetic to logic; cf. Introduction). The statement:

(7)   Necessarily, if there is life on the Evening Star then there is life on the Evening Star

is equivalent to:

(8)   'If there is life on the Evening Star, then there is life on the Evening Star' is analytic

or, as we could also formulate it:

(9)   'There is life on the Evening Star' implies analytically 'There is life on the Evening Star'

(where *analytic implication* stands for the relation one statement bears to another when the conditional formed from the respective statements is analytic).[29] (7) is then true, since the conditional in question is logically true and therefore analytic.

   On the other hand, the statements:

(10)   The number of planets is necessarily greater than 7,

(11)   Necessarily, if there is life on the Evening Star then there is life on the Morning Star

are false, since the statements:

      The number of planets is greater than 7,

      If there is life on the Evening Star, then there is life on the Morning Star

are true only because of circumstances outside logic.

The prefixes 'possibly' and 'it is impossible that' are definable immediately on the basis of 'necessarily' in the fashion 'not necessarily not' and 'necessarily not'. Thus, for example, (3) can be paraphrased in the manner:

(12)   It is impossible that bachelors be married.

§ 37 Intensional Composition of Statements[30]

The statements (4), (6), (8), and (9) are explicitly statements about statements. They attribute the property of analyticity or the relation of analytic implication to statements, referring to statements by use of their names (constructed with single quotes). On the other hand, (3), (5), (7), and (12) do not refer to other statements by use of their names; they are rather compounds of the statements themselves. The prefixes 'necessarily' and 'it is impossible that' are applied, like the sign of denial, to statements to form others.

The contrast between 'necessarily' and 'is analytic' is exactly analogous to the contrast between '~' and 'is false'. To write the denial sign before the statement itself in the manner:

$$\sim 9 < 7$$

means the same as to write the words 'is false' after the name of the statement, in the manner:

'9 < 7' is false.

In the example (7) we can recognize a complex connective, 'necessarily, if – then'. This connective, like 'if – then' or the dot of conjunction, joins statements to form others.

There is nevertheless a striking difference between the compounds reducible to conjunction and denial on the one hand and the compounds (3), (5), (7), and (12) on the other. These latter are *intensional* compounds, in the sense (cf. § 7) that the truth value of the compound is not determined merely by the truth value of the components.

The statements (4), (6), (8), and (9), besides containing names of statements and discussion of these statements,[31] are also literally *compounds* of these same statements, the quotation marks being part of an expression applied to the component statement to form the compound. Just as the statements '~ 9 > 7' and (5) are formed from the component statement '9 > 7' by the application of '~' and 'necessarily', we may consider that (6) is formed from the same component by the application of two quotation marks and the words 'is analytic'. Similarly for (4), (8), and (9).

The way in which such statements occur in the "compounds" (4), (6), (8), and (9) is, indeed, rather irregular and accidental. In general, we know that all matter within a context of single quotes is isolated, in an important sense, from the broader context. We know that a name within a context of single quotes does not occur designatively, and that a pronoun within such a context does not succeed in referring to a quantifier anterior to the quotes (cf. §§ 34–35).

It is in the supposed freedom from these defects that the intensional composition of statements by means of 'necessarily', 'possibly', and 'necessarily if – then', like extensional composition by means of '~' and '•', is thought to constitute composition of statements in a more genuine sense than that which puts the component within quotes. The prefixes 'necessarily' and 'possibly' aspire to such uses as:

> If an object necessarily has one or other of two attributes, then it is not possible that it lack both attributes,

that is:

> $(x)(y)(z) \sim (y$ and z are attributes $\bullet$ necessarily x has y or $z \bullet$ possibly x lacks y and z),

in which a pronoun within the context 'necessarily . . . ' or 'possibly . . . ' refers beyond that context.

However, the cited modes of intensional composition of statements are, in fact, subject to the same defects as the context of quotes. For, in view of the fact that a substitution on the basis of the true identity (1) transforms the truth (7) into the falsehood (11), we have to conclude that the terminal occurrence of the name 'Evening Star' in (7) is not purely designative. Equally, in view of the fact that a substitution on the basis of the true identity (2) transforms the truth (5) into the falsehood (10) we conclude that the occurrence of the name '9' in (5) is not purely designative.

It follows that the context 'necessarily . . . ', at least in the analytic sense which we are considering, is similar to the context of single quotes and to the contexts 'is unaware that . . . ', 'believes that . . . ', etc. It does not admit pronouns which refer to quantifiers anterior to the context.[iv]

[iv] These circumstances must be carefully considered in any appraisal of a calculus of necessity such, for example, as that of C. I. Lewis. (See Bibliography.)

The expression:

Necessarily ~ (x) ~ x > 7,

that is, 'Necessarily something is greater than 7', still makes sense, being in fact a true statement; but the expression:

~(x) ~ x is necessarily greater than 7,

that is, 'There is something which is necessarily greater than 7', is meaningless. For, would 9, that is, the number of planets, be one of the numbers necessarily greater than 7? But such an affirmation would be at once true in the form (5) and false in the form (10). Similar observations apply to the use of pronouns in connection with the example (7).

This resistance to quantification, observed in relation to the context 'necessarily . . . ', is encountered equally in connection with the derivative contexts 'possibly . . . ' etc.

We see, therefore, that the apparent compounds (3), (5), (7), and (12) are compounds of the contained statements only in the irregular or accidental sense noted in the case of contexts that use quotes. It would be clearer, perhaps, to adhere explicitly to the forms (4), (6), (8), and (9), instead of the alternative forms (3), (5), (7), and (12).

These observations apply, naturally, to the prefix 'necessarily' only in the explained sense of analytic necessity; and correspondingly for possibility, impossibility, and the necessary conditional. As for other notions of physical necessity or possibility, the first problem would be to formulate the notions clearly and exactly. Afterwards we could investigate whether such notions involve non-designative occurrences of names and hence resist the use of pronouns referring back to exterior quantifiers.[32]

This question concerns intimately the practical use of language. It concerns, for example, the use of the contrary-to-fact conditional (cf. § 7) within a quantification; for it is reasonable to suppose that the contrary-to-fact conditional reduces to the form 'necessarily, if p then q' in some sense of necessity.[33] Upon the contrary-to-fact conditional depends in turn, for example, this definition of solubility in water: To say that an object is soluble in water is to say that it would dissolve if it were in water. In discussions of physics, naturally, we need the matrix 'x is soluble in water' as a component of various quantifications (or the equivalent context in natural language);[34] but, according to the definition suggested, we should then have to admit within quantifications the expression 'if x were in water then x would dissolve', that is, 'necessarily if x is in water then x dissolves'. Yet we do not know whether there is a suitable sense of "necessity" that admits pronouns referring thus to exterior quantifiers.[v]

The effect of these considerations is to raise questions rather than to answer them. But one important result is the recognition that any intensional mode of statement composition, whether based on some notion of "necessity" or, for example, on a notion of "probability" (as in Reichenbach's system), must be carefully examined in relation to its susceptibility to quantification. Perhaps the only useful modes of statement composition susceptible to quantification are the extensional ones, reducible to '~' and '•'. Up to now there is no clear example to the contrary. It is known, in particular, that no intensional mode of statement composition is needed in mathematics.

§ 38 Existence

The word 'name' has both a *grammatical* and a *semantic* meaning. We can, however, assign to the word 'substantive' the grammatical meaning, reserving for the word 'name' the semantic meaning: *that which is the name of an object*; in short, *that which designates*.

All names designate, although they have at times, as we have had occasion to observe, non-designative occurrences. It is now left to us to consider certain substantives that are distinguished from names, not by some grammatical feature, but simply by lack of designation. An example is the substantive 'Pegasus'.

The question whether a substantive is a name, like the question whether two names designate the same object (cf. § 36), is generally not decided by the study of the mere meaning of the words. From a purely linguistic point of view, the words 'Pegasus' and 'Bucephalus' are similar; it is only an accident of natural history that 'Bucephalus' designates while 'Pegasus' does not.

The question whether two names designate the same object is equivalent, as we know, to the question whether the identity statement formed by two names is true; and this identity can be a truth of natural science, like (1) in § 36. Analogously, the question whether a substantive is a name is equivalent to the question whether the existence statement formed by means of the name is true; and this statement can, like:

---

[v] For a theory of "disposition terms," like 'soluble', see Rudolf Carnap, *Testability*.

(1)   There is such a thing as Bucephalus,

be a truth of natural science (in this case, history).

It is useful, here as it was earlier, to consider verbs as lacking intrinsic temporal determinations. Thus (1) does not affirm that Bucephalus is still alive. Bucephalus is an extended portion of the spatio-temporal world. It has a spatial extension of several hectoliters and a temporal one of several years, although these regions of space and time are far away from here. (1) does not affirm that this temporal extension extends to the year 1942, just as it does not affirm that this spatial extension extends to Brazil. It simply affirms that the supposed portion of the spatio-temporal world does, in fact, exist. The statement:

(2)   ~ there is such a thing as Pegasus

denies that there is, near or far, a section of the spatio-temporal world such as the ancient Greeks assumed under the substantive 'Pegasus'. (2) is, like (1), a truth of natural science.

We must not object to (2) on the basis that Pegasus exists as a mental entity. Perhaps there is an idea of Pegasus, and likewise an idea of Bucephalus. But (1) does not affirm, and (2) does not deny, the existence of an idea, but rather the existence of an animal. The ideas of Bucephalus and Pegasus are not designated by the words 'Bucephalus' and 'Pegasus' in (1) and (2), but by other expressions: 'the idea of Bucephalus', 'the idea of Pegasus'.

Furthermore, I think that we have little to gain in saying that Pegasus exists in the world of Greek mythology and not in the real world. Metaphors aside, there is only one world. It was in relation to this world that the Greeks falsely affirmed – be it by mistake, be it for artistic purposes independent of the question of literal truth – that Pegasus exists; and it is in relation to the same world that the modern scientist affirms (2). It is important to be able to say 'The Greeks affirmed that Pegasus exists', or 'The Greek myths imply that there is such a thing as Pegasus', but we can make such affirmations about cultural history, and even recognize an aesthetic value in the myth of Pegasus, without relativizing the affirmation of (2) under the supposition of a plurality of worlds. As Vicente Ferreira da Silva (p. 33) has written, "These different forms of existence, introduced by certain thinkers, are completely puerile and lead us to absurd conclusions."

We need not conclude from this that everything that exists occupies space and time. We could admit, for example, compatibly with these observations, the truth of the statement:

(3)   There is such a thing as the number 9^{9^9}

even though the number in question is an abstract object, neither spatial nor temporal. Some thinkers believe that (3) is dubious because they adhere to the doctrine that there are only concrete objects; others, not partisans of this doctrine in its complete generality, will find (3) to be dubious for reasons connected to the fact that the total number of the smallest particles in the universe is less than 9^{9^9}; still others, including those who accept the truths of arithmetic as literal truths, will accept (3) as obviously true. Those who doubt (3), as well as those who accept (3), understand the phrase 'there is such a thing as' in (3) in the same sense as in (1) and (2). The difference between the examples does not lie in the phrase 'there is such a thing as', but in the substantives 'Bucephalus', 'Pegasus', and '9^{9^9}'. To deny that there is such a thing as Pegasus means that the object is not found in space and time, but such dependence on space and time comes about only because, if there were such a thing as Pegasus, it would be a spatio-temporal object. To affirm or deny that there is such a thing as the number 9^{9^9} is to affirm or deny that 9^{9^9} is found in the series of numbers, because, if there is such a thing as the number 9^{9^9}, it is an object of this kind.

Certain philosophers think that the phrase 'there is' is used in an essentially different sense when it is applied to objects in space and time, as opposed to when it is applied to abstract objects. They even use different words: 'exist' in one sense, 'subsist' in the other. This tendency is perhaps due to the idea that the methods of investigation are very different in the two cases, the observation of nature being an essential method for determining the existence of an object of space and time, but useless in the case of an abstract object. This idea of a fundamental difference of methods is doubtful, however. The observation of nature is sometimes necessary for determining the existence, or "subsistence," of an abstract object as well. For example, we can introduce the expression 'Paraná fever' as an abbreviation of the expression 'the sickness that annihilated the majority of the inhabitants of Curitiba in the year 1903'. The question whether there is such a sickness – not the question whether cases of Paraná fever can be found, but the actual question whether there is such a sickness as an abstract object – is resolved only by means of the observation of nature. An enquiry into the history of Curitiba reveals, in fact, that *no* sickness *at all* annihilated the majority of the inhabitants of Curitiba in 1903, and, for this reason, Paraná fever does not exist – nor does it "subsist," even as an abstract object.

Many philosophers admit, aside from abstract objects and aside from concrete objects in space and time, certain concrete objects that are more or less similar to objects in space and time, but are only possible and not actual. These philosophers imagine a domain of concrete objects that is broader than that of the actual world. Bucephalus and Pegasus both belong to this wider domain; but Bucephalus has among his attributes that of being actualized, while Pegasus does not have this special attribute. These philosophers limit the word 'exist' to actualized objects, using 'be' in the inclusive sense for concrete objects, actualized or not, and for abstract objects.

One of the objectives of this vast multiplication of objects is, without doubt, to be able to treat statements of the type 'Pegasus does not exist' as statements about objects. If there is not, in some sense, an object that is Pegasus, how can the word 'Pegasus' and its contexts, and even 'Pegasus does not exist', have meaning? How can we say of Pegasus that he does not exist, if there is not an object which is Pegasus that does not exist? However, it must be obvious that extending the universe to include possible objects is no remedy, seeing that we can reproduce the problem in relation to the new, broader universe. In place of 'Pegasus does not exist', we can propose the example 'The spinster wife of Pegasus does not exist'. The spinster wife of Pegasus is not found within the supposed domain of possible objects.

There is not, in fact, anything paradoxical in the statement that Pegasus does not exist – that there is no such object. It is not a statement about a certain object that is Pegasus; and this should not surprise us, as we are already accustomed to see non-designative occurrences of substantives and even of names. As to the question of meaning, it is clear that the word 'Pegasus' remains plainly meaningful independently of the question of existence. Words don't have to be names, or even substantives, to possess meaning. The supposed paradox of non-existence comes from confusing meaning and designation.

§ 39 The Ontological Significance of the Principle of Application

The general question 'What is there?' – the locus, as has just been illustrated, of innumerable philosophical disagreements – is intimately connected to the meaning of the logical notation of quantification. Since the quantifier has the sense of 'whatever x may be', quantification makes an affirmation about everything there is. The logical theory of quantification is, nevertheless, independent of the choice among ontological alternatives – that is, among the alternative answers to the question 'What is there?'. Quantificational truths remain the same regardless of the type of objects – concrete or abstract, actual or possible – admitted into the universe, and regardless of the paucity or multiplicity of objects, as long as there is at least one.

But if the choice of an ontology is indifferent to quantificational truths, it is not indifferent to all truths constructed with the help of quantification. The quantification:

$$(x)\sim(x \text{ results from the multiplication, } 9^9 \text{ times, of 1 by 9}),$$

which denies (3) of § 38, would be false according to the implicit ontology of classical arithmetic, and true according to other points of view mentioned earlier. The quantification:

$$(x)\sim(x \text{ whinnies} \cdot x \text{ flies})$$

is true according to perhaps more reasonable norms, but would be false according to the ontology that counts an object which is Pegasus within the domain of possible concrete objects.

The ontology that one accepts, or that a given context presupposes, is not revealed by an examination of vocabulary alone; for we know that substantives can be used indesignatively without depriving them of meaning. The use of the word 'Pegasus' does not imply acceptance of Pegasus, nor does the mere use of the signs '9' or '9^9' imply that there are abstract objects, numbers, such as 9 and 9^9. It is not the mere use of a substantive, but its designative use, that commits us to the acceptance of an object designated by the substantive. In order to determine whether a substantive is used designatively in a given context we have to look beyond the substantive and observe the behavior of the pronouns.[35]

We have seen (§ 35) that the use of a pronoun in the position of a non-designative occurrence often produces a meaningless expression, but this does not always happen. Corresponding to the (true) statement 'No one has seen Pegasus', for example, we have a matrix 'no one has seen x' that is plainly meaningful and fits in quantificational contexts in the usual way, even though the occurrence of 'Pegasus' in the statement above is, as in any other statement, non-designative.

To see how the non-existence of the designatum of a substantive is revealed by the behavior of pronouns, we must have recourse to the principle of application (§ 28), as it is this principle that links a quantification to its instances, which are constructed by means of a name. The content of the principle is that whatever holds of all objects also holds of the object designated by the name in question, and it is clear that this principle loses its justification when applied to a non-name like 'Pegasus', or even to a non-designative occurrence of a name. From the truth (N) in § 33, that is:

(1) $(x)\sim(y)\sim x=y$,

for example, we must not infer, by the principle of application, the false statement:

(2) $\sim(y)\sim$ Pegasus $= y$,

that is, 'Pegasus is identical to some object'.

What requires the recognition of the designatum of a given substantive is thus not the mere use of the substantive, but its use as a target of the principle of application. What is required is inference by application, which consists in erasing an initial quantifier and substituting the substantive in question for the pronoun.

This becomes especially clear when we consider inference by *existential generalization*, which is the equivalent, and the converse,[36] of inference by application, consisting in the inference of a conclusion of the form '$\sim(x)\sim fx$'; that is, 'There is some object x such that fx', based on a matrix represented by 'fx', except that it contains a certain substantive in the places where the matrix has 'x' as a free pronoun. The idea behind this inference is that whatever holds of the object designated by the substantive in question holds of some object, and it is clear that the inference loses its justification when the substantive does not designate. From the truth:

(3) $(y) \sim$ Pegasus $= y$,

for example, that is, 'There is no object with which Pegasus is identical', we must not infer:

(4) $\sim(x)\sim(y) \sim x = y$,

that is, 'Some object is distinct from every object', the denial of (1).

Note that application and existential generalization are aspects of a single principle. The conditional whose antecedent is (1) and whose consequent is (2), for example, is the same as the conditional whose antecedent is (3) and whose consequent is (4):

(5) $\sim((x)\sim(y) \sim x = y \bullet (y) \sim$ Pegasus $= y)$.

It is the falsehood of (5) that reflects the fact that 'Pegasus' does not designate.

The principle of application (or of existential generalization) is a "principle" only by courtesy, as has now become evident. It is valid only in the case where the substantive in question is a name. Rather than being a logical principle, it is simply the logical content of the idea that a given substantive designates. And this idea is not, in general, founded on logic. The question whether 'Pegasus' designates, for example, is a question of natural science.

Thus the classification of the "principle of application" is explained outside of the pure theory of quantification (cf. § 28). We have also seen the theoretical importance of the fact, to be established shortly, that *every use of names and of the principle of application is theoretically dispensable*, the names being eliminable from all contexts by paraphrase. As a preliminary to the establishment of this fact we must study the theory of

§ 40 Descriptions

We call *descriptions* those substantives that begin with the article 'the' in the singular, for example in the following way:

> the author of *Os Sertões*,[37]

that is:

> the unique object x such that x wrote *Os Sertões*,

or, in symbols:

(1)   (ɪx) x wrote *Os Sertões*.

In general, a description will be a name, that is, it will designate, if and only if the matrix that follows the prefix '(ɪx)' (or '(ɪy)', etc.) is satisfied by a unique object; and this object will be the object designated. *Os Sertões* having one author and no more, the description (1) is that author's name. Another name for the same object is 'Euclides da Cunha'; so we have the identity:

> Euclides da Cunha = (ɪx) x wrote *Os Sertões*.

We now consider any description, represented schematically by '(ɪx)fx', and any matrix that contains the description, represented schematically by 'g (ɪx) fx'. If the description designates, the matrix represented by 'g (ɪx)fx' can be paraphrased step by step in the following way:

There is a unique object y such that fy, and this object is such that gy,

> ~(y)~(gy • y is the unique object such that fy),
> ~(y)~(gy • fy • no object x except y is such that fx),

(2)   ~(y)~(gy • fy • (x)~(fx • ~ x = y)).

It follows that every use of descriptions can be avoided, or considered as a mere abbreviation, the context of the description being expandable in the manner of (2). The description disappears and no other substantive is needed in its place, except the pronouns.[vi]

The intuitive correctness of this mode of paraphrase depends on the supposition that the description designates. But in everyday language we are accustomed to use descriptions only when we think they designate; for this reason the question of the correspondence between (2) and the intuitive sense of 'g $(\imath x)fx$' loses its importance when the description does not designate. We can, therefore, treat every use of a description as an abbreviation, in the manner suggested.

This version is subject to two ambiguities that remain to be eliminated. It may be that the context represented by 'g $(\imath x)fx$' contains two descriptions. The result of eliminating the first of these descriptions in the manner of (2), and afterwards eliminating the other description in the same way, would differ – at least with regard to notational form – from the result of eliminating the descriptions in the reverse order. The other difficulty is that, given a description within a matrix that forms part of another matrix, we do not know if it is the shorter matrix or the longer matrix that must play the role of 'g $(\imath x)fx$' in the previous explanation. These ambiguities can be shown to be logically indifferent when the descriptions designate; nevertheless, a convention of pure abbreviation must preserve the original expression as univocally reproducible in its own notation. It is easy to subject our convention to the necessary additional specifications in the following way: the matrix that plays the role of 'g $(\imath x)fx$' must not contain any shorter matrix that also contains the description in question, and must not contain any other description to the left of the description in question.

It is clear that other pronouns are admissible in the place of the pronouns 'x' and 'y' used in this explanation, and that the pronoun that plays the role of 'y' in (2) must be a pronoun that does not occur in the matrix represented by 'g $(\imath x)$ fx'. In fact, to guarantee that the abbreviation is univocally expandable into the appropriate notation, we can stipulate that the pronoun that plays the role of 'y' be alphabetically the first pronoun that does not occur in the matrix represented by 'g $(\imath x)fx$'.

We have two ways of saying that y is $(\imath x)fx$ (imagining any matrix in place of 'fx'); one is 'y = $(\imath x)fx$', and the other, corresponding to the words 'y and only y is such that fy', is 'fy • $(x)\sim(fx • \sim x = y)$'. The reciprocal conditionals that

---

[vi] This eliminative treatment of descriptions is due to Russell (1905). The first exact treatment of descriptions was perhaps that of Frege (1893).

connect these two formulations are easy to establish on the basis of the theories of identity and quantification.

(O) $\sim(y = (\imath x)fx \bullet \sim (fy \bullet (x)\sim(fx \bullet \sim x = y)))$

Proof:

(a) $\sim(z = y \bullet fz \bullet (x)\sim(fx \bullet \sim x = z) \bullet \sim(fy \bullet (x)\sim(fx$
       $\bullet \sim x = y)))$ (J)
(b) $\sim(y = z \bullet \sim z = y)$ (M)
(c) $\sim(y = z \bullet fz \bullet (x)\sim(fx \bullet \sim x = z) \bullet \sim(fy \bullet (x) \sim$
       $(fx \bullet \sim x = y))$ From (a) and (b) by (i),
(d) $\sim(\sim(z)\sim(y = z \bullet fz \bullet (x)\sim(fx \bullet \sim x = z)) \bullet \sim(fy \bullet$
       $(x)\sim(fx \bullet \sim x = y)))$ From (c) by (iv) and (v).
(O)   Abbreviation of (d).

(P) $\sim(fy \bullet (x)\sim(fx \bullet \sim x = y) \bullet \sim y = (\imath x)fx).$

Proof:

(a) $y = y$ (K)
(b) $\sim((z)\sim(y = z \bullet fz \bullet (x)\sim(fx \bullet \sim x = z)) \bullet a \bullet$
       $fy \bullet (x) \sim(fx \bullet \sim x = y))$ (A)
(c) $\sim(\sim y = (\imath x)fx \bullet a \bullet fy \bullet (x)\sim(fx \bullet \sim x = y))$ Abbreviation of (b).
(P)   From (a) and (c) by (i).

To say that the object $(\imath x)fx$ exists is, naturally, to say that the description designates. The condition for the existence of $(\imath x)fx$ is, therefore, that there be a unique object y such that fy; that is,

$\sim(y) \sim(fy \bullet (x) \sim (fx \bullet \sim x = y)).$

But, given the previous result, this formulation is equivalent to:

(3) $\sim(y)\sim y = (\imath x)fx.$

We can, therefore, read (3) as 'There is $(\imath x)fx$', or '$(\imath x)fx$ exists'. Literally, (3) says 'Some object is identical to $(\imath x)fx$'.

The principle of application depends, as we have seen (§ 39), on the hypothesis that the substantive in question designates. But now, due to the existential formulation of (3), we can express the principle of application explicitly in all cases in which the substantive is a description; and we can prove the principle, in such cases, on the basis of the theories of identity and quantification. The principle to be proved is that all conditionals of the form:

If $(\imath x)fx$ exists, and (y)gy, then g $(\imath x)fx$

are logically valid. That is:

(Q)   ~(~(y)~y = (ıx)fx • (y)gy • ~g(ıx)fx).

Proof:

(a)   ~(~(gy • fy • (x)~(fx • ~ x = y)) • gy • y = (ıx)fx)   From (O) by (i).
(b)   ~((y)a • (y)~(gy • fy • (x)~(fx • ~ x = y)) • ~(y)~   (C)
       (gy • y = (ıx)fx)
(c)   ~((y)a • ~g(ıx)fx • ~(y)~(gy • y = (ıx)fx))   Abbreviation of (b).
(d)   ~((y)~(gy • y = (ıx)fx) • (y)gy • ~(y) ~y = (ıx)fx)   (C)
(Q)   From (a), (c), and (d) by (i) and (iv).

§ 41 The Pronoun as the Only Substantive

Any name, or other substantive such as 'Pegasus' that looks like a name, can be transformed into a description if it does not already have such a form. It is not necessary to laboriously look for a matrix to use in the description; we can have recourse to the following artificial method. Let us consider, for example, the name 'Europe'. We can introduce the verb 'europize' in the sense of 'to be Europe'. We can take this verb as fundamental, instead of accepting the name as fundamental; and this way we can dispense with the name, using in its place the descriptive name '(ıx) x europizes'. This word 'europizes' is not a name, as we do not use it in positions that admit pronouns. Even if there is an attribute of europizing, the word 'europizes' does not designate it; it would be designated by some other word that can be reduced in turn to a description by the same artificial method. This artificial method thus serves for avoiding all names that are not descriptive – in fact, all substantives that are not descriptions or mere pronouns.

Such a transformation does not claim to avoid the presupposition of the existence of objects; the object Europe, for example, remains, being desig-nated by the description '(ıx) x europizes'. The transformation also does not claim to give a more complete analysis of the nature of the objects; the non-analyzed idea of Europe still plays almost the exact same role within the meaning of the new verb 'europize'. What the transformation docs is to reduce all names or other substantives (except the pronouns themselves) to a familiar type, that of the descriptions. The advantage is considerable: the analysis (3) of the singular existential statement of the form 'there is . . . ' or ' . . . exists', like the establishment of the principle of application in form (Q), becomes generally adequate.

Now, however, we can advance another step: eliminate all names and, beyond this, all other substantives except the pronouns! – because we already know how to eliminate descriptions. Descriptions are retained only as convenient abbreviations, safely ignored in theoretical considerations.

We already know that the pronoun is always the main vehicle of reference to objects; this was made apparent by our reflections on the non-designative occurrence of names (cf. §§ 34, 35, 39), and also by the fact that some objects, according to classical mathematics, cannot be named and must be treated only by means of pronouns (cf. § 17). But now the pronoun, which was already the main vehicle of reference, has become the only one.

One result is that the theory of quantification does not have to be supplemented by a principle of application. In general, it is obvious that the considerations about the relation between sign and object, or between language and reality, are simplified considerably. All objects remain as before, but contact between objects and language is concentrated in the pronoun. The ontology to which a given use of language commits us simply includes the totality of objects within the range of the quantifier.

IV

Class, Relation, and Number

§ 42 Attributes and Classes[38]

The use of general terms, like 'man' or 'blue', or of abstract terms, like 'liberty'[39] or '9', does not commit us to recognizing the existence of abstract objects. As is already clear, the question of our ontological presuppositions rests rather on our designative use of such terms, and depends finally on our manner of using pronouns and quantifiers. In fact, as we have just seen, every consideration of names and of the relation of designation is ultimately dispensable,[40] reducing the question of ontological presuppositions completely to the question of the domain that must be covered by the quantifier.

It turns out, nevertheless, that mathematics depends on the recognition of abstract objects – such as numbers, functions, relations, classes, attributes. The abstract objects upon whose recognition mathematics depends are, in fact, reducible to a part that includes only classes or attributes. But abstract objects of some type always[41] have to be admitted in the domain of the quantifier.

The nominalist, admitting only concrete objects, must either regard classical mathematics as discredited, or, at best, consider it a machine that is useful despite the fact that it uses ideograms of the form of statements that involve a fictitious ontology. It remains important, however, to examine the foundations of mathematics, whatever our prior ontological dogma may be.

We must, therefore, begin with a provisional tolerance of classes or attributes.[42] But what is the difference between classes and attributes? It is common to speak of a class as a "mere aggregate," and to imagine it as having its members inside it, according to a spatial analogy; whereas an attribute tends to be imagined rather on the analogy of a power that inheres in the object that has the attribute, or as a feature that the object exhibits. This appeal to opposing analogies is pointless. A class, even of concrete and spatial things, is neither concrete nor spatial. A class of spatial things is not the spatial thing formed by the fusion of the members of the class. This follows from a comparison of the two following classes: One has as its members the thirteen continental countries of South America, and the other has only two members, one member being Brazil and the other the rest of the territory of the continent. The spatial thing that consists of the thirteen members of the first class is the continent, and the spatial thing that consists of the two members of the second class is the same continent. The classes, however, cannot be simply the continent, because the two classes differ; for example, one has Paraguay as a member and the other does not. The two classes, in contrast with the continent, must be recognized as objects of an abstract and intangible character.

We are left with few reasons for the distinction between classes and attributes, or between being a member of a class and having an attribute. If there is a difference, it is only this: Attributes can differ among themselves even if by chance they are attributes of the same things, while classes are always identical when they have the same members.[43]

The opinion is sometimes held that the idea of attribute (or property) is more intuitive than that of class, and that the idea of class should be derived from that of attribute. The derivation presents little difficulty,[i] but the idea that such a derivation is desirable is very curious. It rests perhaps on a confusion between attribute and verbal expression.[44] Certainly, in order to specify a class we usually have to present a matrix that is satisfied by the members of the class and by them only; but in this respect classes and attributes are alike, for the determination of an attribute also depends, usually, on presenting a matrix satisfied by the objects, and only those that have the attribute. The matrix is not the attribute.

Classes, being abstract objects, are less clear and familiar than we might wish, but attributes are even more obscure; for the only difference between classes and attributes resides, as we have seen, in the condition of identity, and in this respect classes are much clearer than attributes. Two matrices determine the same class when satisfied by the same objects; but under what condition do the matrices determine the same attribute?

Usually no criterion is offered. The only one I know is the following: Matrices determine the same attributes if and only if they are logically equivalent. But this criterion leads to awkward results. Consider the attributes determined by the respective matrices:

---

[i] [Same as "Notes on Existence and Necessity" footnote 9, except for added details to references (eds.).] Cf. Whitehead and Russell, *Principia Mathematica*, *20; also my essay "Whitehead and the Rise of Modern Logic."

(1)   x > number of planets,

(2)   x > 9;

that is, the attribute of exceeding the number of planets and the attribute of exceeding 9. Since (1) and (2) are not logically equivalent, it follows that the attributes will not be identical. The statement:

(3)   The attribute of exceeding the number of planets = the attribute of exceeding 9

is false. Still, substitution in the true statement:

The attribute of exceeding 9 = the attribute of exceeding 9

on the basis of the true identity:

The number of planets = 9^{45}

leads to (3). We have to conclude that the occurrence of '9' in the context 'the attribute of exceeding 9' is not purely designative (cf. § 34). Likewise, more generally, we must conclude that the occurrences of names within names of attributes are not in general designative, and that the positions they occupy cannot in general be occupied by pronouns.[46] Expressions of the type that specify attributes are not in general[47] contexts accessible to pronouns referring to anterior quantifiers. Clearly this constitutes a fundamental restriction on the use of attributes. It is, in particular, a restriction that makes attributes inadequate to the ends of mathematics and inadequate even as a basis for the subsequent introduction of classes.

The only recourse would be to adopt another standard for identity of attributes not based on logical equivalence. But what might such an alternative standard be? And would attributes so construed still be as intuitive as classes?

There may still be a reason to maintain that certain attributes are more intuitive than classes – namely, the attributes, properties, or qualities of sense experience, for example, those of color and sound. It is possible to maintain that these attributes are sometimes distinct even though possessed by the same objects, and still to maintain that the difficulty noted in the case of the matrix 'x > 9'[48] does not arise, since this matrix is[49] not among the matrices to which these intuitive attributes[50] correspond. However, such a domain of special attributes, not corresponding to matrices in general, would not suffice for the purposes of mathematics, nor for the derivation of a general theory of classes. It is therefore irrelevant to the present analysis.[51]

§ 43 Membership and Identity

Let us, therefore, begin directly with the notion of class, leaving the distinct notion of attribute aside. To say that an object x is a member of a class y, or that x *belongs* to y, the usual notation is 'x ε y', 'ε' being the first letter of the Greek verb '$\dot{\varepsilon}\sigma\tau\dot{\iota}$'. We must now formulate the fundamental principles that govern this new logical connective, the connective of *membership*.

One principle that arises from earlier considerations is that classes with the same members are identical; that is, whatever x and y may be, if (z) (z ε x if and only if z ε y), then x = y. We can write this principle as follows:

(1)   (x) (y) ~ ((z) (z ε x ≡ z ε y) • ~ x = y)

using '≡' in the sense of 'if and only if' according to the convention of abbreviation:

D1   'p ≡ q' *for* '~ (p • ~ q) • ~ (q • ~ p)'.

(The letter 'D' here stands for 'definition'.)

An apparent exception to principle (1) arises in the case in which x and y are not classes; because, x and y not having members in this case, the condition '(z) (z ε x ≡ z ε y)' is fulfilled vacuously, even though we do not want to conclude from this fact that x and y are always the same thing. It seems that we must limit (1) by adding the condition that x and y are classes. This condition cannot be formulated only by means of the notations already at hand, that is the notations of denial, conjunction, quantification, identity, and membership.

A partial solution to this problem consists in slightly altering the notion of membership, so as to give to 'z ε y' the meaning of 'z is a member of y if y is a class, and z = y if y is not a class'. Having done this, (1) remains true even in the case in which x and y are not classes. In this case (1) affirms that, if the things (the thing, in truth) that are identical to x are identical to y, then x is identical to y.

But the solution is still partial, as the case in which x is a class and y is not (or vice-versa) remains to be proved. In this case the antecedent '(z) (z ε x ≡ z ε y)' within (1) has the meaning '(z) (z ε x ≡ z = y)', that is, the class x has as members exactly the things identical to y, or, in short, the class x has y as its only member. (1) obliges us to conclude from this antecedent that x = y, even though x is a class and y is not. We can, however, avoid this remaining difficulty by denying the antecedent; that is, by refusing to recognize the existence of a class x whose only member is a non-class y.

The exclusion of classes of this type does not create any difficulty in the use of the theory of classes, because it happens that a non-class y is adequate in itself for all the uses of a class whose only member is y. It remains important to preserve, together with the class w, another class whose only member is w;[ii] but as it happens there is nothing useful about preserving both the non-class y and a class whose only member is y.

We have just agreed: (a) to understand 'z ε y' in the manner of 'z = y' when y is not a class, and (b) to repudiate any class whose only member is a non-class.[iii] It is possible, however, to formulate these same innovations in the following quite different form: (c) we agree to assimilate every non-class into the universe of classes, thinking of a non-class as a class that has itself as its only member. (Under this formulation, naturally we must adopt another word in place of 'non-class' – let us say 'individual'.) The conventions (a)–(b) and the convention (c) simply constitute two formulations of an identical system. But formulation (c) represents a more convenient point of view, as under this formulation every object becomes uniformly a class, and the notation 'z ε y' uniformly preserves the meaning 'z is a member of y'. ·

These refinements, whether formulated in the manner of (a)–(b) or in the manner of (c), have the effect of restoring to (1) its full generality. From (1), now, we see that '(z) (z ε x ≡ z ε y)' is equivalent to 'x = y'. (1) establishes as valid the conditional whose antecedent is '(z) (z ε x ≡ z ε y)' and whose consequent is 'x = y'; and the inverse conditional is easy to prove:

(2) $\sim (x = y \bullet \sim (z) (z\ \varepsilon\ x \equiv z\ \varepsilon\ y))$.

Proof:

(a)   z ε x ≡ z ε x   By (i).
(b) $\sim (x = y \bullet (z)\ a \bullet \sim (z) (z\ \varepsilon\ x \equiv z\ \varepsilon\ y))$ (J)
(2)   From (a) and (b) by (i) and (iv).

It follows that the notational form 'x = y' is dispensable, since it admits of the paraphrase '(z) (z ε x ≡ z ε y)'. We can consider the notation of identity as a mere convenient abbreviation.

D2   'x = y' *for* '(z) (z ε x ≡ z ε y)'.

(Naturally, this convention is adopted likewise with any other pronouns in place of 'z' and 'y'; and we may suppose that the third pronoun, in the role of 'z', is chosen on the basis of the other two, following an arbitrary alphabetical rule.)

[ii] As pointed out by Frege in 1879.
[iii] This repudiation can be represented as a convention that consists in limiting the word 'class' in such a way that it does not cover certain cases covered earlier.

In virtue of D2, principle (1) becomes immediately provable, acquiring the form '(x) (y) ~ (fxy • ~ fxy)'. In addition, the principle (K) of identity (§ 33) becomes equally provable.

(a)	y ε x ≡ y ε x	By (i).
(b)	(y) a	From (a) by (iv).
(K)	Abbreviation of (b).	

But (J), the other principle of identity, must be preserved as an (abbreviated) principle of membership. It is an abbreviation, following D2, of:

*1   ~ ((z) (z ε x ≡ z ε y) • fx • ~ fy).

The consequences (L), (M), and (N) follow as above.

§ 44 Pure Matrices. Structure and Content

Certain matrices, which we may call *pure matrices of the theory of classes*, or *pure matrices* for short, consist only in the notations of conjunction, denial, quantification, and membership, without any other content. These matrices consist of the atomic matrices, 'x ε x', 'x ε y', 'y ε y', 'y ε z', etc., varyingly connected and elaborated by the use of conjunction, denial, and quantification. Among these pure matrices, some are statements: *pure statements* of the theory of classes. The shortest one is the false statement '(x) x ε x' (and its alphabetic variants '(y) y ε y', '(z) z ε z', etc.).

The applications of logic and mathematics depend on the use of logical and mathematical signs within *impure* contexts – contexts that also contain signs that are neither logical nor mathematical. For this reason, we will continue to think of matrices of all types, not just pure matrices, as occurring in the positions of 'p', 'q', 'fx ', etc., within the valid forms (A)–(I) of the theory of quantification and likewise within *1 and the ensuing forms. If, on the other hand, we were to continue to consider the pure theory of classes, leaving all impure matrices aside, then we could forego *1 and adopt in its place one of its cases – the statement:

*1'   (w) (x) (y) ~ ((z) (z ε x ≡ z ε y) • x ε w • ~ y ε w).

On the basis of *1' and of the theory of quantification, it is possible (though complicated) to show that every *pure* matrix of the form *1 is valid.[iv]

When we affirm that mathematics reduces to logic, what we mean is that all of the ideas that belong to arithmetic and to the other parts of pure mathematics

---

[iv] Cf. *Mathematical Logic*, §§ 29–30.

are definable on the basis of denial, conjunction, quantification, and member-ship alone (or, on the basis of joint denial, quantification, and membership; cf. § 14). We can continue this series of definitions and conventions of abbrevia-tion initiated with D1 and D2, in such a way that every matrix of pure mathematics is shown to be an abbreviation of a pure matrix of the theory of classes; and, in particular, that every statement of pure mathematics (for example, '2 + 2 = 4', '2 + 2 = 5', the binomial theorem, or Fermat's theorem) becomes an abbreviation of a pure statement of the theory of classes. We will encounter various definitions of this series in the present chapter.

Between the theories of composition and quantification on the one hand, and the theory of classes on the other, there are points of contrast so fundamental that this dividing line can be proposed as a boundary between logic in the strict sense and mathematics itself. In logic in this strict sense – that is, in the theory of composition and quantification, or, in short, in the theory of deduction – matrices are determined only in relation to their external structure, since the atomic components (for example, 'Socrates is mortal' or 'y is mortal') are constructed out of non-logical material. In Chapters I and II, we used schemata to facilitate the treatment of the logical structure of matrices (including state-ments); but the letters 'p', 'q', etc., and the combinations 'fx', 'gxy', etc., should be thought of as placeholders for matrices that contain, naturally, some material beyond the mere structure provided by the notation of conjunction, denial, and quantification. On the other hand, in the theory of classes certain atomic matrices are determined such that it becomes possible to construct entire matrices and statements within the theory itself. We can perhaps say that logic in the strict sense only provides structure, while the theory of classes also provides content.

There exists another sense in which, more literally, the theory of classes has content; the theory requires that the objects covered by the quantifiers include objects of a certain type – classes – that will form the special objects of the study of the theory, while logic in the strict sense is indifferent to the nature and even to the number of objects (assuming that there is at least one; cf. § 39). The theory of classes, in contrast with logic in the strict sense, implies an ontology. It does not imply an exclusive ontology, as it imposes no restrictions on the type of objects remaining, the so-called "individuals"; but it implies a positive ontology of classes. This implication of an ontology of abstract objects is, although indispensable to classical mathematics, repug-nant to many thinkers.

These considerations provide some grounds for a fundamental division between the theory of classes and the aforementioned part of logic, and even, as mentioned earlier, for restricting the term 'logic' to the first part. According to this usage, the concept of *quantificational* truth comes to exhaust *logical* truth. The truths (K)–(N), *1', etc. would be called *mathematical*, and not logical; analogously for the concepts of validity, implication, and equivalence. It would no longer be correct to say that mathematics is reduced to logic; we would have to say instead that mathematics is reduced to that fundamental domain of mathematics that constitutes the theory of classes. However, we will leave this terminological question undecided.

§ 45 The Existence of Classes

The principle according to which classes with the same members are identical is, from the point of view of the existence of classes, a negative principle, as it limits the number of classes with a given assortment of members to one. We still have to formulate the principles that support the existence of classes. The natural principle is that, given any matrix whose free pronoun is 'x', there is a class whose members are exactly the objects x that satisfy the given matrix. It is this principle that we depend on when we use the prefix 'the class of all objects x such that . . . '. It is usual to suppose that this prefix always serves for naming a class.

The principle in question, called *abstraction*, would affirm the truth of every statement, or, more generally, the validity of every matrix, of the form:

(1) $\sim (y) \sim (x) (x \; \varepsilon \; y \equiv fx),$

that is, 'There is a class y to which any object x belongs if and only if fx'. However, the principle is, in fact, false. There are statements of the form (1) that are false, their falsehood being provable even within the theory of quantification. The simplest statement of this type is:

(2) $\sim (y) \sim (x) (x \; \varepsilon \; y \equiv \sim x \; \varepsilon \; x).$

Its denial is proved in the following manner:

(3) $(y) \; \sim (x) (x \; \varepsilon \; y \equiv \sim x \; \varepsilon \; x)$

Proof:
(a) $\sim ((x) (x \; \varepsilon \; y \equiv \sim x \; \varepsilon \; x) \bullet \sim (y \; \varepsilon \; y \equiv \sim y \; \varepsilon \; y))$ (A)
(3)   From (a) by (i).

Intuitively, the argument is the following: there is no class K formed only of the classes that are not members of themselves, for such a class would be a member of itself if and only if it were not a member of itself.[v]

---
[v] Due to Russell (1903, Ch. 10).

Therefore, as intuitive as the principle of abstraction may be, we must subject it to certain restrictions. There are various well-known ways of restricting the principle, so as to avoid contradictions and yet not overly impoverish the theory of classes.[vi] All of these ways are quite artificial. The most convenient among them, it seems to me, depends on the idea (due to von Neumann) that certain classes cannot belong to classes. We call *elements* all objects that are members of classes; that is, 'x is an element' means '$\sim$ (z) $\sim$ x ε z'. Now the new *restricted principle of abstraction* will be that, given any matrix whose free pronoun is 'x', there is a class whose members are exactly the *elements* (instead of 'objects', as earlier) that satisfy the matrix. The validity of every matrix is affirmed, not in the form of (1), but in the more particular form:

*2 $\sim$ (y) $\sim$ (x) (x ε y $\equiv$ (fx • $\sim$ (z) $\sim$ x ε z)).

This restricted principle does not lead to the false statement (2). When we replace 'fx' with '$\sim$ x ε x' in *2, the result is not (2), but:

   $\sim$ (y) $\sim$ (x) (x ε y $\equiv$ ($\sim$ x ε x • $\sim$ (z) $\sim$ x ε z)),

according to which there is a class K' formed only of *elements* that are not members of themselves. This class K', in contrast with the class K supposed earlier, can indeed exist; the only restriction is that K' cannot be an element, as proved in the following manner:

(4)   (y) $\sim$ ((x) (x ε y $\equiv$ ($\sim$ x ε x • $\sim$ (z) $\sim$ x ε z)) • $\sim$ (z) $\sim$ y ε z).

Proof:
(a) $\sim$ ((x) (x ε y $\equiv$ ($\sim$ x ε x • $\sim$ (z) $\sim$ x ε z)) • $\sim$ (y ε y $\equiv$ ($\sim$ y ε y • $\sim$ (z) $\sim$ y ε z))) (A)
(4) From (a) by (i).

The original principle of abstraction has, aside from the contradictory consequence (2), an infinity of other contradictory consequences, more or less analogous to (2) but more complicated.[vii] Restricting the principle of abstraction in the manner of *2 removes such consequences. But, despite being safe, the restricted principle is nevertheless too weak to guarantee all the classes that we want, in the absence of certain supplementary principles regarding the existence of elements. Given a domain of elements, our restricted principle of

[vi] The first two attempts in this regard were those of Russell ("theory of types") and Zermelo, both in 1908. The theory that I will present here is closer to that of Zermelo, but is also influenced in its essence by the theory of von Neumann (1926). For a comparison of these and other theories, see my article "On Existence Conditions," as well as *Mathematical Logic*, pp. 164–166.

[vii] Cf. *Mathematical Logic*, pp. 128–129.

abstraction provides us with all the imaginable classes formed from these elements: but our principle does not guarantee the existence of some element. If there were no elements, no class would have members; the individuals themselves, being classes with a single member (cf. § 43), would not exist; the only object in the universe would be the empty class, 0 – the class without members. Even so, matrices of the forms *1 and *2 would remain valid.[viii] We must therefore adopt supplementary principles to specify which objects are elements. But we can develop a part of the theory of classes before adding such principles. This part is important, even though it does not contain anything incompatible with a universe whose only object is 0.

§ 46 Abstraction

The principle implicit in the use of the prefix 'the class of all objects x such that . . . ' was not, as we have seen, sustainable. The new restricted principle of abstraction serves, however, as the basis for the use of the modified prefix 'the class of all *elements* x such that . . . '. We write this prefix as '$\hat{x}$' for short. The notation '$\hat{x}fx$'[52] (imagining a matrix in the position of 'fx') has the sense of 'the class y whose members are exactly the objects x such that fx, and x is an element'; in short,

$$\hat{x}fx = (\imath y)\,(x)\,(x \; \varepsilon \; y \equiv (fx \bullet \sim (z) \sim x \; \varepsilon \; z)).$$

The notation of the form '$\hat{x}fx$', called the notation of class *abstraction,* can be introduced as an abbreviation. Earlier on we introduced the notation of description. We already know, from § 40, the contextual definition:

D3   'g ($\imath x$) fx' *for* '$\sim (y) \sim (gy \bullet fy \bullet (x) \sim (fx \bullet \sim x = y))$',

'fx', 'gx', etc., being replaced by matrices subject to the restrictions noted in § 40. Now the *abstract* is introduced as an abbreviation of a description:

D4   '$\hat{x}fx$' *for* '($\imath y$) (x) (x ε y $\equiv$ (fx $\bullet \sim$ (z) $\sim$ x ε z))'.

It is by means of the abstract that we introduce notations for specific classes, such as the following definitions:

D5   'V' *for* '$\hat{x}$ (x = x)',
D6   '0' *for* '$\hat{x} \sim x = x$',
D7   '$\imath x$' *for* '$\hat{y}$ (y = x)'.

[viii] As pointed out by Rosser (1941).

It must be understood that the pronouns that are free in the defined expressions, as for example 'x' in D7, can be replaced not only by other pronouns, but equally by descriptions and in particular by abstracts, without the convention of abbreviation ceasing to hold.

V, defined as the class of all elements x such that x = x, is simply the class of all elements. 0, defined as the class of elements x such that '~ x = x', is the empty class mentioned earlier. ιx, defined as the class of all elements y such that y = x, is obviously 0 if x is not an element; but if x is an element, then ιx is the *unit class* of x, that is, the class whose only member is x. In the case in which x is an individual, ιx = x (cf. § 43); but in all other cases ιx ≠ x. For example ιV ≠ V, as ιV has no more than one member, while V must have many; and ι0 ≠ 0, as ι0 has one member (if 0 is an element), while 0 has none.

We first began proving theorems on the basis of *1 and *2 with (K)–(N) in § 33, these being incorporated into the theory of classes as indicated at the end of § 43. The same thing happens to principles (O)–(Q) of the theory of descriptions, given D3. Various principles regarding abstraction remain to be proved, the most important of which affirm that all matrices of the forms:

(5) $y \, \varepsilon \, \hat{x}fx \equiv (fy \bullet \sim (z) \sim y \, \varepsilon \, z)$,

(6) $\sim ((y) \, gy \bullet \sim g \, \hat{x}fx)$

are valid. The proof of these principles, on the basis of *1, *2, D1–4, and the intermediate results (K) (Q), by means of the known techniques of the theory of quantification, can be an interesting exercise for the reader. After that, various theorems about the notions defined in D5–7 follow easily, including:

(7) $(x) \sim x \, \varepsilon \, 0$,

(8) $(x) \, x \, \varepsilon \, V \equiv \sim (y) \sim x \, \varepsilon \, y$,

(9) $(x) \, x \, \varepsilon \, V \equiv \sim \iota x = 0$,

(10) $(x) \, x \, \varepsilon \, V \equiv x \, \varepsilon \, \iota x$.

Note in particular that (8) provides us with a shorter way of saying that x is an element; namely, 'x ε V'.

§ 47 The Algebra of Classes

The following definitions determine the *complement* x of a class x and the *logical product* x⌒y of classes x and y.

D8   '$\bar{x}$' *for* '$\hat{y} \sim y \; \varepsilon \; x$',
D9   '$x \frown y$' *for* '$\hat{z} (z \; \varepsilon \; x \bullet z \; \varepsilon \; y)$'.

$\bar{x}$ is the class of all elements except the members of x, and $x \frown y$ is the class of all elements that are common members of x and y. Given that all the members of x and y are elements, we can describe $x \frown y$ simply as the common part of x and y. If x is the class of lawyers and y the class of Brazilians, $x \frown y$ is the class of Brazilian lawyers.

By means of the signs of complement and product, we can express various other classes: $x \frown \bar{y}$ is the class of the members of x that do not belong to y; $\bar{x} \frown \bar{y}$ is the class of elements that belong neither to x nor to y; $\overline{x \frown y}$ is the class of elements that are not common to x and y; $\overline{\bar{x} \frown y}$ is the class of the members of x and of all elements that do not belong to y; $\overline{\bar{x} \frown \bar{y}}$ is the class that covers all members of x and all members of y. If x is the class of lawyers and y of Brazilians, then $\overline{\bar{x} \frown \bar{y}}$ has as its members all lawyers, Brazilians and foreigners alike, and also all other Brazilians.

The complement and the product are the subject of a small algebra of classes,[ix] among whose laws (provable on the basis of *1, *2, and D1–9, but not proved here) are found the following:

(11)   (x) $x = \bar{\bar{x}}$,

(12)   (x) $x = x \frown x$,

(13)   (x)(y) $x \frown y = y \frown x$,

(14)   (x)(y)(z) $(x \frown y) \frown z = x \frown (y \frown z)$,

(15)   (x)(y) $x \frown y = \overline{\bar{x} \frown \bar{y}} \frown y$.

It is possible to establish a parallelism between this algebra and the theory of composition, in the following sense: each identity of this algebra corresponds to a compositional equivalence, and vice-versa, the terms of the identities containing the signs of complement and product where the statements of the equivalences contain '$\sim$' and '$\bullet$'. The identities of this algebra are, for this reason, subject to the same mechanical criterion that was used for compositional equivalence.

The classes V and 0 fit within the same algebra, in virtue of the laws:

(16)   (x) $x \frown \bar{x} = 0$,

(17) $\bar{0} = V$.

[ix] Founded by Boole (1847) and developed by Peirce and Schröder. This algebra is foreshadowed in the writings of Leibniz (1690 and afterward).

other algebraic laws about V and 0 are:

(18)   (x) $x \cap 0 = 0,$

(19)   (x) $x \cap V = x.$

The class '$\overline{\overline{x} \cap \overline{y}}$', described above, is customarily referred to as the *logical sum* of x and y, having a special notation:

D10   '$x \cup y$' *for* '$\overline{\overline{x} \cap \overline{y}}$'.

Introducing an abbreviation in general creates a need for setting down a few more laws – laws that, written without the use of the abbreviation, would be mere cases or minor corollaries of the other laws already set down. In this way the multiplication of conventions of abbreviation creates, beyond the liquid content of mathematics, a great volume of foam, almost without substance. But the role of logical sum is perhaps central enough to justify the adoption of D10. Some of the laws that then appear are the following:

(20)   (x) $x = x \cup x,$

(21)   (x)(y) $x \cup y = y \cup x,$

(22)   (x)(y)(z) $(x \cup y) \cup z = x \cup (y \cup z),$

(23)   (x)(y)(z) $x \cup (y \cap z) = (x \cup y) \cap (x \cup z),$

(24)   (x)(y)(z) $x \cap (y \cup z) = (x \cap y) \cup (x \cap z),$

(25)   (x) $x \cup \overline{x} = V,$[53]

(26)   (x) $x \cup V = V,$

(27)   (x) $x \cup 0 = x.$

The notation of logical sum combines with that of the unit class to provide a notation for specification of a finite class by enumeration of its members; thus, x, y, z, . . . being any elements whatever, the class whose members are x, y, z, . . . is $\iota x \cup \iota y \cup \iota z \cup$ .... This formulation does not, however, belong to the algebra of classes itself, which is only a fragment of the theory of classes. The notion of the unit class ιx is foreign to the algebra, just as the general notion of abstraction and the fundamental notion of membership are foreign to the algebra.

That a class x is *included* in a class y, in the sense that all the members of x are members of y, is expressed as '$x \leq y$'. We could define '$x \leq y$' as an abbreviation of '(z) ~ (z ε x • ~ z ε y)'; but the following equivalent definition accentuates that the notion of inclusion is an integral part of the algebra of classes.

D11   'x $\leqq$ y' *for* 'x = x ^ y'

Another related notation is suggested according to an analogy with arithmetic

D12   'x < y' *for* 'x $\leqq$ y • ~ x = y'.

These notions of inclusion are in fact generalizations of, not mere analogies to, the notions thus expressed in arithmetic. When x and y are numbers, it results from the definitions of numbers (§§ 52–53) that x $\leqq$ y in the numerical sense if and only if x $\leqq$ y in the "inclusive" sense of D11; and the same is true for D12. D11–12 are definitions of the two familiar arithmetical notions, in a generalized sense so as to admit no less important uses outside the field of numbers. In addition, the empty class 0 defined in D6 presents itself in arithmetic in the role of the number 0.

Among the easily provable theorems, we highlight the following. Note that the first is at the same time a generalization of an arithmetical principle and a formulation of the syllogistic principle 'If every member of x is a member of y, and every member of y is a member of z, then every member of x is a member of z'.

(28)   (x) (y) (z) ~ (x $\leqq$ y • y $\leqq$ z • ~ x $\leqq$ z),

(29)   (x) (y)   ~ (x $\leqq$ y • y $\leqq$ x • ~ x = y),

(30)   (x)   x $\leqq$ x,

(31)   (x)   0 $\leqq$ x,

(32)   (x)   x $\leqq$ V,

(33)   (x) (y) (z) (x $\leqq$ y ^ z) $\equiv$ (x $\leqq$ y • x $\leqq$ z),

(34)   (x) (y) (z) (x ⌣ y $\leqq$ z) $\equiv$ (x $\leqq$ z • y $\leqq$ z).

The arithmetical principle that y $\leqq$ x (and, in fact, y < x) whenever it is not the case that x $\leqq$ y holds within the domain of numbers but fails in the more general case. If x is the class of lawyers and y that of Brazilians, for example, it is not the case that x $\leqq$ y (some lawyers being foreigners); nor is it the case that y $\leqq$ x.

§ 48 Relations

The notion of *relation* is as necessary to mathematics as that of class or attribute. *Functions*, so often referred to in mathematics, are simply relations.

The function 'half of', for example, is the relation of each number to its double. The function expressed by '$3x^2 + 2x + 5$' is the relation that holds between the numbers $3x^2 + 2x + 5$ and x, for every number x. *Series*, so prominent in mathematics, are also relations; the clearest notion of a series identifies it with the relation that holds between each element x of the series and each element of the series not preceding x. The series of numbers, for example, is identified with the relation of every number x to every number y such that $x \leqq y$.

Just as it was natural to suppose that every matrix with a free pronoun determines a class, now it is also natural to suppose that every matrix with two free pronouns 'x' and 'y' determines a relation: the relation of any object x to any object y such that x and y satisfy the matrix. That is, it is natural to suppose that all matrices of the form:

(35) $\sim$ (z) $\sim$ (x) (y) (z relates x to y $\equiv$ fxy)

are valid, as it was natural to suppose that all matrices of the form (1) in § 45 were valid. We saw, however, that this supposition in the case of classes was not sustainable. The same occurs in the case of relations, for one of the statements of the form (35) is:

(36) $\sim$ (z) $\sim$ (x) (y) (z relates x to y $\equiv$ $\sim$ x relates x to y),

even though the denial of (36) is provable in the theory of quantification in the same manner as the denial (3) of (2) in § 45.[x]

The solution, in the case of relations as in that of classes, consists of a restriction of the elements. Just as we limit (1) in the manner of *2, we must limit (31) in the manner:

(37) $\sim$ (z) $\sim$ (x) (y) (z relates x to y $\equiv$ (fxy • x ε V • y ε V)).

Classes of *ordered pairs* of elements are sufficient for all of the purposes of relations. Writing 'x;y' to designate the ordered pair that consists of x and y in the order indicated, we can, for example, consider the function 'half of' as the class of ordered pairs 1/4;1/2, 1/3;2/3, 1/2;1, 3;6, etc., in short, the class of ordered pairs x/2;x for all numbers x. The function expressed by '$3x^2 + 2x + 5$' is the class of ordered pairs $(3x^2 + 2x + 5)$;x, for all numbers x. The relation of being a son of is the class of ordered pairs x;y, for all animals x and y such that x is a son of y.

It is essential that pairs are conceived as ordered in such a way that the pairs x;y and y;x are distinct for all distinct elements x and y; for we want the pair 3;6 to belong to the relation 'half of', and the pair Isaac;Abraham to belong to the

[x] Example (36), like (2) in § 45, is due to Russell (1903, Appendix A).

relation 'son of', but we do not want the opposite pairs 6;3 and Abraham;Isaac to belong to these relations, 6 not being half of 3, nor Abraham the son of Isaac. More generally, it is essential that any elements x and y be uniquely determined and distinguished by x;y. The fundamental principle of ordered pairs must be, for this reason, the following:

(38) $(x)(y)(z)(w) \sim (x \varepsilon V \cdot y \varepsilon V \cdot z \varepsilon V \cdot w \varepsilon V \cdot x;y = z;w \cdot \sim (x = z \cdot y = w)).$

Any definition of ordered pair that satisfies (38) would be adequate. As it happens, it is possible to construct such a definition purely on the basis of the theory of classes.

D13[xi]   'x;y' *for* '$\iota x \smile \iota(\iota x \smile \iota y)$'.

The ordered pair of any elements x and y is, therefore, the class whose members are the unit class of x and the class whose members are x and y. This formulation, although artificial, satisfies (38). On the basis of D13 and of the theory of classes founded earlier, it is possible to prove (38) as a theorem.

To say that w relates x to y is to say that x and y are elements such that x;y ε w. Therefore, writing 'w (x,y)' in the sense of 'w relates x to y', we adopt the following definition:

D14   'w (x,y)' *for* 'x;y ε w $\cdot$ x ε V $\cdot$ y ε V'.

It is useful to adopt a relation abstract prefix '$\hat{x}\hat{y}$', parallel to the class abstract prefix '$\hat{x}$'. The prefix '$\hat{x}\hat{y}$', read as 'the relation of any element x to any element y such that', admits a definition analogous to D4:

D15   '$\hat{x}\hat{y}fxy$' *for* '$(\iota z)(x)(y)(z(x,y) \equiv (fxy \cdot x \varepsilon V \cdot y \varepsilon V))$'.

Relations in this sense are *dyadic*, in the sense of relating elements in pairs. On the other hand, the relation of *giving* (x gives y to z) is *triadic*, and the relation of *paying* (x pays y to z for w) is *tetradic*, constituting classes of ordered triples and quadruples, respectively, in place of pairs. We can construct triples, quadruples, etc. on the basis of the notion of pair, in the manner x;(y;z), x;(y;(z;w)), etc., and then construct definitions exactly analogous to D14–15 for triadic relations, tetradic relations, etc. The definitions for the triadic case are:

D16   'w (x, y, z)' *for* 'x;(y;z) ε w $\cdot$ x ε V $\cdot$ y ε V $\cdot$ z ε V'.
D17   '$\hat{x}\hat{y}\hat{z}fxyz$' *for* '$(\iota w)(x)(y)(z)(w(x, y, z) \equiv (fxyz \cdot x \varepsilon V \cdot y \varepsilon V \cdot z \varepsilon V))$'.

[xi] Due to Wiener (1914), with a simplification by Kuratowski (1921).

The fundamental laws of relational abstraction are exactly analogous to the two fundamental laws (5) and (6), § 46, of class abstraction. For the dyadic case, they are:

(39) $\hat{x}\hat{y}fxy$ (z, w) ≡ (fzw • z ε V • w ε V),

(40)   ~ ((y) gy • ~ g $\hat{x}\hat{y}fxy$).

For the triadic case, they are:

(41) $\hat{x}\hat{y}\hat{z}fxyz$ (u, v, w) ≡ (fuvw • u ε V • y ε V • w ε V),

(42)   ~ ((y) gy • ~ g $\hat{x}\hat{y}\hat{z}fxyz$).

The same is true correspondingly in cases of quadruples, quintuples and so on.

These laws are not, however, provable purely on the basis of *1 and *2. Their proofs depend on another additional principle, according to which the ordered pairs of elements are elements: as it is the pairs, and not the elements within the pairs, that must be the members of relations. To found the theory of relations we must add to *1 and *2 the axiom:

*3.   (x) (y) ~ (x ε V • y ε V • ~ x;y ε V).

This principle of pairs also works for triples, as *3 gives us these two cases:

        ~ (y ε V • z ε V • ~ y;z ε V),

        ~ (x ε V • y;z ε V • ~ x;(y;z) ε V),

whose conjunction compositionally implies:

        ~ (x ε V • y ε V • z ε V • ~ x;(y;z) ε V).

The extension to quadruples, quintuples, etc. follows in the same way. It is possible to prove (39)–(42), and analogous principles for cases which are tetradic, etc., on the basis of *1–*3.

Our observation, made in § 45, that *1 and *2 are satisfied in a universe whose only object is 0, also holds for *1–*3. This observation is useful as a methodological note of caution, since it means it is always a waste of time to look for a proof on the basis of *1–*3 when the theorem to be proved implies that some class has members. This nearly empty ontology naturally does not provide a serious interpretation of the theory of classes and relations. The theory would be reducible, under this ontology, to the single principle '(x) (y) ~ x ε y'.

§ 49 Converse, Projection, and Relative Product

Three notions of the theory of relations that usefully apply as much outside as inside mathematics are the following:

D18   'x̆' *for* 'ŷẑ x (z, y)',
D19   'x"y' for 'ẑ ~ (w) ~ (w ε y • x (z, w))'
D20   'x | y' *for* 'ẑŵ ~ (v) ~ (x (z, v) • y (v, w))'.

x̆, called the *converse* of x, is the relation that consists of the inverse pairs of the pairs that belong to x. The converse of the relation 'half of' is the relation 'double of', and the converse of the relation of parents to children is the relation of children to parents.

x"y, called the *projection* of y by x, is a class of objects that are related by x to the members of y. If x is the relation 'square of' and y is the class of prime numbers, then x"y is the class of the squares of prime numbers. If x is the relation of son to father and y is the class of lawyers, then x"y is the class of the sons of lawyers.

x | y, called the *relative product* of x and y, is the relation of any object z to any object w such that z is related by x to some object that is related by y to w. If x is the relation of being a brother, and y is the relation of being a mother, x | y is the relation of being a maternal uncle. If x is the relation of being a father and y is the relation of being a mother, then x | y is the relation of being a maternal grandfather; y | x is the relation of being a paternal grandmother; x | y̆ is the relation of a man to the mother of some of his children; y | x̆ is the relation of a woman to the father of some of her children; x̆| y is 0, being the relation of z to w such that the father of z is the mother of w; and y̆ | x is likewise 0.

The importance of these notions is obvious. In particular, it is interesting to observe the variety of meanings expressible by the combination of the notion of projection with that of complement. Suppose that x is the relation each person bears to each moment of that person's life, and that y is the class of moments in the year 1930. It is easy to establish the following:

x"y = the class of people alive during at least a part of 1930.
x"ȳ = the class of people whose lives are not limited to the year 1930.
x̄"y = the class of people whose lives end before 1930 (and of all elements that are not people).
x̄"ȳ = V (not in general, but in this example).
‾x"y‾ = the class of people whose lives do not include 1930 (and of all elements that are not people).

$\overline{x\text{``}\overline{y}}$ = the class of babies alive only within 1930 (and of all elements that are not people).

$\overline{\overline{x}\text{``}y}^{54}$ = the class of people who were born at the beginning of 1930 or before, and died at the end of 1930 or afterwards.

$\overline{\overline{x}\text{``}\overline{y}} = 0$.

Preserving the same relation x and taking y^{55} to be the class of Bandeirantes,[56] we further observe that:

$\check{x}\text{``}y$ = the class of moments during which one or more of the Bandeirantes lived,

$\check{x}\text{``}\overline{y}^{57}$ = the class of moments during which some people who are not Bandeirantes lived (that is, the lifetime of the entire human race).

I leave the six remaining cases to the reader.

It is clear that $\breve{\breve{x}} = x$, for every relation x; not, however, for every object x, as $\breve{x}$ is a relation (a class of ordered pairs) even when x contains some members that are not pairs. The condition 'x = $\breve{x}$', serves, in fact, as a convenient means of affirming that x is a relation.

Among the various theorems that govern converse, projection, and relative product, note the following:

(1)   (x) $x\text{``}V = \hat{y} \sim (z) \sim x\,(y, z)$

(2)   (x) $x\text{``}V = \hat{z} \sim (y) \sim x\,(y, z)$

(3)   (x) (z) $x\text{``}\imath z = \hat{y}\; x(y, z)$

(4)   (x) (y) $\breve{x}\text{``}\imath y = \hat{z}\; x(y, z)$

(5)   (x) (y) (z) $(x \smile y)\text{``}z = (x\text{``}z) \smile (y\text{``}z)$

(6)   (x) (y) (z) $x\text{``}(y \smile z) = (x\text{``}y) \smile (x\text{``}z)$

(7)   (x) (y) (z) $(x \mid y) \mid z = x \mid (y \mid z)$

(8)   (x) (y) $(x \mid y) = \breve{y} \mid \breve{x}$

(9)   (x) (y) (z) $x\text{``}(y\text{``}z) = (x \mid y)\text{``}z$.

The classes $x\text{``}V$ and $\breve{x}\text{``}V$, described in (1) and (2), are called respectively the *domain* and *co-domain* of x. The domain of the relation 'uncle of', for example, is the class of all uncles, and its co-domain is the class of all people who have uncles – that is, the class of all nephews and nieces.

x being the relation 'uncle of', $x\text{``}\imath z$, is, following (3), the class of all uncles of z, and $x\text{``}\imath y$ is, following (4), the class of all nephews (and nieces) of y.

Law (5) indicates, for example, that the class of all persons who are the fathers or friends of lawyers consists of the fathers of lawyers and of the friends of lawyers; and (6) indicates that the wives of classicists covers the wives of Hellenists and the wives of Latinists. Note that the corresponding laws fail for logical products. If x is the relation 'older than', y the relation 'brother of', and z the class of sailors, then

$$(x^\frown y)\text{``}z \neq (x\text{``}z)^\frown (y\text{``}z);$$

as $(x^\frown y)\text{``}z$ is the class only of the older brothers of sailors, while $(x\text{``}z)^\frown (y\text{``}z)$ also covers every person who is older than some sailor and is the younger brother of another sailor. If x is the relation of helping, y is the class of musicians, and z is the class of disabled people, then

$$x\text{``}(y^\frown z) \neq (x\text{``}y)^\frown (x\text{``}z),$$

as $x\text{``}(y^\frown z)$ is the class only of the benefactors of disabled musicians, while $(x\text{``}z)^\frown (y\text{``}z)$ also covers every person who helps some musician and some disabled non-musician.

Law (7) shows that grouping does not make a difference to iterated relative products. If x is the relation of brother, y that of father, and z that of mother, what (7) says is that the paternal uncles of the mother of someone are the brothers of that someone's maternal grandfather. Note, on the other hand, that order does make a difference to the relative product; for example, a maternal grandfather is not a paternal grandmother.

The converses of the relations of employer to employee and of father to son being the relations of employee to employer and of son to father, (8) indicates that the converse of the relation 'employer of the father of' is the relation 'son of an employee of'. Finally, (9) indicates that brothers of fathers of lawyers are uncles of lawyers.[xii]

§ 50 Types of Relations

Leaving aside the qualities and nature of the members of a class, the only character that remains by which we may compare and contrast classes to each other is that of cardinality – number of members. In the case of dyadic relations, on the other hand, one feature is left to us as a basis for important contrasts and

---

[xii] The calculus of relations, which concerns the notions discussed in § 49 and certain of those in § 50, was founded by De Morgan and Peirce (1860–70).

classifications, even after we've abstracted away from the nature and the number of the related elements.

A relation x is called *symmetric* if, whenever x (y, z), it follows that x (z, y); and *asymmetric* if, whenever x (y, z), it follows that $\sim$ x (z, y). The relation of being a colleague of is symmetric and the relation of being the father of asymmetric. The relation of being a sister of is neither symmetric nor asymmetric, as there are people y and z such that y is the sister of z and vice-versa, and there are others such that y is the sister of z but not vice-versa.

A relation x is called *transitive* if, whenever x (y, z) and x (z, w), it follows that x (y, w); and *intransitive* if, whenever x (y, z) and x (z, w), it follows that $\sim$ x (y, w). The relation of inclusion, for example – that is, $\hat{u}\hat{v}$ (u $\leqq$ v) – is transitive, and the relation of being the father of is intransitive. The relation of being a brother of is, however, neither transitive nor intransitive, as y being a brother of z and z a brother of w, y can be either a brother of w or w himself.

An example of a jointly symmetric and transitive relation is provided by the relation of identity, I, defined as follows:

D21   'I' for '$\hat{x}\hat{y}$ (x = y)'.

Note that 'I' names the relation, while '=' is not a name. In addition, 'I(x, y)' and 'x = y' are not equivalent; for 'I (x, y)' implies that x and y are elements, but 'x = y' does not. The same contrasts hold between '$\hat{u}\hat{v}$ (u $\leqq$ v)' and '$\leqq$'.

A relation x is called *anti-symmetric* if, whenever x (y, z) and x (z, y), it follows that y = z. The relations $\hat{u}\hat{v}$ (u $\leqq$ v) and I, for example, are both anti-symmetric.

Aside from the symbolic formulation '(y) (z) $\sim$ (x (y, z) • $\sim$ x (z, y))', that corresponds directly to the verbal definition of 'x is symmetric', there is a shorter formulation that is equivalent, and the same is true for asymmetry, anti-symmetry, transitivity, and intransitivity:

x is symmetric:	$\check{x} \leqq x$,
x is asymmetric:	$\check{x}^\frown x = 0$,
x is anti-symmetric:	$\check{x}^\frown x \leqq I$,
x is transitive:	$x \mid x \leqq x$,
x is intransitive:	$x^\frown (x \mid x) = 0$.

A relation x is called reflexive if, whenever y belongs to the domain or co-domain of x, it follows that x (y, y). The relation I, for example, is reflexive, and the same is true for the relation of inclusion $\hat{u}\hat{v}$ (u $\leqq$ v). But a reflexive relation need not necessarily, like I and $\hat{u}\hat{v}$ (u $\leqq$ v), relate every element to itself. The relation that holds between people who are contemporaries is still reflexive even though it holds only between people.

As a preparation for compact formulations of reflexivity and the other notions, let us adopt the following definition:

D22   'x$_y$' *for* 'ẑŵ (x (z, w) • z ε (ў"V) ‿ (y"V) • w ε (y"V) ‿ (ў"V))'.

If x and y are relations, x$_y$ is the relation x limited to the members of the domain and co-domain of y. I$_y$, in particular, is the relation of every member of the domain or co-domain of y to itself. Reflexivity can now be formulated as follows:

x is *reflexive*:   I$_x$ ≦ x.

A relation x is called *completely connexive* when it holds, in one direction or other, among all the objects of the domain or co-domain. The following formulation is equivalent:

x *is completely connexive*:[xiii]   V$_x$ ≦ x ‿ x̆.

The relation between numbers y and z, such that y ≦ z, is connexive, as any objects y and z in the domain or co-domain of this relation – any numbers, in short – are such that y ≦ z or z ≦ y.

A series is identified, as mentioned earlier (§ 48), with the relation between each element y of the series and each element of the series not preceding y. To define the idea of a series, however, we must determine what properties a relation must possess in order to be the relation between each element y of series (in the vague and intuitive sense of the word) and a non-preceding element. There are three such properties: *transitivity, anti-symmetry*, and *complete connection*.[xiv] The relation between numbers y and z, such that y ≦ z, is an example of this combination of three properties. This is the relation with which the series of numbers is identified.

A generalization of the notion of series, ever more important in the mathematical literature, is the notion of *partial order*: the notion of a transitive, antisymmetric, and reflexive relation. Every series is a partial order, as complete connection implies reflexivity; but not every partial order is a series. The general relation of inclusion, ûv̂ (u ≦ v), is a partial order but not a series. It is not connexive, as was observed in the example of Brazilians and lawyers (end

---

[xiii] I use the adverb to distinguish between this type of connection and connection in the sense of Russell (1901 [*recte* 1903]):V$_x$ ≦ x ‿ x ‿ I. Calling his notion *quasi-connection*, we can dispense with our adverb.

[xiv] Russell identified series with the relation of each element to each posterior element – thus identifying a series of numbers with the relation between the numbers y and z such that y < z. The properties that he enumerates as a definition of series differ, however, from these three. But the present method is more convenient and is becoming ever more usual.

of § 47). The notion of partial order is significant for being perhaps the most general type that deserves the name of order.

The notion of series is divided, for its part, into an innumerable number of kinds. There are *discrete* series, *dense* series, *continuous* series, *well-ordered* series. The study of the series of this last kind has become an important chapter in mathematics, namely, the theory of infinite ordinal numbers.[xv] We will leave this fecund field aside, however, to study two more classifications of relations.

A relation x is called *univocal* (or, in mathematics, the univocal function of a variable) if, whenever x (y, w) and x (z, w), it follows that y = z; in short, x never relates two objects to the same object. The compact formulation is the following:

x is *univocal*: $x \mid \breve{x} \leq I$.

The relation 'mother of', for example, is univocal, but the relation 'son of' is not. The relation 'double of' is univocal, and so also the other 'polynomial functions of a variable' of mathematics – for example, the function corresponding to the expression '$x^2 + 4x + 4$', that is, the relation $\hat{y}\hat{x}(y = x^2 + 4x + 4)$. A relation is univocal if, given w, the fact that y maintains this relation with w is sufficient for determining y.

A relation x is called a *transformation* in mathematics if it and its converse are univocal and have the same domain.

x is a *transformation*: $x \mid \breve{x} \leq I \cdot \breve{x} \mid x \leq I \cdot x``V = \breve{x}``V$

The relation 'square of', that is, $\hat{y}\hat{x}(y = x^2)$, thought of as a relation that does not hold only between positive numbers, is not a transformation; for its converse $\hat{x}\hat{y}(y = x^2)$ is not univocal, given that it relates 2 and -2 to the same number 4. The relation of husband to wife, when limited to persons who have not married twice, is univocal and has a univocal converse, but is still not a transformation. for its domain consists of men while its co-domain (the domain of the converse) consists of women. But the relation 'double of', that is, $\hat{y}\hat{x}(y = 2x)$, considered as a relation not only between whole numbers, is a transformation, for it is univocal, and so is its converse $\hat{x}\hat{y}(y = 2x)$ (the relation of half), and the domains of both exhaust the numbers.

An already classic branch of mathematics, called the *theory of groups*, studies the notions of converse, relative product, and limited identity (I_y above), in their applications to transformations. A group consists of any assortment of transformations, with equal domains, together with all the

---

[xv] Good introductions to this area, whose principal pioneer was Cantor, are found in Huntington, *Continuum*, and Russell, *Introduction to Mathematical Philosophy.* See also my "Element and Number."

transformations obtainable from the given transformations by means of the formation of relative products and converses. One of the transformations of a group is always I_y, y being any transformation of the group, for when y is a transformation, $I_y = y \mid \breve{y} = \breve{y} \mid y$. The theory of groups is a part of the theory of relations that has been fruitfully applied many times, for example in the theory of equations, in quantum mechanics, and in crystallography.

§ 51 The Virtual Theory of Classes and Relations

The theory of classes, together with its part, the theory of relations, was developed above in such a way that it depends on the acceptance of an ontology that admits abstract objects – classes – as real. The fundamental sign 'ε', of membership, was used between pronouns of quantification, and this required that classes, to which members were attributed, were counted as objects in the universe covered by the quantifiers. It is unsurprising, indeed, that the theory of classes requires recognition of classes in this way. As it happens, however, an important part of the so-called theory of classes (and of relations) can be developed in an alternative way, so as to form part of the theory of quantification or identity itself, completely avoiding all ontological suppositions.

   The method consists in introducing the following conventions of abbreviation, analogous to D2, D8–12, and D18–20, for direct application to the schematic letters 'f', 'g', etc., used in the theory of quantification:

D2'   'f = g' *for* '(x) (fx ≡ gx)' (*or* '(x) (y) (fxy≡ gxy)', etc., according to the context).

D8'   '$\overline{fx}$' *for* '~ fz', '$\overline{fxy}$' *for* '~ fxy', etc.

D9'   '(f⌢g)' *for* '$\overline{\overline{fx} \cdot \overline{gx}}$', '(f⌢g) xy' *for* 'fxy • gzy', etc.

D10'   'f⌣g' *for* '$\overline{\overline{f} \_ \overline{g}}$'.

D11'   'f ≤ g' *for* 'f = f⌢g'.

D12'   'f < g' *for* 'f ≤ g • ~ f =g'.

D18'   'f̆xy' *for* 'fyx'.

D19'   '(f"g) x' *for* '~ (y) ~ (gy • fxy)'.

D20'   '(f | g) xy' *for* '~ (z) ~ (fxz • gzy)'.

   Corresponding to statement (5) of § 49, for example, in this new notation we have the schema:

(1)   (f⌣g)"h = (f"h)⌣(g"h),

which is an abbreviation of the quantificationally valid schema:

(2)   (x) $\sim$(y)$\sim$(hy $\bullet$ $\sim$($\sim$ fxy $\bullet$ $\sim$ gxy)) $\equiv$ $\sim$((y)$\sim$(hy $\bullet$ fxy) $\bullet$ (y)$\sim$(hy $\bullet$ gxy)).

All matrices of the form represented by schema (2) are quantificationally valid, as is easily proved within the theory of quantification.

(a) $\sim$ (y) $\sim$ (hy $\bullet$ $\sim$ ($\sim$ fxy $\bullet$ $\sim$ gxy)) $\equiv$ $\sim$ (y) $\sim$ (hy $\bullet$ $\sim$ ($\sim$fxy $\bullet$ $\sim$ gxy))   By (i).

(b) $\sim$ (y) $\sim$ (hy $\bullet$ $\sim$ ($\sim$ fxy $\bullet$ $\sim$ gxy)) $\equiv$ $\sim$ (y) ($\sim$ (hy $\bullet$ fxy) $\bullet$ $\sim$ (hy $\bullet$ $\sim$ gxy))
                                                                                From (a) by (ii).

(2) From (b) by (iii).

Something analogous occurs with statements (6)–(9) of § 49 and (11)–(15), (20)–(24), (28)–(30), (33), and (34) of § 47. All of those statements, although they depend on the notation, the principles, and the ontology of the theory of classes, correspond to schemata provable within the pure theory of quantification.

We can also obtain schemata of the theory of quantification analogous to (7) and (8) of § 46 and (16)–(19), (25)–(27), (31), and (32) of § 47, if we treat '0' and 'V' as abbreviations of the schematic expressions 'f$^\frown$$\bar{\text{f}}$' and 'f$\smile$$\bar{\text{f}}$'. In particular, the algebra of classes is reproduced in this manner within the theory of quantification.

It is also easy to accommodate abstracts. The schema analogous to (1) of § 49, for example, can be:

$$(g``V) \ y \equiv \sim (z) \sim gyz,$$

an abbreviation of:

$$\sim (z) \sim (\sim (\sim fz \bullet fz) \sim gyz) \equiv \sim (z) \sim gyz.$$

The case of (2) in § 49 is similar.

Statements (9) and (10) of § 46 and (3) and (4) of § 49 use the notation of the unit class, omitted from the list of D2′–D20′. The reason for this omission was that the sign '=', used between pronouns and not between schematic letters as in D2, resists definition within the pure theory of quantification. Nevertheless, if we consider the theory of quantification augmented by the theory of identity (adopted as in §§ 32–33, independently of the notion of membership), then we can insert into the list D2′–D20′ the definition:

D7′   '(ιx) y' *for* 'x= y'.

Then we can formulate, as corresponding to (3) of § 49, the schema:

$$(f''\iota z) \cong fyz,$$

an abbreviation of:

$$\sim (x) \sim (z = x \bullet fyx) \equiv fyz$$

– a valid schema, not of the pure theory of quantification, but of the theory of identity, as in schema (J). Cases (4) of § 49, and (9) and (10) of § 46, are similar.

In the theory of identity, if not in the pure theory of quantification, we can thus formulate and establish schemata that correspond to the thirty-seven statements mentioned as theorems of the theory of classes (and relations): (7)–(34) of §§ 46–47 and (1)–(9) of § 49. The material in § 50 can be incorporated in the same way.

We thus have, parallel to the real theory of classes (and relations) developed earlier, a virtual theory of classes and relations that does not depend on the ideas of class or of membership, and does not imply ontological issues. This virtual theory does not really invoke classes or relations; the letters 'f', 'g', etc., although they behave more or less as though they refer to classes and relations, are schematic letters, incapable of occurring in quantifiers or statements. The expressions that contain such letters are schemata, instruments of discourse about statements in a general way. We can thus preserve all of the practical advantages of the algebra of classes, and of some other branches of the theories of classes and relations, without abandoning the terrain of logic in the stricter sense: the theory of quantification. Only four of the thirty-seven statements cited require the addition of the theory of identity, and even with this addition the theoretical basis remains independent of ontological presuppositions – in contrast to what was affirmed earlier (§ 42) about mathematics.

Let us now note the limits of the virtual theory. The transition from a theorem of the real theory to a schema of the virtual theory depends on the use of the schematic letters 'f', 'g', etc. in place of the pronouns that play the role of 'x' in the context 'y ε x' or 'x (y, z)'. Thus we avoid the ontological acceptance of classes among the objects covered by the quantifiers. Given that the schematic letters cannot occur in quantifiers, any quantifier whose pronoun is replaced by a schematic letter must, in the course of such a transition, be dropped from the context. Such a quantifier may be dropped either as a result of the transformations implicit in the abbreviations D2′–D20′, or because it is initial to the entire context, as, for example, the quantifiers '(x)', '(y)', and '(z)' are dropped in the course of the passage from theorem (5) in § 49 of schema (1) above. If, on the other hand, the quantifier '(x)' of a theorem of the form ' … (x) … y ε x … ' is not dropped, in any of the ways mentioned above, in the course of the search for a schema corresponding to the theorem, then (before terminating in a pseudo-schema of the type ' ... (f) ... fx ... ') we must simply recognize that the theorem depends on the ontology of classes in such an essential way that it is not able to correspond to any schema in the virtual theory of classes and relations. Arithmetic involves theorems of this type, although the quantifiers in question are sometimes covered by abbreviations. Arithmetic depends on the real theory of classes, with all of its ontological presuppositions.

The important fact remains that the algebra of classes and other considerable sections of the theory of classes and relations fit within the firm and indisputable basis of the virtual theory. Among the theorems of the real theory that have corresponding schemata that can be formulated in the virtual theory, however, there are some such that the corresponding schemata are not valid. One example is:

(3)   (x) $\sim$ (y) y ε x,

which is deducible from *2. The corresponding schema '$\sim$ (y) y = y' is not valid; on the contrary, the statement '$\sim$ (y) y = y', which has the form '$\sim$ (y) fy', is false. But such divergences between the virtual theory and the corresponding part of the real theory are only peripheral differences that do not reflect on the practical applications of the two theories.

The existence of example (3) as a theorem of the real theory is a result of the restrictions imposed on the principle of abstraction in order to avoid contradictions of the type in (2) of § 45. Therefore, since they cannot be formulated in the virtual theory by any schema corresponding to contradictions of this type, the restrictions that lead to (3) in the real theory are not reflected in the virtual theory.

§ 52 Natural Numbers

The positive integers are used to measure multiplicity when we add up or enumerate objects. To determine that the class of American republics has 21 members, we name each of the members of this class in turn, and match each to one of the succession of integers starting with 1 – we thereby bring about a correlation between the 21 countries and the first 21 numbers. It is natural, for this reason, to consider the number 21 as a class of the first 21 numbers themselves; then the process of the enumeration of the countries is thus a method of establishing that the class of the republics and the class 21 are equal with regard to multiplicity. The number 21 is a class of 21 members which is convenient as a comparative standard of measurement. The other numbers are analogous.

It would be circular to try to define the number 21 as a class whose members are the numbers 1, 2, . . ., 21. We can, however, break this circle by taking the number 0 as initial. Now each number n can, without circularity, be defined as the class of the n first numbers. The number 0, as the class of the first 0 numbers, must be the empty class – revealing, thereby, the motive of our having chosen the sign '0' earlier to designate the empty class. The number 1, as the class of the first number, is the class ı0; the number 2, as the class of the first two numbers, is the class ı0 ‿ ı1 whose members are 0 and 1; the number 3 is ı0 ‿ ı1 ‿ ı2, and so on. More briefly, 2 is 1 ‿ ı1, 3 is 2 ‿ ı2, and, in general, the number that succeeds n is n ‿ ın. (This is true even when n = 0, as 0 ‿ ı0= ı0 = 1; cf. (27) of § 47.) We adopt, therefore, the series of abbreviations:

D23   '1' *for* 'ı0', '2' *for* '1 ‿ ı1', '3' *for* '2 ‿ ı2', etc.

Each of the *natural numbers* thus has its definition. But we still have to construct a definition of the general notion of natural number – that is, to define the class Nn whose members are 0, 1, 2, etc. The definition:

        'Nn' *for* 'ı0 ‿ ı1 ‿ ı2 ‿ etc.'

will not do, as it determines 'Nn' as the abbreviation of an expression that contains the word 'etc.', which we have not defined. The problem is to formulate this same idea, avoiding the word 'etc.'. The solution, due to Frege (1879), depends on the consideration that Nn *has 0 as a member and also has the successor z ‿ ız of each of it members z as a member*. This condition on Nn still does not completely determine Nn, as the same condition is also satisfied by every class that has as members both the natural numbers and also some additional objects. However, Nn is the smallest class that satisfies the given condition. It is the smallest of the classes y, such that

(1)   0 ε y • (z) ~ (z ε y • ~ z ‿ ız ε y).

It is the common part of all classes y that satisfy (1). We can define Nn, therefore, as the class of elements x that belong simultaneously to all classes y that satisfy (1). That is:

D24   'Nn' *for* 'x̂ (y) ~ (0 ε y • (z) ~ (z ε y • ~ z ‿ ız ε y) • ~ x ε y)'.

Given that every natural number is, according to the given definitions, a class included in each of the numbers that succeed it, the notations 'x ≦ y' and 'x < y' of class inclusion regain their original arithmetical meanings when x and y are natural numbers.

The definitions of arithmetical *addition, multiplication,* and *exponentiation* depend on the notion of the *relative power* of a relation w, in the following sense:

$$w^0 = I, \ w^1 = w, \ w^2 = w \mid w, \ w^3 = w \mid w \mid w, \text{ etc.}$$

w being the relation of being the father of, for example, w^2 is the relation of being the grandfather of, and w^3 is the relation of being the great-grandfather of. The characteristic of arithmetical sum, now, is that x + y is the successor of the successor of the successor ... (y times) of x; that is, where w is the successor relation (the relation $\hat{u}\hat{v}$ (u $= $ v $\smile$ ιv)), x + y is the object that is related to x by w^y. We thus arrive at the definition:

'x + y' *for* '(ιz) $\hat{u}\hat{v}$ (u $=$ v $\smile$ ιv)^y (z, x)'.

On the basis of this notion of sum, the notion of product admits in turn of an analogous definition; for x·y is the result of adding x, y times, to 0.

'x·y' *for* '(ιz) $\hat{u}\hat{v}$ (u = x + v)^y (z, 0)'.

Finally, the arithmetical power x $\wedge$ y (using this notation temporarily to avoid confusion with the relative power x^y) is the result of multiplying 1, y times, by x.

'x $\wedge$ y' *for* '(ιz) $\hat{u}\hat{v}$ (u = x·v)^y (z, I)'.

The notion of relative power, on which these three definitions depend, still lacks a formal definition. Such a definition, adequate not only for the separate cases 'w^0', 'w^1', 'w^2', etc., but for the general case w^y with a pronominal exponent, is constructed in a manner similar to the construction that led to D24; however, this being a very much more complicated definition, we will omit it here.[xvi]

A central principle of the arithmetic of the natural numbers, used to prove familiar identities such as 'x + y = y + z', 'x + 0 = x', etc., is that of *mathematical induction,* according to which 'fx' is followed by the conjunction of 'f0', '(z) ~ (fz • ~ f ($\sim$ z $\smile$ ιz))', and 'x ε Nn'. The fundamental form of this principle is the theorem:

(x) (y) ~ (0 ε y • (z) ~ (z ε y • ~ z $\smile$ ιz ε y) • x ε Nn • ~ x ε y).

whose proof, given D24, is immediate.

But this principle does not permit its usual applications without the support of the theorems '0 ε Nn', '1 ε Nn', '2 ε Nn' etc.; and these theorems depend on

_____

[xvi] See *Mathematical Logic,* § 47.

the fact that 0, 1, 2, etc. are elements. To found arithmetic, however, we must add to *1–*3 two more axioms:

(2)   0 ε V,

(3)   (x) ~ (x ε V • ~ x ⌣ ɩx ε V).

From these axioms we may conclude that 0 ⌣ ɩ0 ε V, that is, 1 ε V; from this result, together with (3), we can conclude that 2 ε V; and so on. The two axioms require us to accept an infinity of elements, and in consequence also to accept certain infinite classes (whether or not they are elements), for example Nn and V. It is thus that arithmetic – even that of the natural numbers – makes stronger ontological presuppositions than do those of the branches we have looked at so far.

In place of adopting *3 and (2)–(3), it is more elegant to adopt:

*3′.   (x) ɩx ε V,

*4.   (x) ~ (x ε V • y ε V • ~ x ⌣ y ε V).

The proof of (3), on the basis of *3′ and *4, is immediate. The proof of *3 is also easy, given D13. The proof of (2), intuitively outlined, is the following: Non-elements exist in virtue of *2 and (4) of § 45, and, x being that non-element, 'ɩx ε V' is reduced to (2).

Note that *3′ and *4 imply that every finite class ɩx ⌣ ɩy ⌣ ɩz ⌣ … is an element. On the other hand, *3′ and *4 do not imply the existence of any infinite element.

To establish the enumerative use of the natural numbers, we must still formulate what it means to say that a class x has y members. As we noted at the beginning, x has y members if there is a correlation between the members of x and the members of the number y. This correlation consists in any relation z, between the members of x and the members of y, such that it never relates two members of x to a member of y, nor a member of x to two members of y; in short, a relation z such that z and ž are univocal (cf. § 50) and x = z"y. Therefore, we adopt the definition:

'x sm y' *for* '~ (z) ~ (z | ž = I • ž | z = I • x = x"y)'.

In general, 'x sm y', pronounced 'x is similar to y', means that the classes x and y have the same number of members; and if, in particular, y ε Nn, then 'x sm y' means simply that x has y members.

§ 53 Further Constructions

The most important further construction is that which introduces the real numbers, that is, the rational and irrational numbers. Among various alternative definitions, the one that is perhaps the most convenient[xvii] interprets real numbers as certain relations between natural numbers. The real number $\sqrt{2}$, for example, is identified with the relation $\hat{y}\hat{z}$ (y ε Nn • z ε Nn • y·y < 2·z·z). Another example: The real number 2 – or r2, to distinguish it from the natural number 2 – is interpreted as the relation $\hat{y}\hat{z}$ (y ε Nn • z ε Nn • y < 2·z). In general, the intuitive idea is the following: Each real number x is identified with the relation of each natural number y to each natural number z such that, according to intuitive notions, y/z < x. The considerations that guide the general construction must be left out here; I will limit myself to presenting without comment the definition of the class of real numbers:

'Nr' *for* '$\hat{x}$ (x = $\hat{y}\hat{z}$ ~ (u) (v) ~ (y ε Nn • z ε Nn • x (u, v) • y·v < u·z) • ~ x = $\hat{y}\hat{z}$ (y ε Nn • z ε Nn))'.

The notations 'x ≦ y' and 'x < y' of the inclusion of classes regain their former arithmetical meanings when x and y are real numbers. Sum, product, and power receive new definitions for application to the real numbers (distinct signs such as '$_r$+', etc., being introduced during the theoretical considerations).

Until now we have ignored the negative numbers. We could continue the constructions so as to include the negative numbers and the imaginary numbers, as well as the infinite cardinal and ordinal numbers, and the notions of differential and integral, central to "analysis." [xviii]

With the arrival of the real numbers, the two axioms *3' and *4 about what counts as an element must be supplemented. We must prove why the real numbers are elements. To this end we only need an axiom according to which every relation between natural numbers is an element:

*5   (x) ~ (x ≦ $\hat{y}\hat{z}$ (y ε Nn • z ε Nn) • ~ x ε V).

While *3' and *4 imply that there exist certain infinite classes, but not that there exists an infinite element, *5 implies that there exist certain infinite elements. This contrast is fundamentally the same one that was expressed earlier, in vague terms, in the following manner: The arithmetic of natural numbers rests only on the *potential* infinite, while that of the real numbers rests on the *actual* infinite.

[xvii] Due to Whitehead and Russell. Cf. *Principia*, vol. III, p. 336.
[xviii] See *Mathematical Logic*, § 52.

We have, for the theory of classes and for the mathematics constructible within this theory, an infinite body of axioms. Each of the matrices of the form *1–*2, or, better, each statement formed by the application of initial quantifiers to one such matrix, constitutes an axiom; and, in addition to these, we have the three separate axioms *3′–*5. The statements implied quantificationally by the conjunctions of these axioms are the theorems. But these axioms are still not enough to imply or contradict each of the pure statements (cf. § 44) – that is, each of the statements expressible in the given notation. There remain mathematical statements – even arithmetical statements – whose proof or refutation would require the adoption of even stronger axioms than those that we have adopted until now.

§ 54 Another Crisis

It would be desirable to complete this list of axioms, but, as Gödel has proved (1931), we cannot complete it. We shall now look at the general nature of this result and of the reasoning that supports it.

For a systematization of logic or mathematics to be used for proving theorems, it is not necessary that it provide a *mechanical method* for the discovery of proofs (such as, for example, the one we have for truth-table proofs in the theory of composition), but it is necessary that every theorem have a proof (even if it has not been discovered) and that there be a *mechanical method* by which every proof, once found, can be authenticated. An exact formulation of the idea of "mechanical method" is available,[xix] but we will omit it here.

Now let us consider the elementary arithmetic of the natural numbers. We will limit ourselves to a very minimal mathematical notation, consisting only in the notations of addition, multiplication, and identity, together with the usual notations of denial, conjunction, and quantification. Take any systematization of this arithmetic. Suppose, in conformity with what has just been pointed out, that there is a mechanical method for authenticating the proofs of theorems.

The first step in Gödel's framing is to number, in a systematic but arbitrary way, each of the statements of the elementary arithmetical language we have adopted. One result of this numbering is a parallelism between the formal properties of statements and certain properties of the natural numbers. The property of being a theorem, for example, corresponds to the numerical property possessed exactly by those numbers that are correlated, according to our

---

[xix] Cf. Rosser, "Informal Exposition."

general numbering, to theorems. An additional result is that this numerical property is purely arithmetical and expressible even within the elementary language of arithmetic we have assumed. That is, in this language we can construct a certain long and complicated matrix – let us abbreviate it as 'Θx' – that will hold of exactly those numbers x that are correlated to theorems.

Clearly, the way to construct such a matrix, within the given arithmetical language, will depend on the following circumstances: 1st, on the details of the systematization of arithmetic that is adopted, as it is the notion of theorem under this systematization that we must copy in order to construct the arithmetical matrix 'Θx'; 2nd, on the nature of our arbitrary numbering of the statements, as it is the numbering convention that determines how to "copy" the notion of theorem in the construction of 'Θx'. Gödel established, however, that this numbering can be done in such a way as to facilitate the construction of 'Θx' within the elementary arithmetical language, *whatever may be* the adopted systematization of arithmetic – given that it allows for a mechanical method for authenticating proofs (as we supposed before). Gödel's reasoning is based on the exact formulation (mentioned above, but not outlined) of the concept of mechanical method.

Then, given the numbering of statements, the systematization of arithmetic, and the construction of 'Θx', Gödel shows how we can calculate a natural number k with the following attribute: The number correlated to the statement '$\sim \Theta k$'[58] of the arithmetical language is k.

This is what Gödel's brilliant construction achieves. All we have to do next is interpret the result. '$\sim \Theta k$' will be true if and only if k is not the number of a theorem. But k was the number of the statement '$\sim \Theta k$' itself. We see, therefore, that this statement is true if and only if it is not a theorem. The supposed systematization of arithmetic is either defective, admitting the false theorem '$\sim \Theta k$', or not complete, omitting from the theorems an arithmetical truth '$\sim \Theta k$' that is expressible by means of the given rudimentary language of arithmetic.[xx]

No formulation of the notion of theorem can cover all of the true statements that can be formulated even in this very restricted notation of elementary arithmetic, without also covering false statements. The same is true *a fortiori* for our logical notation, since it is capable of expressing arithmetic and much more.

It may be said that the truth of a mathematical statement itself consists in the possibility of its proof. However, Gödel's result shows that there can be no coherent systemization of mathematics such that whatever true mathematical statement you may select always admits of proof. There will always be

---

[xx] For the details of the construction that has just been outlined, see *Mathematical Logic*, Ch. 7.

mathematical statements that are neither provable nor refutable. What do we mean when we call them *statements* – and therefore true or false? Here we have a crisis in the philosophy of mathematics. We cannot put the blame on our favorite scapegoat, the actual infinite, for the difficulty still exists in the arithmetic of the natural numbers, which involves only the potential infinite.

This is a second victory for those who obstinately refuse to recognize abstract objects. Their first victory was realized when we found difficulties with the principle of abstraction (§ 45) and had to qualify the principle in one or another artificial way. Nevertheless, to abandon classical mathematics, including elementary arithmetic, would be an overly quixotic remedy. We must in any case preserve classical mathematics because it is a useful tool, even if we judge that the ideograms this tool can draw are not literally statements in the full sense of the word.

This notion of mathematics as a tool, without content in the full sense, is very helpful in dispelling the air of mystery that surrounds the subject. That these pseudo-statements behave as though they have meaning is still guaranteed, within limits, by the use of the methods of the theory of quantification (whose meaning still remains unquestioned) in deriving theorems from the axioms we assume. It is not strange, from this point of view, that several of the axioms, as for example those which constitute the restricted principle of abstraction (*2), seem especially artificial; and if we cannot, compatibly with our purposes, come up with axioms capable of settling the pseudo-truth or pseudo-falsehood of each one of these pseudo-statements, this is an accident that does not shake any of our preconceptions. The pseudo-statements thus left undecided will still be treated as if they were true or false, even though we are unaware which of these values they possess. We can add to the axioms as much as we like, when we find it useful to attribute a pseudo-truth to some of these remaining pseudo-statements.

List of Principles Most Often Referred to in the Text

(i)   *inference of what is compositionally implied*
(ii)   *interchangeability of compositional equivalence*
(iii)   *interchangeability of clauses of the forms '(x) (fx • gx)' and '(x) fx •*
        (x) gx'
(iv)   *quantification*
(v)   *interchangeability of sentences of the forms '~ (p • ~ (x) fx)' and '(x)*
        ~ (p • ~ fx)'
(vi)   *alphabetic variance of pronouns*
(vii)   *commutativity of adjacent quantifiers*
(A)   ~ ((x) fx • ~ fy)
(B)   ~ ((x) fx • (x) ~ fx)
(C)   ~ ((x) ~ (fx • gx) • (x) fx • ~ (x) gx)
(D)   ~ (~ (x) ~ (fx • gx) • (x) ~ fx)
(E)   ~ (~ (p • ~ (x) fx • ~ (x) ~ (p • ~ fx))
(F)   ~ ((x) (y) fxy • ~ (y) (x) fxy)
(G)   ~ (~ (y) ~ (x) ~ fxy • ~ (x) ~ (y) fxy)
(H)   ~ ((x) ~ (gx • hx) • (x) ~ (fx • ~ gx) • ~ (x) ~ (fx • hx))
(I)   ~ ((x) ~ (gx • ~hx) • (x) ~ (gx • ~fx) • ~ (x) ~ gx • (x) ~ (fx • hx))
(J)   ~ (x = y • fx • ~ fy)
(K)   (x) x = x
(L)   (x) (y) (z) ~ (x = y • y = z • ~ x = z)
(M)   (x) (y) ~ (x = y • ~ y = x)
(N)   (x) ~ (y) ~ x = y
(O)   ~ (y = (ıx)fx • ~ (fy • (x) ~ (fx • ~ x = y)))
(P)   ~ (fy • (x) ~ (fx • ~ x = y) • ~ y = (ıx)fx)
(Q)   ~ (~ (y) ~ y = (ıx)fx • (y)gy • ~ g(ıx)fx)
*1   ~ ((z) (z ε x ≡ z ε y) • fx • ~ fy)
*1'   (w) (x) (y) ~ ((z) (z ε x ≡ z ε y) • x ε w • ~ y ε w)

139

*2 $\sim (y) \sim (x)\ (x\ \varepsilon\ y \equiv (fx \bullet \sim (z) \sim x\ \varepsilon\ z))$

*3 $(x)\ (y) \sim (x\ \varepsilon\ V \bullet y\ \varepsilon\ V \bullet \sim x;y\ \varepsilon\ V)$

*3′ $(x)\ \iota x\ \varepsilon\ V$

*4 $(x) \sim (x\ \varepsilon\ V \bullet y\ \varepsilon\ V \bullet \sim x \smile y\ \varepsilon\ V)$

*5 $(x) \sim (x \leqq \hat{y}\hat{z}\ (y\ \varepsilon\ Nn \bullet z\ \varepsilon\ Nn) \bullet \sim x\ \varepsilon\ V)$

Definitions

D1	'p ≡ q' *for* '~ (p • ~ q) • ~ (q • ~ p)'.
D2	'x = y' *for* '(z) (z ε x ≡ z ε y)'.
D3	'g (ɿ x) fx' *for* '~ (y) ~ (gy • fy • (x) ~ (fx • ~ x = y))'.
D4	' x̂fx' *for* '(ɿ y) (x) (x ε y ≡ (fx • ~ (z) ~ x ε z))'.
D5	'V' *for* ' x̂(x = x)'.
D6	'0' *for* ' x̂ ~ x = x'.
D7	'ɿ x' *for* ' ŷ(y = x)'.
D8	'x̄' *for* 'ŷ ~ y ε x'.
D9	'x ⌒ y' *for* 'ẑ(z ε x • z ε y)'.
D10	'x ⌣ y' *for* ' x̄ ⌒ ȳ'.
D11	'x ≦ y' *for* ' x = x ⌒ y'.
D12	'x < y' *for* 'x ≦ y • ~ x = y'.
D13	'x;y' *for* 'ɿɪ x ⌣ ɿ (ɿ x ⌣ ɿ y)'.
D14	'w (x,y)' *for* 'x;y ε w • x ε V • y ε V'.
D15	' x̂ŷfxy' *for* '(ɿ z) (x) (y) (z (x,y) ≡ (fxy • x ε V • y ε V))'.
D16	'w (x, y, z)' *for* 'x;(y;z) ε w • x ε V • y ε V • z ε V'.
D17	' x̂ŷẑfxyz' *for* '(ɿ w) (x) (y) (z) (w(x, y, z) ≡ (fxyz • x ε V • y ε V • z ε V))'.
D18	'x̆' *for* ' ŷẑ x(z, y)'.
D19	'x"y' for ' ẑ ~ (w) ~ (w ε y•x(z, w))'.
D20	'x	y' *for* ' ẑŵ ~ (v) ~ (x(z, v)•y(v, w))'.
D21	'I' for ' x̂ŷ(x = y)'.
D22	'x_y' *for* ' ẑŵ (x (z, w) • z ε (y̆"V) ⌣ (y"V) • w ε (y"V) ⌣ (y̆ "V))'.
D23	'1' *for* 'ɿ0', '2' *for* '1 ⌣ ɿ1', '3' *for* '2 ⌣ ɿ2', etc.
D24	'Nn' *for* ' x̂ (y) ~ (0 ε y • (z) ~ (z ε y • ~ z ⌣ ɿz ε y) • ~ x ε y)'.

141

Bibliography

Ackermann, see Hilbert.

Behmann, Heinrich. "Beiträge zur Algebra der Logik, insbesondere zum Entscheidungsproblem". *Mathematische Annalen*, volume 86 (1922), pp. 163–229.

Berkeley, E. C. "Boolean algebra and applications to insurance". *Record* (American Institute of Actuaries), vol. 26 (1937), Part III, pp. 373–414.

Bernays, see Hilbert.

Boole, George. *The Mathematical Analysis of Logic*. London and Cambridge, England, 1847. Reprinted in *Collected Logical Works*, Chicago and London, 1916.
An Investigation of the Laws of Thought. London, 1854. Reprinted ibidem.

Cantor, Georg. *Gesammelte Abhandlungen mathematischen und philosophischen Inhalts*, edited by Ernst Zermelo. Berlin, 1932.

Carnap, Rudolf. *The Logical Syntax of Language*. London and New York, 1937.
"Testability and meaning". *Philosophy of Science*, vol. 3 (1936), pp. 419–471, vol. 4 (1937), pp. 1–40.

Church, Alonzo. *A Bibliography of Symbolic Logic*. Providence, 1938. Reprinted from *Journal of Symbolic Logic* (1936, 1938).
"A note on the Entscheidungsproblem", *Journal of Symbolic Logic*, vol. 1 (1936), pp. 40–41, 101–102.

Cooley, J. C. *A Primer of Formal Logic*. New York: forthcoming.

Curry, H. B. "Grundlagen der kombinatorischen Logik". *American Journal of Mathematics*, vol. 52 (1930), p. 509–536, 789–834.

De Morgan, Augustus. *Formal Logic: or, the Calculus of Inference, Necessary and Probable*. London, 1847.
"On the syllogism and on the calculus of relations". *Transactions of the Cambridge Philosophical Society*, vol. 10 (1864), pp. 331–358. (1860).

Ferreira da Silva, Vicente. *Elementos de Lógica Matemática*. S. Paulo, 1940.

Frege, Gottlob. *Begriffsschrift*. Halle, 1879.
Die Grundlagen der Arithmetik. Breslau, 1884. Reprinted 1934.
Grundgesetze der Arithmetik. Vol. 1, 1893; vol. 2, 1903. Jena.
"Ueber Sinn und Bedeutung". *Zeitschrift der Philosophie und philosophischer Kritik*, n.s. vol. 100 (1892), pp. 25–50.

Gödel, Kurt. *On Undecidable Propositions of Formal Mathematical Systems.* Mimeograph. Princeton, 1934.

   The Consistency of the Axiom of Choice and of the Generalized Continuum Hypothesis with the Axioms of Set Theory. Princeton, 1940.

   "Die Vollständigkeit der Axiome des logischen Funktionenkalkuls". *Monatshefte für Mathematik und Physik*, vol. 37 (1930), pp. 349–360.

   "Über formal unentscheidbare Sätze der *Principia Mathematica* und verwandter System I". Ibidem, vol. 38 (1931), pp. 173–198.

Grelling, Kurt and Leonard Nelson. "Bemerkungen zu den Paradoxien von Russell und Burali-Forti. Bemerkungen zur Vorstehenden Abhandlung von Gerhard Hessenberg". *Abhandlungen der Frieschen Schule*, n.s. vol. 2 (1907–8), pp. 300–334.

Hilbert, David and Wilhelm Ackermann. *Grundzüge der theoretischen Logik.* Berlin, 1928. 2nd edition, 1938.

   and Paul Bernays, *Grundlagen der Mathematik*, 2 vols. Berlin, 1934 and 1941.

Huntington, E. V. *The Continuum.* Cambridge, Mass., 1917.

Kuratowski, Casimir. "Sur la notion de l'ordre dans la théorie des ensembles". *Fundamenta Mathemeticae*, vol. 2 (1921), pp. 161–171.

Langford, see Lewis.

Lewis, C. I. *A Survey of Symbolic Logic.* Berkeley, 1918.

   and C. H. Langford. *Symbolic Logic.* New York, 1932.

Löwenheim, Leopold. "Über Möglichkeiten im Relativkalkul". *Mathematische Annalen*, vol. 76 (1915), pp. 447–470.

Łukasiewicz, Jan. "O logice trojwartosciowej". *Ruch Filozoficznej*, vol. 5 (1920), pp. 169–171.

   "Uwagi o aksyomacie Nicod'a i o 'dedukcyi uogólniajacej'". *Ksiega Pamiatkowa Polskiego Towarzystwa Filozoficznego we Lwowie*, Lwów 1931.

Neumann, J. V. "Eine Axiomatisierung der Mengenlehre". *Journal für die reine und angewandte Mathematik*, vol. 154 (1925), pp. 219–240. Correction in vol. 155, p. 128.

Nicod, Jean. "A reduction in the number of primitive propositions of logic". *Proceedings of the Cambridge Philosophical Society*, vol. 19 (1917–20), pp. 32–41.

Peano, Giuseppe. *Formulaire de Mathématiques.* Introduction, 1894; vol. 1, 1895; vol. 2, 1897–9. Torino. Vol. 3, 1901, Paris. Vol. 4, 1902–3; vol. 5 (s. v. *Formulario Mathematico)*, 1905–8. Torino.

Peirce, C. S. *Collected Papers.* Edited by C. Hartshorne and P. Weiss. 6 vols. Cambridge, Mass., 1931–5.

Post, E. L. "Introduction to a general theory of elementary propositions". *American Journal of Mathematics*, vol. 43 (1921), pp. 163–185.

Quine, W. V. *A System of Logistic.* Cambridge, Mass., 1934.

   Mathematical Logic. New York, 1940.

   Elementary Logic. Boston, 1941.

   "Truth by convention". *Philosophical Essays for A. N Whitehead* (New York, 1936), pp. 90–124.

   "Relations and reason". *Technology Review*, vol. 41 (1939), pp. 299–301, 324–327.

   "Designation and existence". *Journal of Philosophy*, vol. 36 (1939), pp. 701–709.

"Completeness of the propositional calculus". *Journal of Symbolic Logic*, vol. 3 (1938), pp. 37–40.

"Element and number". Ibidem, vol. 6 (1941), pp. 135–149.

"On existence conditions for elements and classes". Ibidem; forthcoming.

"Whitehead and the rise of modern logic". *The Philosophy of A. N. Whitehead*, Evanston, Illinois, 1941. pp. 127–163.

Reichenbach, Hans. *Wahrscheinlichkeitslehre*. Leyden, 1935.

Rosser, Barkley. "The independence of Quine's axioms *200 and *201". *Journal of Symbolic Logic*, vol. 6 (1941), pp. 96–97.

"An informal exposition of proofs of Gödel's theorems and Church's theorem". Ibidem, vol. 4 (1939), pp. 53–60.

Russell, Bertrand (also see Whitehead). *The Principles of Mathematics*. Cambridge, England, 1903. second edition, New York, 1938.

Introduction to Mathematical Philosophy. London, 1919 and 1920.

"On denoting". *Mind*, vol. 14 (1905), pp. 479–493.

"Mathematical logic as based on the theory of types". *American Journal of Mathematics*, vol. 30 (1908), pp. 222–262.

Schröder, Ernst. *Vorlesungen über die Algebra der Logik*. Vol. 1, 1890; vol. 2, 1891–1905; vol. 3, 1895. Leipzig.

Shannon, C. E. "A symbolic analysis of relay and switching circuits". *Transactions of the American Institute of Electrical Engineers*, vol. 57 (1938), pp. 713–723.

Sheffer, H. M. "A set of five independent postulates for Boolean algebras". *Transactions of the American Mathematical Society*, vol. 14 (1913), pp. 481–488.

Skolem, Thoralf "Ueber einige Grundlagenfragen der Mathematik". *Skrifter utgitt av Det Norske Videnskaps-Akademi i Oslo*, I. klasse, 1929, N.º 4.

Tarski, Alfred. *Introduction to Logic*. New York, 1941.

Whitehead, A. N. *Universal Algebra*. Cambridge, England, 1898.

"On cardinal numbers". *American Journal of Mathematics*, vol. 24 (1902), pp. 367–394.

and Bertrand Russell. *Principia Mathematica*. 3 vols. Cambridge, England, 1910–1913. second edition, 1925–1927.

Wiener, Norbert. "A simplification of the logic of relations". *Proceedings of the Cambridge Philosophical Society*, vol. 17 (1912–14), pp. 387–390.

Wittgenstein, Ludwig. *Tractatus Logico-Philosophicus*. New York and London, 1922.

Zermelo, Ernst. "Untersuchungen über die Grundlagen der Mengenlehre I". *Mathematische Annalen*, vol. 65 (1908), pp. 261–281.

Appendix: The United States and the Revival of Logic

Willard Van Orman Quine

Within the last seven or eight decades, logic has evolved to the point of becoming a new science. Perhaps it would be better to say, simply, that it has become a science. In this development, which is of capital importance for mathematics and philosophy – and whose benefits also promise to extend to other sciences, the United States has until recently played only a secondary role. During the last twenty years, however, the situation has changed significantly, to the point of making that country the main center of activity in the field of logic.

Naturally, in my lecture this evening, I will concern myself more with logic than with the United States.

What, then, is logic? I tried to define it at the beginning of my course at the Free School of Sociology and Politics, but the definition and preliminary considerations which I then expressed lasted for almost an hour. You may relax, ladies and gentlemen, as it is not my intention to repeat that lecture here.

We will take as our starting-point the rather vague idea that logic, in one way or another, is related to reasoning, and then go on to consider the most significant contrasts between this science and other ways of approaching the study of reasoning.

On the one hand, quite separate from logic, there is psychology. Like physics or astronomy, this is a science that observes nature, recording uniformities, looking for causes and effects, and formulating natural laws. For example, an individual picks up his hat and looks toward the window. The rays of light that strike his retina are distorted by drops of water on the glass. The person turns around and picks up his umbrella. Psychologists look for a chain of causes and effects, whatever they may be, that connect the two physical events: that of the distorted light striking the retina and that of picking up the umbrella. When psychologists ask "How do we know this?", they ask it in the same spirit in which astronomers enquire "Why do the planets follow elliptical paths?" – seeking a causal chain, still unknown to us, that connects known and observable facts in the natural world.

145

We leave to the psychologist the task of searching for the unknown chain between the two known facts: the striking of light on the retina and the picking up of the umbrella. How is it that we know that there is light striking the person's retina, and that the person picks up the umbrella? How is it that we can know the world in general and, in particular, the circumstances of light, drops of water, man, and umbrella, before raising the psychological question of a chain connecting these apparently known facts?

The question of the foundations of psychology, like those of any other science, cannot be answered within psychology itself (according to some authors) without our falling into an infinite regress. The problem of avoiding this regress, if indeed it exists – or of explaining why it doesn't exist, in the negative case – belongs to philosophy rather than to any of the natural sciences. It constitutes a typical problem, if not the only one, of the part of philosophy called epistemology, that is, the theory of knowledge. This field may quite briefly – and quite vaguely – be described as dedicated to the philosophical examination of the general foundations of knowledge.

Psychology has the singular trait of constituting an important and interesting science without being part of logic. The same cannot be said of epistemology. Many people, at least, consider epistemology a subdivision of logic. Accordingly, the study of reasoning in general contains a part which belongs to psychology, with the rest belonging to logic in the broadest sense of the term. With regard to logic we have, so far, only considered the part called epistemology. There are two further parts to take note of, known as *inductive* and *deductive* logic. The most current and correct sense of the word "logic" is that which comprises only inductive and deductive logic, leaving aside epistemology as a separate and independent field. Logic, be it inductive or deductive, has as its practical aim the establishment of rules destined to guide and facilitate reasoning. It is for this reason that logic is commonly referred to as the "art of reasoning." In the natural sciences we boldly propose laws of a general character based on a few observed cases, and it is this type of mental action that logic, particularly inductive logic, strives to make possible. Theoretically, given some collection of observed facts, there are an infinite number of general laws, and any of them can be made to fit the facts. In the same way, if we take some discrete points on a geometric plane, we can connect them by means of a continuous curve which may take any one of an infinite variety of forms. The curve must touch the points, but it can wander wildly in between them and beyond them. Analogously, a general law must fit the observed facts, but beyond them it enjoys an unlimited latitude. To pick out from among so many laws the law which will fit not only the observed facts, but also facts not yet observed, relies on intelligent conjecture. It is the job of inductive logic to further such conjecture. To carry out this practical function, however, inductive logic must concern itself in large part with pure theory; and this theory, which is in fact a branch of mathematics, is called *statistics*.

Deductive logic, qua art of reasoning, concerns the type of reasoning that is not content with mere conjecture. It concerns the type of reasoning that leads us from given sentences, be they known truths or assumed hypotheses, to other sentences which are inexorable consequences of the given ones. This type of reasoning is characteristic of mathematics. But it also plays a role in the natural sciences, given that even a conjectural law, suggested inductively on the basis of a small set of data, must be tested with its consequences in mind. If we can derive from the hypothesis, in a strictly deductive manner, a sentence which conflicts with established facts, then we know that we will have to abandon the hypothesis.

It is in deductive logic that great progress has recently been achieved; and the word "logic" tends to be more and more restricted to deductive logic. The theoretical part of inductive logic – statistics – has its place among the other branches of mathematics; and the practical or technological part is usually referred to as *scientific methodology*, not "logic." A considerable part of published writings on inductive logic, or scientific methodology, belongs in fact to epistemology – fortunately, these fields are not fenced off from one another.

In order to carry out its practical task of guiding deductive reasoning, deductive logic must concern itself in large part with pure theory. In fact, it is so much concerned with general and abstract structures, which form the basis of all rules of deductive reasoning, that the designation "art of reasoning" seems strange. Far from being principally a technology, deductive logic is as theoretical and abstract as possible. This becomes especially clear in the new logic, which today constitutes the theoretical basis of pure mathematics in general. But even the ancient form of deductive logic – the formal logic of Aristotle – was mainly a theoretical study, perhaps because its development was insufficient to allow for applications of great practical value.

Aristotle's formal logic, consisting primarily of the theory of the syllogism,[59] survived the Middle Ages intact without undergoing any major changes or progressive development. Even in the second half of the eighteenth century, the famous philosopher Kant could speak of formal logic as a science that had already been perfected, and completed, two thousand years earlier. Nevertheless, people habitually engaged in fruitful deductive arguments of a kind almost completely unrelated to the existing logic. Consider the following example: We know that everyone who enters a given building, without being accompanied by a member of a certain firm, is stopped by the guard. Beyond this, we know that some of Fiorecchio's subordinates entered the building without being accompanied by another person. We know, in addition, that the guard has never stopped any of Fiorecchio's subordinates. We conclude, without great difficulty, that one or more of Fiorecchio's subordinates belong to the firm. Our ancestors concluded the same thing, without the benefit of modern logic. Nevertheless, who could have reduced this deduction to successive steps within the traditional logic? And if one tries to reduce this or another typical example of slightly complicated reasoning to the traditional logic, one must generally resort not only to the methods of Aristotle, but also to those of Procrustes. Ancient logic always used as illustrations reasoning for which a guide was not necessary; for example, if all men are mortal and Socrates is a man, therefore Socrates is mortal. Complex reasoning, for which a guide would be welcome, had to be executed in the primordial light of reason. In particular, great advances in mathematics were made this way. Still, mathematicians, and people in general, engaged in reasoning freely without redressing the theoretical inadequacy of the formal logic of the time, or, at least, without concerning themselves with any attempt to reform or extend this logic. Perhaps they had become accustomed to not thinking of logic when they were engaged in proper reasoning.

And why not continue that way? If we can perform mathematical and deductive reasoning about Fiorecchio's subordinates without the use of logic, old or new, what is its benefit? But the need for a new examination of the techniques of deduction was made apparent principally by mathematics itself, as we will now see.

Mathematicians were so busy reasoning and making discoveries about numbers, functions, and other mathematical entities, that they did not have time to reason about reasoning itself. But mathematical progress reached a stage where the role of deductive methods had to come in for special scrutiny. This occurred principally with the arrival on the scene of the higher infinities.

At the end of the nineteenth century, the German mathematician Georg Cantor (whose theories are rejected at present in Germany as belonging to Jewish mathematics)[60] discovered that there are multiple degrees of infinity. It is possible for two classes to be infinite, even though one is larger than the other. It became necessary to accept transfinite numbers, in addition to the usual numbers, to measure the difference in size between some of these infinite classes. Cantor showed that the collection of transfinite numbers is also infinite, and of a higher level of infinity than the infinity which any of the transfinite numbers can be used to measure.

This theory has several peculiar consequences. For example, Cantor showed that there are just as many even numbers as there are integers, and that there are just as many integers as there are integers and fractions combined, but that there are more real numbers than there are integers. The usual type of mathematical reasoning, relying on "intuition" or on "good sense," fails in the study of the higher infinities. The faculty of the imagination becomes useless when one goes beyond finite numbers and classes, or, in any case, beyond the first degree of infinity. We must explore the ocean that Cantor discovered by navigating blindly, depending only on the rigorous use of valid rules of deduction, and accepting the consequences. After Cantor, the techniques of modern logic have continued to prove useful in this respect, for instance in their deployment by the German Löwenheim, the Norwegian Skolem, and the Austrian Gödel.

But why should we concern ourselves with this outlandish theory of transfinite numbers? Recall the March Hare in *Alice in Wonderland*. He explained to Alice that he was constantly drinking tea with his two friends because it was always 6 o'clock, his watch being broken; and that many places had been set around the table so that they could change places after each sitting. But when Alice asked him what they did when they had finished going around the table, the Hare complained that the subject was becoming tiresome. Mathematicians who turn their backs on transfinite numbers behave exactly like the March Hare. We must concern ourselves with this theory for the sake of coherence. Cantor established his theory on the basis of principles already accepted and employed in the development of other parts of mathematics, and by means of methods of deduction equally well-entrenched and commonly employed. We cannot coherently repudiate the theory of transfinite numbers, as strange as it may be, without sacrificing at the same time familiar and useful parts of mathematics that share the same foundations.

Perhaps we could break free from parts of that theory without such sacrifice in the following way. Perhaps we could arrive at a formulation of the fundamental principles of mathematics, and the methods of deduction, in such a way that they would be sufficient for familiar and useful mathematical theories, but not for the more outlandish parts of Cantorian theory. But we will see that, even setting aside transfinite arithmetic in a mathematical rather than a political way, we must make the methods of deduction explicit and study them intensively.

An even more pressing motivation for such logical enquiries arose at the beginning of this century, with the discovery by the British logician Bertrand Russell that the principles of reasoning tacitly accepted and used in mathematics, and perhaps outside of it, could involve us in contradiction. This discovery precipitated a crisis. The principles of deductive logic had to be made explicit and carefully formulated, and even revised, for mathematics in general to be properly supported.

These contradictions or paradoxes are curious and entertaining. A characteristic contradiction, for example, involves the notion of *denotation* in the sense that the adjective 'human' denotes every human being, the adjective 'green' every green thing, the adjective 'long' every long thing, and so on. Let us use the term *heterological* for every adjective that does not denote itself. For example, the adjective 'long' is heterological, because it does not denote itself, that is, it is not long. The adjective *'inglês'* is heterological, because it is not English – it is Portuguese. The adjective 'monosyllabic' is heterological, because it is not monosyllabic, it is pentasyllabic. On the other hand, the adjective 'short' is not heterological, because it denotes itself – it is short. The adjective *'português'* is not heterological, because it is a Portuguese adjective. The adjective 'pentasyllabic' is not heterological, because it is pentasyllabic. Now, the paradox appears when we ask, with respect to the adjective 'heterological' itself, if it is heterological. It is heterological if and only if it does not denote itself, that is, if and only if it is *not* heterological.

This paradox, which we owe to the German logician Kurt Grelling, is not a purely logical paradox, because it depends on the non-logical notions of adjective and denotation. But the original paradox of Russell, which is very much analogous to it, *is* purely logical. It is about the *class* whose members are exactly the classes that are not members of themselves. This class is a member of itself if and only if it is not.

These paradoxes and other, more complex ones, are entertaining enough, but they result in very serious problems. Their repercussions in mathematics are still being felt today. And, as we have noted, the discovery of the paradoxes created a need for the current revival of logic.

Another motivation for this revival is the search for more perspicuous foundations for some of the dubious ideas used in mathematics. The arrival on the scene of the heterodox theory of transfinite numbers naturally led to an attempt to give a general definition of the notions of number, and infinity, on the basis of other more fundamental notions. Long before Cantor's transfinite numbers, there were other mathematical notions standing in need of clarification by means of definitions in terms of perspicuous notions. One of these notions was that of the *infinitesimal*, fundamental to the differential calculus since the time of Newton and Leibniz. It was an absurd notion: that of a positive number which is infinitely small, but nevertheless greater than zero. It was Weierstrass, in the past century, who eliminated this absurdity and found a solid foundation for the differential calculus, called the theory of limits. Yet another notion that stood in need of clarification was, naturally, the notion of imaginary number – the square root of negative one.

Mathematicians are entitled to make senseless pronouncements if they like, as their work provides many fruitful applications to the natural sciences regardless. But it would be interesting, at least from a philosophical point of view, to make sense of such notions, to understand the content of mathematics. Even mathematicians themselves may find this useful.

This program of reducing one mathematical notion to another, moving toward greater clarity, may seem independent of the development of the new logic. As it happened, however, analysis became dependent on the increasingly exact understanding and employment of the kind of auxiliary notions central to the very principles of logic: the notions of class and of relation, and those that correspond to the words 'if', 'then', 'not', 'and', 'is', 'all', 'some', and various others. The most surprising result was that which showed all mathematical notions to be reducible, not only to some of those same mathematical notions, but reducible entirely to auxiliary logical notions. Apart from this the discovery was also made that these logical notions are reducible, in turn, to just three: one corresponding to the phrase 'neither ... nor', another to the word 'is', and a third to the word 'all', supplemented by a system of pronouns. So, by these reductions, every single mathematical statement turns out to be a mere abbreviation of a purely logical statement written exclusively in terms of these three notions, with nothing more to be added.

To say that the theorem '2 + 2 = 4', when written out in this tiny vocabulary, would be several meters long, and that the binomial theorem would reach from the North to the South Pole, is not to take away from the theoretical importance of this reduction. Despite this, it remains the case that every mathematical law is an abbreviation of a logical law. Pure mathematics is reducible to logic.

The old logic is not repudiated by the new. The former corresponds to the infancy, and the latter to the adulthood, of the same science. As Whitehead said eight years ago in the preface he wrote to my first book: "In the modern development of Logic, the traditional Aristotelian Logic takes its place as a simplification of the problem presented by the subject. In this there is an analogy to arithmetic of primitive tribes compared to modern mathematics."[61] Whitehead's analogy is exactly right, because the new logic, like mathematics, makes essential use of a schematic and powerful language of symbols.

However, despite being more general and more powerful than the old logic, the new logic has achieved new extremes of economy – not only for itself but for pure mathematics in general, as we have just observed.

A no less important feature is that it has achieved new heights of rigor and exactness, even to the point of establishing new norms for mathematics in this respect.

The new logic has become integrated with the body of mathematical theory, not only as a theoretical basis in the manner just considered, but also as a practical instrument of research within various special branches of mathematics. To give just one example: The celebrated mathematical problem known as the continuum problem was solved three years ago, with regard to one of the two parts into which it is subdivided, by the Austrian refugee Kurt Gödel, making use of the technical means of the new logic.

One of the most important effects of the new logic over the last two decades has been a series of discoveries about the reach and the limits of mathematical method. One of these discoveries is due to this same Gödel. This logician discovered that no deductive system can be coherent and at the same time sufficient for mathematics, or sufficient for logic or the arithmetic of the whole numbers. For any system of arithmetic, Gödel showed how to construct a sentence of purely arithmetical character that would be a theorem of the system if, and only if, it were false, such that the theorems of the system either include a falsehood or exclude a true arithmetic statement.

This is a truly surprising result. One might have thought that the truth of a mathematical sentence itself consists in the possibility of its proof. Gödel's result, however, shows that there cannot exist a coherent systemization of mathematics such that any true mathematical statement admits of proof. What can be said, then, about the rest? What do we mean when we call them true or false? Here there is a crisis, indeed, in the philosophy of mathematics. This crisis still hangs over us today.

This fundamental discovery was only possible in virtue of the rigorous formulation, within the new logic, of rules of deduction in the explicit form of rules for the permutation, substitution, etc., of the ideograms that appear written in mathematical theories. It is only under such an explicit formulation that methods of proof in mathematics become susceptible to such penetrating investigations as those of Gödel – research which consists, in fact, of an application of mathematical methods to the study of mathematical methods themselves.

The fact that rules of deduction can be formulated in a way so explicitly framed as rules for manipulation of signs is one of the most significant features of the new logic, and one which has notable repercussions for epistemology. It has inspired a conventionalism according to which all logical and mathematical truths depend, not on the character of reality or on an essential structure of the mind, but only on certain linguistic conventions that cover the use of words. This conventionalism served, for its part, to revive the radical type of empiricism, that of the philosophical school that insists that all knowledge is based on the recording of observations. An obstacle to this point of view is found in the problem of logical and mathematical knowledge: but conventionalism averted this obstacle, accepting logical and mathematical knowledge as purely verbal and without content. The new modified empiricism, called *logical empiricism* or *logical positivism*, is identified with the name of the Vienna Circle, having been developed in that city between the two world wars.

All of the representatives of this school admired the new logic, and some of them understood it as well. The new logic played an important part in the writings of the school, especially in those of Carnap, the school's leader, who is as much a logician as an epistemologist. Thus, in the minds of philosophers who understood the new logic well, it was identified with the philosophy of logical empiricism and became the target of attacks directed against that philosophy. It is important to remember that, in fact, the new logic does not imply this philosophy, nor even the doctrine of conventionalism. Perhaps the greater part of mathematical logicians, I myself among them, do not share the principal conclusions of the Vienna Circle. I believe, however, that many of Carnap's contributions have great value. It cannot be denied that the philosophical movement of which he is the principal representative is the most vital and significant of the present time.

The care that the new logic takes gives to signs, and the operations on them, has once again called attention to the linguistic, philosophical, and logical problems concerning the relation between signs and objects: in short, the problems of semantics. Even though the consequences of conventionalism are not at all clear, the fact remains that semantics ended up making scientific progress of the first order, due in large part to the Polish logician Tarski. I am, besides, convinced that these clarifications with regard to semantics have very important consequences for philosophy itself, consequences that are still almost unknown and that differ from the conclusions of the Vienna Circle. I think that ancient questions of an ontological character, such as "What is there?" and "What is real?", have only now begun to acquire some meaning and even to admit certain partial solutions.

We must return, however, from these heights. We would like, in the little time that remains, to form some idea of the social environment of the new science of which we have just obtained knowledge. It is clear that its development has been a cosmopolitan enterprise, given that I have already had occasion to mention Englishmen, Germans, Austrians, a Pole, and a Norwegian. With regard to its origin, the new logic represents quite diverse cultures, being the fruit of the union of the Aristotelian tradition with the algebraic tradition. It was the Irish mathematician George Boole who, in the middle of the nineteenth century, undertook to frame formal logic in a form analogous to that of algebra. The new logic thus had crude beginnings, only later being stimulated and enriched by a growing interest in the methods and foundations of mathematics. The calculus of classes and propositions developed by Boole and his immediate successors had much in common not only with the Aristotelian and algebraic traditions, but also with a third tradition, the Stoic – even though the latter was not known to these researchers. It was only in the past decade that the Polish logician Łukasiewicz called attention to important similarities between the most elementary part of modern logic and the logic that was founded by the Greek Stoics and continued in the Middle Ages by Petrus Hispanus.

The nine most important pioneers of the new logic, up to the second decade of this century, represented five countries: Ireland, Germany, England, the United States, and Italy. In the seventeenth century, the celebrated German philosopher and mathematician Leibniz had already envisaged a project somewhat similar to that of modern logic; and even though he did not realize this project, he anticipated, in writings that were not published at the time, some of the ideas that would be developed anew and more systematically in the logic of Boole.

A pioneer who was a contemporary of Boole, but whose work was less definitive, was the Englishman Augustus De Morgan, who concerned himself with the problem of constructing a calculus for reasoning about relations. This work was continued with greater success a few years later by the American Charles Peirce, who also made progress in the calculus of classes and propositions that Boole founded. Other important progress in this direction was made by the German Schröder in the same era, that is, in the last decades of the nineteenth century. But of these pioneers the most important was the German Gottlob Frege, whose books appeared between the years 1879 and 1921. It was he who made logic the subtle and powerful science that we have today. It is mainly to him, as well, that we owe the reduction of mathematics to logic. It is perhaps Frege, and not his predecessor Boole, who deserves the title of the founder of modern logic.

Another important pioneer, whose works took the same direction as those of Frege, was the Italian mathematician Peano. Finally, in the years 1911 to 1912, the period of the pioneers ended with the appearance of the monumental work in three large volumes by the Englishmen Whitehead and Russell: *Principia Mathematica*.

Later developments took place in equally diverse countries. We owe much to Poland, Warsaw and Lvov having been centers of great activity in the study of logic from the year 1920 up to the date of the invasion. Much has also been done in Germany, especially through the work of the great mathematician Hilbert and several of his students. Hungary has for its part furnished various researchers, one of them being John von Neumann, a logician and mathematician of great distinction. Austria and Norway have furnished, as noted earlier, Gödel and Skolem.

In the United States the activity of Charles Peirce ended at the beginning of this century, and publications on the new logic were scarce during the following three decades. From this era, I know only of one article by the mathematician Edward Huntington and another by the philosopher Josiah Royce, both more or less from the year 1904, a third frequently cited article by Henry Sheffer from the year 1913, and a fourth very important article by Emil Post from the year 1921.[62] During this interval, that is, in 1918, the book *A Survey of Symbolic Logic* by Clarence Lewis also appeared, which is a theoretical and historical treatise on the new logic.

It was in approximately 1931 that, in the United States as in Europe, logic began a secondary period of revival within its principal revival. It was at this time that Gödel's sensational discovery about the limits of mathematics was made known in Europe, and that more intense activity began in Poland and Germany. Since then, research and publications on modern logic have continued with an ever-growing intensity in the United States. So as not to refer to persons present, I shall mention only two of the researchers of this recent period: the mathematicians Alonzo Church, of Princeton, and Haskell Curry, of Pennsylvania State College. Both have published very substantial research. Church, in particular, has solved a problem that had become a classic in modern logic, and had been the subject of much research in Germany and Hungary.

In America as in Europe, an increasing number of articles on logic are being published, partly in mathematical journals and partly in philosophical journals. It was in the United States, in the year 1935, that an association was founded for the publication of a journal devoted to logic: *The Journal of Symbolic Logic*. This journal, under the able direction of Church, has served as the means of dissemination of important articles in English, French, and German, originating from the United States, England, Poland, Hungary, Switzerland, and Palestine. A very important feature of the *Journal* is the inclusion of critical reviews of all books and articles published on this science since 1935. The record of material on the subject was completed with the publication in the *Journal* of an excellent bibliography by Church of publications from Leibniz until the year 1935. As you may see, the volumes of this journal are indispensable to every library that has a section devoted to logic, that is, every good library.

In the United States, a third revival of logic has occurred as a result of the events in Europe.[63] We now have Gödel, von Neumann, and Tarski, the most important representative of the great Polish school. Carnap, the principal representative of the Vienna Circle, has become an American citizen, as I, a witness to the act of his naturalization, can attest. This concentration of foreign logicians is only one aspect of the fact that the United States has become, in virtue of international disagreements, the repository of world science and scholarship. I well remember a walk on the slopes of Mount Monadnock, when I observed that a match carelessly thrown in the forest would almost eliminate the principal logicians of the day.

I cannot mention the present concentration of logicians in the United States without adding that, independently of the war, we also have the English pioneers Whitehead and Russell. Both are, however, rather removed at present from the scientific aspect of the new logic. It is possible that when Whitehead directed my doctoral studies in logic in the years 1931 to 1932, that was the first time in fifteen years that he had thought about logic.

General and elementary courses on logic in the United States increasingly recognize the existence of the new logic. The first elementary text on logic in general that was concerned, in part, with the new theories, was that of Ralph Eaton, which appeared in the year 1931. Since then, it has been the custom to include in each general text on logic at least some chapters about the new logic, and in the last few years two elementary texts have appeared in the United States, written exclusively from this point of view: one by Tarski and one of my own authorship. It seems ever more probable that the university student who decides to take a course on logic will find it devoted to modern logic.

Unfavorable comments persisted in the United States as in other places. One force in this regard was the Catholic Church, based on the idea that the destiny of Aristotelian logic is connected to the destiny of religious doctrine. A good example of this point of view is provided by the religious writer Jacques Maritain. It is curious, however, to observe that in Belgium and Poland, both Catholic countries, there were priests who became interested in the new logic. In Poland, the current explanation for its vast logical movement was that logic constituted one of the few permissible subjects, being too abstract to disturb the government or the church. Some admirers of Aristotle received the new logic eagerly, considering it evidence that the logic founded by Aristotle was capable of becoming, like his biology, an important science.

Further resistance to the new logic was based, as I have mentioned earlier, on objections to Viennese epistemology. Still another objection was based on the idea that the new logic was frivolous and inconsequential – an objection that, incidentally, is justified with respect to the writings of some logicians who are more interested in symbolic apparatus than in central problems. The recent progress, however, as for example the contribution of Gödel to the continuum problem, has decisively silenced the skeptics. Its trial period, and the lack of trust placed in it, may effectively be considered as past. The new logic has been established among the respectable sciences. And, from the practical point of view, the techniques of the new logic have already begun to find application in daily life, as they are being applied today even in electrical engineering and in the study of the clauses of insurance policies.

Notes

1. Quine's Portuguese here literally translates as "The Revival of Logic in the United States," but Quine's lecture was eventually published under a title better translated as "The United States and the Revival of Logic." Our translation of Quine's lecture appears on pp. 145–157 of this volume.
2. For publication details of these works, see Bibliography. The translation of the lecture in question is included in this volume.
3. Willard Van Orman Quine, 1943, "Notes on Existence and Necessity," *Journal of Philosophy*, vol. 40, no. 5, 113–127.
4. An obscure term for "theory of knowledge"; Thomas Uebel tells us that it was sometimes used by members of the Lvov–Warsaw School, for instance in the title of T. Kotarbinski's book *Gnoseology*. See also "Willard Van Orman Quine's Philosophical Development in the 1930s and 1940s" in this volume (p. xx). A fondness for rare and obscure words is characteristic of Quine's writing style, especially the later Quine.
5. Quine here expresses an early version of what he was later to call "eternal sentences"; cf. Willard Van Orman Quine, 1960, *Word and Object*, Cambridge, MA: MIT Press, §§ 36, 40. He expressed a similar view in his 1941 publication *Elementary Logic*, Boston, MA: Ginn & Co., 6.
6. By "long conjunction" Quine means '$(\sim (p \bullet \sim q \bullet r) \bullet \sim (p \bullet \sim r) \bullet q)$', and by "long denial" '$\sim (\sim (p \bullet \sim q \bullet r) \bullet \sim (p \bullet \sim r) \bullet q)$'. He is probably resorting to calling them "long conjunction" and "long denial" respectively because the full formulae wouldn't fit onto the page.
7. This remark indicates Quine's interest in algebraic-combinational methods for minimization of Boolean functions. The Quine–McCluskey method (or prime implicants algorithm) is a method for minimization of Boolean functions developed by Quine in "The Problem of Simplifying Truth Functions," *The American Mathematical Monthly*, 59 (8): 521–53, 1952, and extended by Edward J. McCluskey in 1956.
8. Quine is using a rare variant of the less-than-or-equals sign here, with two lines underneath the '$<$'.
9. The 'unless' + negative construction used in Quine's original sentence is permissible in Portuguese ('a menos que não'), but sounds unnatural in English. We have chosen to preserve the negative in our translation in order to retain the overall logical form of the Portuguese original, but have opted for a negative construction that does not contain an explicit 'not', in order to make the sentence read a little less awkwardly.

10. That is, we're looking for the logical operator with the widest scope. In *Elementary Logic*, centripetal translation is called "paraphrasing inward" (35).

11. Quine's claim here is puzzling, because the usual sense of English 'p unless q' is not 'p if q', but 'p if not-q': 'I will be there unless the train is late' is equivalent to 'I will be there if the train is not late', but not at all equivalent to 'If the train is late then I will be there'. This is no less true of the Portuguese connective 'p a menos que q'. (Quine's original text uses an obscure variant, 'ao menos que'.) Even more bafflingly, Quine had asserted just one year earlier, on p. 19 of *Elementary Logic* (1941), that 'unless' in English means 'or' and shares with it the ambiguity between the inclusive and the exclusive sense.

12. Corrected from Quine's original Portuguese, which reads "quantificador" – "quantifier," a typographical error. Quantifiers cannot be true or false, and '(x)' just is the quantifier, not what the quantifier begins with.

13. A misprint in the first edition, repeated and further confounded in the second, resulted in the first line of the following paragraph being repeated as the first line of this paragraph. We have amended the text based on the typescript in the W. V. Quine Papers: held in the Houghton Library at Harvard University, folder number 2550, *O Sentido da Nova Lógica* MS, 1944, p. 64.

14. Corrected from Quine's 1944 original, which has instead the ungrammatical 'hx fx' without parentheses or a dot.

15. Corrected from Quine's 1944 original, which has 'b' instead of '8' – a typographical error.

16. Corrected from Quine's 1944 original, which has "recorra" – "recurs," where we would expect to find "occurs."

17. With small changes and additions, Quine translated the first two paragraphs of § 31 from his 1939 article "Relations and Reason," *Technology Review*, vol. 41, 327. The text as presented here is our own translation of Quine's Portuguese back into English.

18. In Quine's typescript of the book, there is a marginal note, "(5.5303)," obviously referring to the *Tractatus*. It is not clear that Quine is being entirely fair to Wittgenstein here, who was of course talking about logical syntax in his *Tractatus*; nor is it obvious that Quine's translation of Wittgenstein into Portuguese is wholly accurate. Wittgenstein's original text says, "Von zwei Dingen zu sagen, sie seien identisch, ist ein Unsinn, und von Einem zu sagen, es sei identisch mit sich selbst, sagt gar nichts" *(Tractatus* 5.5303). Ogden and Ramsey's translation, the only one available in 1942, renders this as "to say of two things that they are identical is nonsense, and to say of one thing that it is identical with itself is to say nothing." Quine, a fluent speaker of German, was probably thinking of the original. Quine's dismissal of Wittgenstein on identity may have been motivated by his opposition to the Wittgenstein-influenced anti-metaphysics of the Vienna Circle; see "Willard Van Orman Quine's Philosophical Development in the 1930s and 1940s" in this volume (p. xxxv).

19. The Paranaiba river is located in the southeast and centre-west of Brazil in the Paraná river basin, and faces south with the Rio Grande basin, to the east with the São Francisco Basin, to the north with the Araguaia–Tocantins Basin, and to the west with the state of Mato Grosso do Sul. It is over 1170 kilometers in length.

20. With the exception of the first sentence and a few words noted below, this paragraph is identical to pp. 113–115 of "Notes on Existence and Necessity."

21. The second half of this sentence does not appear in Quine's English translation in "Notes on Existence and Necessity."

22. "Purely" is omitted from "Notes on Existence and Necessity."

23. This section corresponds roughly to "Notes on Existence and Necessity," bottom of p. 116 to top of p. 118.
24. The first three paragraphs of this section are identical with those on "Notes on Existence and Necessity," 119; the next three largely overlap with the last three paragraphs of p. 120 of "Notes on Existence and Necessity," except where otherwise indicated; and the remainder largely overlaps with "Notes on Existence and Necessity," 121 and the first paragraph of p. 122.
25. "Perhaps" replaced with "No doubt" in "Notes on Existence and Necessity."
26. The final two sentences of this paragraph do not appear in "Notes on Existence and Necessity."
27. "and . . . statement:" omitted in "Notes on Existence and Necessity."
28. In "Notes on Existence and Necessity," "spinster" is used consistently throughout these paragraphs wherever *The Significance of the New Logic* has "bachelor."
29. Parenthetical differs slightly from "Notes on Existence and Necessity."
30. This section contains all of "Notes on Existence and Necessity" section 4 (122–125), "Non-Truth-Functional Composition of Statements."
31. "and discussion of these statements" omitted from "Notes on Existence and Necessity."
32. "the use . . . quantifiers" omitted from "Notes on Existence and Necessity."
33. "Notes on Existence and Necessity" has "p and q" here, a typographical error.
34. "the matrix . . . natural language" omitted from "Notes on Existence and Necessity."
35. This paragraph is Quine's own translation, appearing on p. 118 of "Notes on Existence and Necessity."
36. Quine's claim here is apt to strike us as a little odd. He does not appear to be using "converse" in its usual sense, where the converse of 'p → q' is 'q → p' – or, in the notation of *The Significance of the New Logic*, the converse of '~(p • ~q)' is '~(q • ~ p)'. These are obviously not normally equivalent. The best interpretation of this remark, we suggest, is that Quine intends for it to make the same point as the following passage from his 1939 article "Designation and Existence," *Journal of Philosophy*, vol. 36, 707: "The other, which may be called specification [i.e. inference by application, eds.], is the form of inference whereby a variable is replaced by a name and a universal prefix is dropped . . . if existential generalization is valid with respect to a given term, say 'Paris,' then specification is likewise valid with respect to that term."
Quine's point, then, is the following:

    Inference by application is the law: '(i) ~((x) F(x) • ~F(a))'
    and existential generalization is the law: '(ii) ~(G(a) • ~ ~(x)~ G(x))'.

    Assuming, as Quine says, that the substantive designates, (i) is equivalent to (ii), since (i) is the same as '~(~ F(a) • ~ ~ (x)F(x))' and is also the same as '~(~ F (a) • ~ ~ (x)~ ~F(x))'.
Now suppose we use the alternative notation 'G(. . .)' for '~ F(. . .)' above. We then obtain (ii).
    Since (i) moves from 'F(x)' to 'F(a)', and (ii) moves from 'G(a)' to 'G(x)', dropping quantifiers, they can be viewed as mutual converses, in a looser sense of "converse."
37. *Os Sertões*, published in 1902, was written by the Brazilian engineer and journalist Euclides da Cunha (1866–1909). It is considered one of the classic works of Brazilian literature. The lengthy book chronicles the extermination, at the hands of the army of the nascent Brazilian Republic, of a messianic movement that arose

in the country's arid northeastern backlands (Euclides da Cunha, 1902, *Os Sertões*. Rio de Janeiro: Laemmert).

38. This section is for the most part the same as part 5 of "Notes on Existence and Necessity."
39. "liberty" is replaced with "justice" in "Notes on Existence and Necessity."
40. "as ... dispensable" added to the corresponding sentence of "Notes on Existence and Necessity."
41. "of some type always" is replaced with "these or others" in "Notes on Existence and Necessity."
42. These two sentences are replaced by a single sentence in "Notes on Existence and Necessity," which is in the third person rather than the first person plural, and with "prior" changed to "private."
43. Instead of the paragraph and a half running from "A class, even of concrete and spatial things" to "when they have the same members," "Notes on Existence and Necessity" has only "Classes are as abstract and non-spatial as attributes, as I have emphasized elsewhere [ref. to his 1940 publication *Mathematical Logic*, New York: Harvard University Press, 120], and there is no difference between classes and attributes beyond perhaps this: classes are the same when their members are the same, whereas attributes may be regarded as distinct even though possessed by the same objects."
44. "verbal expression" is replaced with "matrix" in "Notes on Existence and Necessity."
45. "Notes on Existence and Necessity" substitutes "on the basis of (15)," where '(15)' refers to 'The number of planets = 9'.
46. "Notes on Existence and Necessity" has "Likewise, more generally, we must conclude that the occurrences of names within names of attributes are not designative" here.
47. "in general" is omitted from "Notes on Existence and Necessity."
48. "Notes on Existence and Necessity" substitutes "the matrices (26) and (27)," where '(26)' stands for 'x > number of planets' and '(27)' for 'x > 9'.
49. "Notes on Existence and Necessity" has "(26) and (27) are."
50. "Notes on Existence and Necessity" has "the simple attributes of sense experience."
51. "Notes on Existence and Necessity" omits this final sentence.
52. Corrected from Quine's 1944 original, which reads 'xfx', a typographical error.
53. Corrected from Quine's 1944 original, which renders this formula as 'x ∪ x = V'; plainly a typographical error since it, jointly with (20) above, would entail 'x = V' by the transitivity of identity.
54. Corrected from Quine's 1944 original, where this formula looks the same as the second formula on p. 209.
55. Corrected from Quine's 1944 original, which has 'z' instead of 'y'.
56. The Bandeirantes were Brazilian-Portuguese settlers of mixed racial background who in the seventeenth and eighteenth centuries ventured into the interior of the country to colonize land, seek mineral wealth, and enslave native populations. They played an essential role in drawing the map of Brazil as it is today.
57. Corrected from Quine's 1944 original, where this formula appears as 'x"ȳ'.
58. Corrected from Quine's 1944 original, which omits the '∼'.
59. Pages 150–153 of the lecture are almost identical with pp. 9–13 of the Introduction of *The Significance of the New Logic*.
60. Quine is alluding to the Nazi regime here, whose actions horrified him; see also section 2 of "Willard Van Orman Quine's Philosophical Development in the 1930s and 1940s" in this volume (pp. xviii–xxi).

61. See p. 9 of *The Significance of the New Logic*, where this quotation also appears.
62. Sheffer's and Post's articles are cited in the bibliography of *The Significance of the New Logic* (H. M. Sheffer, 1913, "A Set of Five Independent Postulates for Boolean Algebras," *Transactions of the American Mathematical Society*, vol. 14, 481–488; E. L. Post, 1921, "Introduction to a General Theory of Elementary Propositions," *American Journal of Mathematics*, vol. 43, 163–185).
63. Quine is here referring to the fact that, following the Nazi occupation of parts of Europe, several European logicians, many of whom were Jewish or left-wing and politically active, fled to the United States. For further details, see section 2 of "Willard Van Orman Quine's Philosophical Development in the 1930s and 1940s" in this volume (pp. xviii–xxi).

Index

Printed in Great Britain
by Amazon

48423370R00126